MISCONCEPTIONS OF MIND AND FREEDOM

Irving Thalberg
University of Illinois at Chicago

UNIVERSITY
PRESS OF
AMERICA

LANHAM • NEW YORK • LONDON

150.1
T365m

Copyright © 1983 by

University Press of America,™ Inc.

4720 Boston Way
Lanham, MD 20706

3 Henrietta Street
London WC2E 8LU England

All rights reserved
Printed in the United States of America

ISBN (Perfect): 0-8191-3540-2
ISBN (Cloth): 0-8191-3539-9
LCN:

All University Press of America books are produced on acid-free paper which exceeds the minimum standards set by the National Historical Publications and Records Commission.

86-3124

ACKNOWLEDGEMENTS

I make use of some previously published material in various chapters. Chapter One incorporates part of my essay "The Discovery of Nonsense", <u>Midwest Studies in Philosophy</u>, VI (1981), edited by Peter French et al., and published by University of Minnesota Press. Chapter Two is an expansion of my paper "Immateriality", <u>Mind</u>, XCII (1983), edited by David W. Hamlyn, and published by Blackwell's. Chapter Three is a revision of my article "A Novel Approach to Mind-Brain Identity", <u>Philosophical Studies</u>, XXXV (1978), edited by Keith Lehrer, and published by D. Reidel. Chapter Four is a revision of "Freud's Anatomies of the Self", in <u>Philosophical Essays on Freud</u>, edited by James Hopkins and Richard Wollheim, and published by Cambridge University Press (1982). Chapter Five contains elements from "Motivational Disturbances and Free Will", in <u>Mental Health: Philosophical Perspectives</u>, edited by Tristram Englehardt and Stuart Spicker, and published by D. Reidel (1976); from "Hierarchical Analyses of Unfree Action", <u>Canadian Journal of Philosophy</u>, VIII (1978), edited by Brian Chellas et al., and published by the Canadian Association for Publishing in Philosophy; and from "Socialization and Autonomous Behavior", <u>Tulane Studies in Philosophy</u>, XXVIII (1979): Studies in Action Theory, edited by Robert C. Whittemore, and published by Tulane University. Chapter Six is based on my survey of action theory, which appeared in <u>Modern Trends in Philosophy</u>, edited by Asa Kasher and Shalom Lappin, and published in Hebrew by Yachdav (1982). Chapter Seven is a re-thinking of "How Does Agent-Causality Work?", in <u>Action Theory</u>, edited by Myles Brand and Douglas Walton, and published by D. Reidel (1976). Chapter Eight is a much-improved version of "Mental Activity and Passivity", <u>Mind</u>, LXXXVIII (1978), edited by David W. Hamlyn, and published by Blackwell's.

I am grateful to Hogarth Press for allowing me to quote, in Chapter Four, many passages from <u>The Standard Edition of the Complete Psychological Works of Sigmund Freud</u>, edited by James Strachey (London: 1953-74).

I thank these editors and publishers for letting me take material from the works above. I am also grateful to numerous philosophers with whom I've had the pleasure of discussing either the issues or previous drafts of my chapters. Donald Gustafson kindly offered reactions to my penultimate typescript of the whole book. Kent Bach, Myles Brand, Arnold Levison, Hugh McCann, Michael Stocker, and Richard Wollheim made particularly valuable criticisms or suggestions on drafts of one or more chapters. Finally, I thank Sarah Shaftman for careful typing of the manuscript and valuable last-minute editorial suggestions.

TABLE OF CONTENTS

Acknowledgements		iii
Introduction		vii
Chapter One:	Do Orthodox Theories of Mind Make Sense?	1
Chapter Two:	Could Mental Events be Non-Physical?	27
Chapter Three:	Could Mental Events be Physical?	45
Chapter Four:	Freudian Models of Mental Life	63
Chapter Five:	The Problem of 'Alien Desires'	93
Chapter Six:	Do We Control our Behavior through Volition?	127
Chapter Seven:	Are Actions Caused by Agents, Not by Events?	153
Chapter Eight:	Can our Mental States be Active or Passive?	185
References		211
Index		223

INTRODUCTION

Two facts about human beings are indisputable, highly significant, yet unexpectedly difficult to analyze. People have a mental life; and they also have the power to carry out various actions, if they choose. These traits distinguish people from all inanimate objects, and probably from such 'lower', entirely instinctive creatures as termites. When I speak of our mental life, I mean that we often feel chilled or sore, that we ruminate, worry, rejoice, become indignant or nostalgic, and map out our future undertakings. When I talk of our power to act, I mean that it is sometimes up to us what we do. At this moment I have a choice whether to remain ensconced before my desk, or instead to amble across the hall to a coffee lounge and refill my cup. It is not up to me whether I stay seated, or walk across the ceiling like a human fly. These examples highlight an obvious linkage between mentality and power to act. Our short- and long-term planning, our decisions as well as our expectations, have a crucial bearing on whether or not we eventually do various things that are up to us. The contrast I mentioned, between people and inanimate objects, comes out starkly again here. My desk lamp has a high-intensity bulb, and is capable of lighting up the entire room. It will do so if you switch it on; otherwise it won't. But it scarcely has a choice in the matter. In fact, what could we mean if we said that it is up to the lamp whether or not it goes on? Even if, <u>per impossibile</u>, there were no causal conditions that determine whether the lamp shines or stays dark, I would be unsure what to make of the statement that this lamp is able to go on or off, as it pleases.

Few metaphysicians would dream of doubting these truisms about human mentality and ability to do things. Those who believe that a computing machine or a robot might have the power of acting or refraining would also, I think, attribute consciousness, goals, perhaps scruples, to these contraptions. Despite this near-unanimity as to the crucial facts, there is endless, though still fascinating, debate about why they are so, and what theoretical implications they have. Moreover, some of the most intuitively striking analyses of mind and freedom to act seem vulnerable to straightforward counter-examples. Other <u>prima facie</u> plausible schemes yield apparent nonsense when we subject them to scrutiny.

I do not say this in a censorious or mocking spirit, particularly when I am alluding to some of the grand, deeply tempting confusions that have shaped our theoretical outlook for centuries. Strawson is right to say that

> one of the marks . . . of a really great philosopher is to make a really great mistake . . . to give a persuasive and lastingly influential form to one of those fundamental misconceptions to which the human intellect is prone when it concerns itself with the ultimate categories of thought. So today, more than three hundred years after the death of Réné Descartes, philosophers struggling with one of those fundamental misconceptions think of it under the name of Cartesian dualism . . . [I]f it did not represent a way of thinking about mind and body which has a powerful intellectual appeal, it would not be worth struggling against (1966, p. 89).

In order to keep things up to date, and deal seriously with the best arguments of contemporary analytical philosophers, I shall quote the leading debaters rather copiously. When I occasionally criticize what I consider to be their instructive mistakes, I intend not to score points or have fun at their expense, but to devote to their reasoning the sort of close attention that it deserves. What I am interested in are the problems; however, I believe we are most likely to achieve clarity about the issues and the alternative positions on them if we start from controversies that are in progress. No doubt I shall now and then unwittingly misconstrue some philosopher's utterance or argument. I apologize in advance if this happens. Nevertheless we may learn something from these erroneous interpretations; they may represent positions that deserve a hearing.

Now for a somewhat more detailed prospectus. My first chapter spells out the novel criticism--the charge not of falsity but of unintelligibility--that Ryle and Wittgenstein made against so-called Cartesian dualism. This eternally compelling doctrine was of course originally formulated by Plato, then ingeniously elaborated by Descartes and his followers, including some eminent twentieth-century neurophysiologists. In outline, the dualistic view is that each person has--or simply is <u>identical</u> with--a conscious, non-physical, mind-substance. This mind is somehow associated with, perhaps hitched to or caged inside, what we call the person's body. All mental events unfold within the private sanctum of this psyche, frequently in conjunction with outward corporeal happenings. If a wound is inflicted upon the person's body, probably severe discomfort occurs in his or her psyche. If a decision to act appears within the mental arena, you can be reasonably confident that appropriate behavior is going to ensue.

After I expound the principal Wittgensteinian and Rylean arguments that this doctrine makes no sense, I evaluate some counter-arguments by distinguished post-Wittgensteinian thinkers, most of them opponents of dualism who have perhaps incautiously borrowed one or another of its conceptual underpinnings. I suppose the hottest quarrel is over Cartesian certainty--in particular, the assumption that each person has exclusive, complete, and unerring knowledge of at least some of her or his mental goings-on, notably his pains and thoughts. Such astute philosophers as Ayer, Castañeda, Aune, and Searle reject this Wittgensteinian-Rylean thesis that it is meaningless to claim knowledge of one's mental state or its alleged contents. I attempt to understand and adjudicate this wrangle. Whether or not I am correct in declaring Ryle and Wittgenstein unrefuted, my elucidation of their nonsense-charge should come in handy when we grapple with the problems of succeeding chapters.

My hope is confirmed when I move to my next, closely related question: What do Cartesians and some unaffiliated thinkers mean when they insist that mental events--and minds, if there are any--must be non-physical? Not only defenders of dualism, but materialists who argue that its tenets are false, presumably have an idea about what mental goings-on are, or are not. Here are examples we'll study: The esteemed neurophysiologist Sherrington says his experience of seeing a blue sky is "wholly unlike" the physical changes that "led up to it". I should welcome a few specifics as to how his experience is "unlike" its bodily accompaniments, and especially on just what his visual caper *is* like. Similarly, when Shaffer assures us that a person is "a nonphysical entity", I want to hear what features this entity has, in addition to those it lacks. When the materialist Smart says that his concern is "to deny that . . . there are nonphysical entities", we should expect to learn more about the alleged characteristics of the entities that Smart believes <u>do</u> <u>not</u> exist, and Shaffer believes <u>do</u> exist. Curiously, these questions about what dualists mean by their key descriptive term have seldom come up for discussion. Thus Chapter Two is a plunge into relatively uncharted depths. It is indisputable that most reflective people, when they pay attention to their current psychological states--their suffering, rejoicing, or scheming--feel driven to exclaim, "These can't be merely brain processes; they do not seem physical at all!" Do such episodes seem nonphysical, however? If they do, can you describe their non-physical characteristics? Generally, how do things seem when they seem to be non-physical?

Whether or not we are able to make sense of the claim that mental events are incorporeal, we still run into difficulty with the contrary view that they are really physical--probably nothing but electro-chemical states of our brain. One commentator on Smart's influential version of materialism--the claim that "sensations are brain processes"--finds it no more cogent than Cartesian dualism. D. L. Gunner explains,

> I reject Smart's . . . position and . . . also . . . the alternative dualist position . . . for the same reasons . . . [Both lack] a statement of the . . . procedures . . . for identifying an experience as a distribution of ghost stuff [or a brain process], and therefore [both lack] the means whereby to establish the thesis as true or false. The thesis that sensations are distributions of ghost stuff is like the thesis that sensations are brain processes in lacking truth value. . . . I have not said that <u>any</u> and <u>every</u> brain process thesis must be unintelligible, only that that thesis as formulated . . . by Smart . . . is, as it stands, nonsense (1967, p. 16).

Gunner's attack seems to depend rather heavily on a verificationist construal of meaningfulness and nonsense. My criterion is more relaxed. Instead of branding a statement or thesis unintelligible if its defender cannot tell us what "procedures" or "means" would "establish" its truth or falsity, I so stigmatize it only if nobody can tell us, using a whole cluster of normally intermeshing terms, how things might be if the statement were true or false. For instance, you might say that each person has exclusive ownership of her or his pains, thoughts, intentions, and so forth. I would ask what more can be said of this ownership: Can you acquire and lose this kind of possession? by purchase, inheritance, government grant? Can you dispose of these items as you do your old clothes and furniture--giving them away or auctioning them off? What would it be like if we did not exclusively own our mental states? Could they be collectively owned instead, or shared? Might they not belong to anyone? If none of these things which we can say about everyday ownership and non-ownership situations fits the present case, then by my test your statement is at this juncture meaningless. But my verdict, in contrast with Gunner's, has nothing directly to do with your failure to state methods that establish your exclusive-ownership thesis as true or false.

Actually this is only background for the problem of Chapter Three, whether it makes sense--and therefore might be true--to say mental events are physical. Obviously we should ask specifically what or which physical events constitute our after-imaging, thinking, and deciding. The answer of Smart and most present-day materialists is that certain neural events are the only physical goings-on that count. Unfortunately this kind of mental-physical identity doctrine invites at least three serious accusations of nonsense. Opponents of materialism have objected that our mental states cannot be any of our brain states because things we can say truly, hence meaningfully, of the one make no sense when transferred to the other. For example, it is true to describe any neural event as having a fairly precise anatomical location more or less within one's skull. Since it sounds unintelligible to ascribe this or any other habitat to one's thinking or deciding, how can such psychological events be identical with some spatially pinpointed neural episodes? Another disparity between our brain processes and our mental states is that our authority to say what is happening in our brain is entirely based upon empirical investigation and theorizing by ourselves and mostly by trained experts. It is therefore true, and consequently meaningful, to cite evidence for any report we make of our brain processes, to say why we think it is true. We might also confess that we are ignorant of our current brain states, and it will make sense for other people to say that we are honestly mistaken about what is happening now in our nervous system. But can you intelligibly say any of these things about our candid disclosures of our thoughts, desires, and sensations? Finally, many of our psychological states are <u>about</u> this or that. A lottery winner gloats over his or her windfall. Yet what could it mean to say that the person's brain state is 'over' or 'about' winning the lottery prize? In response to these anomalies, I propose independently plausible alterations of the materialistic doctrine that each mental state or episode is identical with some brain process or other. The upshot, I hope, is that it will sound no more incoherent to classify an event as both mental and physical than to describe a melon as both round and green.

Of course materialists are not home free. They still owe us an intelligible, moderately detailed account of the neural and other bodily goings-on that constitute the incidents and phases of our mental careers. For centuries, two models have been favorites: the operation of rudimentary mechanical gadgets or processes, and the social transactions that occur between two or more individuals. The former appear regularly in pre-Socratic speculation on what happens when we perceive, remember, have emotions, and decide how to behave. Plato began refining animistic similes. For instance, he several times likened the supposed incorporeal process of silent reasoning to an overt conversation between two speakers. The sociopolitical dealings and power-relationships of Plato's <u>Republic</u> are explicitly introduced to help us understand how a just person's immaterial psyche functions. Whether dualists or materialists, nearly all the great philosophers of mind--such as Lucretius, St. Augustine, St. Anselm, St. Thomas, Descartes, Hobbes, Spinoza, Locke, Leibniz, Hume, Kant--tried out mechanistic and interpersonal accounts. But I think some of the most suggestive and painstakingly elaborated comparisons appear in the work of a materialist who seldom deigned to offer philosophical arguments for his outlook. I refer to Freud, whose theorizing also deserves attention because he systematically rejected a fundamental premise of the leading dualists and materialists alike. This is the assumption that underpins Descartes' theories of absolute certainty and of mind-body distinctness. In brief, Descartes says, I have unimpeachable knowledge via the <u>cogito</u> argument that my mind exists. I also have infallible awareness of all events that occur 'in' my mind. But since I might be dreaming or deluded by a powerful trickster, I lack comparable knowledge of physical things, including my own body.

So it seems to follow, inter alia, that the mind and the mental happenings which I am unerringly conscious of cannot be physical. Ironically, most opponents of this dualistic conclusion nevertheless agree with Descartes that I unfailingly cognize at least such archetypal goings-on as my current itching, thinking, or dreaming. Freud's revolutionary doctrine of repressed unconscious mental processes is completely at odds with the Cartesian tradition.

Philosophers of mind are beginning to understand this aspect of Freud's genius; so I explore another, more problematical feature of his thought. My fourth chapter is an appreciative but critical study of Freud's mechanistic, anthropomorphic, and 'mixed' analogies for those mental events we are conscious of, but especially for our dark, brutish, repressed unconscious. I expect to run across some significant nonsense along with many insights.

Chapters Five through Eight all take up fundamental issues about our control over what we do. Here are sample questions from Chapter Five: Ordinary coercion, some of the neurotic and other unconscious pressures described by Freud, and ultimately our social conditioning may deprive us of freedom; but how should we analyze these forms of unfreedom? Suppose you say that in those disagreeable circumstances we act unfreely because, inter alia, we are prevented from doing what we want; in more general terms, if you do what you want--with reasonably complete information about consequences and alternatives, having the opportunity, means, and ability to pursue alternatives--your action is free. The hypothesis is meaningful enough, but seems to be downright false. For imagine that someone threatens you or another person--a hostage, say--with grievous harm unless you empty out your employer's safe. You reluctantly comply because you think compliance is the lesser evil as things stand. Haven't we got a counter-example to the hypothesis? You wanted to minimize suffering in this case; and you cooperated as a result of having that desire and belief. Apparently you did what you wanted, yet your action was clearly unfree. By the same token, if you unconsciously act on a repressed neurotic impulse, aren't you once again doing what you want--however unconscious and irrational your desire is--though in some sense you do not act freely? Along the same lines, perhaps you have been conditioned since childhood by the people of your living group to think and act in accordance with custom. Eventually you need no guidance; you yourself want to behave that way. Yet again, contrary to the hypothesis, it is not at all evident that your tradition-bound behavior is free. But maybe the proposed analysis is incomplete. I consider a widely acclaimed modification of Frankfurt's and Gerald Dworkin's, which defines acting freely as doing what you want, plus having a second-order desire to be motivated by the ground-floor desire that you have. Does this take care of our puzzle cases?

More basic mysteries about action await us in Chapter Six. For instance, how do we manage to act at all? That is, how do we get our limbs moving? You find unequivocal replies in the work of Lucretius, the Scholastics, and modern theorists before Wittgenstein and Ryle. The nearly unanimous opinion was that we bring about movement of our limbs by willing it. Prichard noticed a snag in this answer: Is our willing itself something we do? If it is, then we cannot define action as the result of willing--for such a definition implies that we must engage in higher-level willing in order to produce our original act of willing; and so on ad infinitum. Prichard's solution was to say that our body's movement is not an action of ours, and that all we really do is will. However, neither a Prichardian nor an old-fashioned volitional account seemed defensible against the charges of nonsense brought by Wittgenstein, Ryle, and their adherents. These criticisms of course follow the pattern of Rylean and Wittgensteinian attacks on the orthodox, dualistic theory of mind. It is worth noting, incidentally, that one can be a volitionist without being a dualist, and vice versa. At any rate, after the initial onslaught, volitionism appeared to be moribund. But, like the broadly Cartesian picture of mind that it kept company with, it has been resuscitated by some distinguished present-day metaphysicians. No wonder, since it is an almost irresistible doctrine. All in all, then, we have an ideal occasion to adjudicate a tough controversy.

You might try to stay out of the quarrel about volitionism and similar accounts of what we must do or undergo in foro interno when we move our bodies. Why assume there must be any such occurrences when we act? One small but highly respected group of contemporary action-theorists, led by Roderick Chisholm and Richard Taylor, have articulated a clear alternative. So I devote Chapter Seven to their analyses of how a person just <u>causes</u> her or his behavior, perhaps by just causing the requisite cerebral antecedents. The new twist in this doctrine of "agent causality" is that one is supposed to make behavioral or neural events happen "directly"; they do not have to be caused by previous or contemporary events, such as episodes of volition, wanting, second-order desire--even forethought. The behavior or the brain process just springs from the agent. Champions of this theory also promise a rich dividend. They believe their doctrine will help us put an end to the age-old fracas over determinism, indeterminism, and our ability to act in alternative ways. Agent-causationists hold that when your behavior results from preceding or simultaneous events, you cannot act otherwise than you are caused to act. On the other hand, if your behavior is simply <u>uncaused</u> by existing circumstances, then it is random, and you certainly have no control of it, no power to act differently. But if you are the sole author, originator, agent, or cause of your bodily movement or brain process, doesn't that place you in charge, and enable you to choose between genuine options? These large questions ought to keep us busy. We must give agent-causationists a sympathetic hearing, and decide how cogent their doctrine is, as well as what consequences it has--particularly in the feud over determinism and free will.

Throughout our inquiries regarding free and unfree action, and simply what it is to act, we have to consider mental events. A creature or a mechanism without desires and aversions, likes and dislikes, cannot be said to act either freely or unfreely, willingly or unwillingly. The main theory of free action we must evaluate in Chapter Five is that we act freely just in case we do what we want, and have a higher-level desire to act for such reasons. Volitional doctrines either define action as the bodily movement produced by a mental occurrence--willing--or else reduce action to the mental event of willing. I suppose agent-causationists could follow suit; they could say that the bodily occurrence we directly bring about is our action, or else that our only action is <u>agent-causing</u> the bodily occurrence. Presumably this unusual form of causing is mental--and if I am right in Chapter Three, it could be physical too. So could willing. But another resemblance between willing and agent-causing absorbs me in Chapter Eight: whether or not these are the <u>only</u> actions we perform, they do seem to be <u>actions</u>. Are they, however? What other categories might they belong in? Speaking more generally, what could we mean if we classified psychological goings-on as either active, passive, or something else?

These ruminations lead me to probe the familiar antithesis between mental activity and passivity. It was part of the Scholastic heritage, and Descartes seems to have taken it for granted when he says that our thinking comprises a voluntary mental act of "assent" to an "idea"; similarly when he explains that you risk falling into error if you wilfully assent to an idea that you have not established to be true--or clear and distinct. Locke also appears to accept the dichotomy--for example, when he says that some ideas "force themselves on me", and infers from this that there "must needs be some exterior cause . . . that produces those ideas in my mind, whether I will or no" (1690, IV, xi, 5). Berkeley starts from similar premises, though he would never endorse Locke's conclusion that material objects produce any of our ideas. Berkeley declares, "I can excite [some] ideas in my mind at pleasure . . . But whatever power I have over my own thoughts, I find the ideas actually perceived by sense have not a like dependence on my will . . . [T]herefore some other will or spirit . . . produces them" (1709, §§28-29). Neither his nor Locke's reasoning interests me here--only the contrast Berkeley draws between "operations of the mind, wherein the mind is active" and operations wherein "the mind is passive" (1708?, §286). It is still casually assumed though it has yet to be elucidated. Besides attempting to make sense of the claim that various antecedents of action--willing, agent-causing, desiring--are active, passive, or neither, I shall consider an argument that thinking is active; finally I shall assess two *prima facie* cases of passivity--the emotions, and those repressed unconscious happenings we worried about in Chapter Four.

From this short preview of what I plan to discuss in the next eight chapters, several things must be evident. No world system, no synoptic vision of mind, freedom, and their place in nature, is likely to await us at the end of these inquiries. Nevertheless each puzzle or debate I am going to work through is intrinsically fascinating and linked with most of the others. Though each has received some discussion, the relevant literature is manageable, and rival claims have not yet become obfuscated as a result of too many defensive qualifications. Last but not least, the kind of nonsense I shall be looking for in most chapters is far from trivial; often it represents an overwhelmingly strong temptation to misconstrue ourselves and our surroundings. I shall try to illustrate this methodological point straightaway.

CHAPTER ONE

DO ORTHODOX THEORIES OF MIND MAKE SENSE?

Throughout this book I shall deploy what I call 'arguments from nonsense' against a number of quite appealing doctrines about mind and freedom. This form of argument begins to appear systematically in the work of analytical philosophers--notably Ryle and Wittgenstein--from the 1930s onward. Ryle says that by this time he believed "the philosopher's proprietary question is . . . 'Why does this . . . expression make nonsense? and what sort of nonsense does it make?'" (1970, pp. 6 ff.). For his part, Wittgenstein declares it his objective "to pass from a piece of disguised nonsense to something that is patent nonsense" (1953, §464; see §119). John Wisdom adds a salutary emphasis. Wisdom agrees that the theories Wittgenstein debunks are indeed "specimens of the whoppers philosophers can tell"; yet such doctrines are not "merely symptoms of linguistic confusion"; they are "symptoms of linguistic penetration" as well (1936-37, p. 104). I believe Wisdom means that some of the wildest theories derive from at least a partial insight into our established patterns of speaking--for example, our tendency to depict consciousness as a hidden, subterranean waterway, carrying with it our aches, itches, thoughts, moods, and impulses, all of which are somehow revealed to our inward gaze.

Before I explore such themes, I should remark that prototypical arguments from nonsense antedate our century. They are scattered throughout Plato's dialogues-- as in Theaetetus when Socrates denies that knowing could be the same as perceiving, because we can perceive dimly or vividly, but it makes no sense to characterize knowledge as dim or vivid. For a paradigm of this early genre, however, I would take one of Berkeley's pithy objections to Locke's account of physical things. In brief, Locke holds that such items consist of matter or material substance, plus the specific qualities or "accidents" that make them the kind of thing they are. In response to the Lockean view that "matter supports or stands under accidents", Berkeley wonders, "How? Is it as your legs support your body?" Naturally followers of Locke would reject this crudely literal reading. But what other interpretations are there for the key verb "supports"? Berkeley says, "Pray let me know any sense, literal or not literal, that you understand it in"; generally, "let me know what it is you would have me believe" (1713, pp. 199, 218). Of course Berkeley's challenge does not constitute a full-fledged disproof of the Lockean analysis. Nevertheless it places an obligation on votaries of matter and accidents to set forth what they mean. My aim will be analogous when I look at the not altogether dissimilar, and equally enticing, theory of our mental life that Wittgenstein, Ryle, and their sympathizers have belabored.

1. <u>A warmup exercise</u>. To get the hang of arguments from nonsense, we should begin with a less controversial and really almost facetious example from Ryle's early paper, "Systematically Misleading Expressions". Ryle takes a statement that many of his contemporaries would have assumed was about a Platonic universal--a property, an attribute, or in Locke's terminology an "accident". The statement, "Unpunctuality is reprehensible", seems to be as much about unpunctuality as "Jones merits reproof" is about Jones. Yet Ryle wants that if we assume these statements are on a part,

> absurdities soon crop up. It is silly to speak of a universal meriting reproof. You can no more praise or blame a universal than you can make holes in the Equator. Nor . . . do we . . . suppose that unpunctuality ought to be ashamed of itself. What we . . . mean is . . . "Whoever is unpunctual deserves that other people should reprove him for being so" . . .

> . . . all statements [that] seem to be "about universals" are analysable [thus] . . . So universals are not objects . . . and therefore the age-old question what <u>sort</u> of objects they are is . . . bogus (1931-32, pp. 90 f.).

This rather trumped-up case exhibits many salient features of an argument from nonsense. First we have to imagine a setting for the statement that unpunctuality is reprehensible. Perhaps the believer in universals has offered to provide us information on his favored entities. He (or she) might explain that we can describe them in various terms. We could say, for instance, that the universal unpunctuality is something reprehensible. But shouldn't we make sure what the familiar adjective 'reprehensible' means in this context? So we recall everyday situations where someone judges other people--or their behavior--to be reprehensible. It is not germane that we happen to be dealing with a moral or normative term, 'reprehensible'. Ryle's procedure would be the same if unpunctuality were being characterized in morally neutral terms.

Perhaps we envisage this situation: Jones's conduct has been reprehensible. That cannot be the end of the story; more can be said and done. Jones himself ought to be contrite and make amends. Other people can admonish Jones, ostracize him, impose penalties on him. He certainly should not exult over his misdeeds, and we should not encourage or reward him. The further terms we have introduced, and the activities they denote, help to flesh out our literal, everyday use of the adjective 'reprehensible'.

Now we should turn to the alleged universal, unpunctuality. Could it or any other universal be ashamed? Could it make restitution? How might we go about condemning this universal, isolating it from society, punishing it? What might we do to insure that its untoward behavior does not get reinforced? If we were still discussing Jones or his misconduct, replies would be easy. But any answer we give regarding the universal, unpunctuality, is going to sound capricious--no more plausible than its negation.

The would-be proponent of universals may retreat, explaining that all he really meant was that individuals who are not on time ought to be censured. I would interpret this as a confession that his original statement did not in fact concern the universal unpunctuality. On the other hand, if he persists in describing this universal as literally reprehensible, his assertion must be consigned to the same basket as the news report that someone has drilled holes in the Equator. More precisely, his statement carries equally unintelligible implications--for example, that the universal might display or fail to display remorse, that it might receive or escape chastisement, and so on. We show the original statement to be disguised nonsense because we get bare-faced nonsense as soon as we try to develop the parallel between it and the clearly meaningful assertion that Jones, or Jones's behavior, is reprehensible.

One immediate consequence is that until the

booster of universals can produce a more satisfactory model for his characterization of them, we should not waste time debating "what <u>sort</u> of objects they are". That would be like quarreling about what size holes mar the Equator. Perhaps Ryle overstates his case when he concludes that universals definitely are "not objects"--reprehensible or otherwise. But I think his line of critical reasoning explains why the type of claim made by a devotee of universals is not literally meaningful, and therefore not worth disputing. Ryle has placed the onus upon the advocate of universals to devise a more cogent account of them, if that is possible.

    2. <u>The analysis of unintelligibility so far</u>. The Rylean mini-argument I have put together hardly proves that our subject term, 'unpunctuality', much less our predicate expression, 'is reprehensible', are mere nonsense sounds. Unlike the babbling of a six-month-old infant, they belong to the English phonetic system. They also differ markedly from several of the phonemes in Lewis Carroll's beloved verses:

        The Jabberwock, with eyes of flame,
    Came whiffling through the tulgey wood,
          And burbled as it came!

Our phonemes, 'unpunctuality', 'is', and 'reprehensible', are all English words. Moreover, their concatenation, 'Unpunctuality is reprehensible', conforms to English syntax, and ranks as a declarative sentence. Incidentally, the sentence is not unintelligible through being wildly out of place, disconnected with other things that have been said and done in the context we imagined. Wittgenstein gives two particularly striking examples of such incongruity: I abruptly say "'Good morning' . . . to someone in the middle of a conversation" we are having; or I suddenly tell a close friend whom I've been chatting with, "I knew all along that you were so-and-so" (1969, §354). The statement, "Unpunctuality is reprehensible", diverges from these cases. How then is it nonsensical?

    3. <u>Comparisons with falsity and unverifiability</u>. Sometimes people react to an outrageously untrue statement by saying "Nonsense!" On occasion statements that are self-contradictory or analytically false are called 'nonsensical'. However, our statement, "Unpunctuality is reprehensible", cannot fall into these categories. If it were either a glaring empirical falsehood like

"Pigs are carnivorous", or a necessary falsehood like "You can jog without moving your legs", then its denial would be true. But its standard negations—"Unpunctuality is not (in the least) reprehensible" and "It is not the case that unpunctuality is reprehensible"—are as puzzling as their affirmative counterpart. For what would things be like if either of these negative statements were true? Specifically, what do you rule out—as a matter of fact, or else a priori—when you deny that unpunctuality is reprehensible? You ought to tell us what it is that you are denying to be the case. Wittgenstein has an apt illustration of this requirement. He compares the negative statements, "A goose has no teeth" and "A rose has no teeth", wondering ironically if the second is not "obviously true"—even "surer" than its companion. Yet he muses, "Where should a rose's teeth have been? The goose has none in its jaw. And neither . . . has it any in its wings; but no one means that when he says it has no teeth" (1953, pp. 221 f.). What then are you excluding when you deny that a rose has teeth? I think it is just as obscure what you mean if you deny that unpunctuality is reprehensible.

Thus far I have distinguished philosophically interesting nonsense from mere gibberish: from sounds that are not phonemes of English or whatever language is being spoken; from phonemes that are not words of English; from strings of English words that violate syntax, and fail to qualify as a sentence; from utterances that are glaringly inappropriate to the rest of the interchange during which they occur; and from statements that are either contingently or necessarily false. I should also mention unverifiability and unfalsifiability, which positivists between the 1920s and the 1950s took as their criteria for deciding whether a statement is empirically meaningful.

In brief, most positivists held that an unverifiable and unfalsifiable statement is a purportedly factual assertion that no evidence that you can describe, no experiment or other testing procedure, would either corroborate or disconfirm to any degree. No observation you make would contribute toward proving the statement true—or false either.

From the little I have said, it is plain that 'unverifiable' and 'unfalsifiable' are epistemological notions, having to do with sense-perception, the gathering of evidence, proof and disproof. Notions belonging to this epistemological clan were altogether absent from Ryle's critique of the statement that the universal unpunctuality is reprehensible. He did not complain that we are unable to prove or disprove by observation that unpunctuality is reprehensible. Instead the central issue for Ryle was: What else can we assert or deny about unpunctuality, using terms that otherwise keep company or clash with the predicate 'is reprehensible'? In particular, do we produce downright bizarre combinations when we bring in terms from the same cluster as 'reprehensible'? If we get such plainly incoherent results, then we have to assume that our original statement was camouflaged nonsense. I suppose it will also turn out that no observational test you can dream up will count either for or against the truth of "Unpunctuality is reprehensible". But this would be a separate defect of that statement, over and above its unintelligibility.

I think we have had enough target practice on universals. It sounds plausible to connect nonsense with other things that can be said, after you assume for the sake of argument that a given utterance is true. At all events, we are ready to gun for the ever-popular general theory that human beings consist of non-physical minds which are somehow tethered to a material body.

4. What do we mean when we attribute minds to people? Enemies as well as defenders of universals would agree that an ontologically noncommital assertion, such as "Whoever is unpunctual deserves to be scolded", makes perfectly good sense. By the same token, both opponents and aficionados of mind would consider it meaningful--and platitudinously true--to say that people are often conscious or 'mindful'. Statements such as "Jane is mentally computing her tax deductions" and "Sam is planning what to do over the holidays" are clearly intelligible. None of the contending theorists of mind doubts that human beings enjoy a rich mental life--that they become infatuated or indignant, and daydream or deliberate. Thus Wittgenstein exclaims, "Why should I deny that there is a mental process?" This is altogether uncontroversial--for instance, if we assume that "'There has just taken place in me the mental process of remembering [such-and-such]' means nothing more than 'I have just remembered [such-and-such]'" (1953, §306). In the same vein, Ryle assures us that he is not "denying there are mental processes. Doing long division is [one] and so is making a joke"

(1949, p. 22). But the metaphysical crux is how we should analyze these "processes" and our reports of them. Must we summon up a container-like mind or consciousness, and fill it to the brim with elusive images, sensations, thoughts, and urges? When a psychological occurrence takes place, must something go on that resembles the meshing of gears, the rolling of pulleys, the tugging of cables--or even digestive processes? Maybe; but we should make certain that it increases our understanding of human mentality if we postulate such goings-on. Before we plunge too deeply into this kind of theorizing, we ought to investigate whether the whole mind-hypothesis makes sense.

Wittgenstein puts his finger on the issue when he asks, "What am I believing in when I believe that men have souls?" He appears to contrast this with the ostensibly straightforward empirical belief that some chemical compound has two rings of carbon atoms among its ingredients. But surprisingly, Wittgenstein's verdict seems to be that in both cases it is unclear what we are "believing in" (1953, §§422 ff.). Elsewhere, however, he tries a simpler model for attributing a mind to someone: the statement that a certain tribe of people has a chief. Wittgenstein asks if we say something analogous when we add that "the chief must surely have consciousness" (§419). I doubt it. The leader may have inherited his office; perhaps he was elected by the tribal elders; possibly he usurped authority. Inheriting, selecting, and usurping are all deliberate transactions between conscious human agents. We understand what it is for people to interact in these ways. On the other hand, we have no clear idea what it would be like for similar goings-on to occur between the chief himself--or his body--and the "consciousness" he is said to "have". How would he proceed to nominate and elect his mind? How might it defeat its rivals who also aspire to be the chief's mind? Our suggested para-political model of 'having a mind' seems to stir up as much nonsense as the claim that unpunctuality is reprehensible. What you can meaningfully say of the relationship between a tribe and its leader does not carry over to people and their minds. Incidentally, we can deny that a tribe has a ruler, and mistakenly believe that it has one. But, as Wittgenstein remarks, "What would it mean for me to be wrong about his having a mind, having consciousness? . . . [or] to be wrong about _myself_ and not have any?" (1967, §394). The difficulty is not trivial. Insofar as we cannot specify what alternatives it rules out, the mind-hypothesis remains a mystery.

I object similarly to theories about the putative denizens of our mind: the sensations, images, thoughts, and desires that we supposedly 'have' by virtue of their transitory or long-term presence in our mental arena. My own eclectic argument from nonsense against the doctrine that such items reside 'in' or march 'before' our consciousness is mainly a request for details. At what coordinates, or in what regions of your mind, do your aches, beliefs, and yearnings hang out? Are some of them located above or below, in front of or behind others? How many of them can a given mental district accommodate at a time? Do some crowd out others? Do some get compressed, like foam rubber? If they are sometimes 'present' to your consciousness, are they at other moments 'absent' from it while nevertheless continuing to exist? We have no difficulty at all furnishing this kind of information about the keys and coins that happen to be--or not to be--in our pocket; but anything similar that we say of our mind's alleged contents will sound quite daft.

Wittgenstein inquires along such lines about the relationship between people and the mental contents they are said to 'have'. He supposes that a mind-philosopher has declared, "When I imagine something, or even actually _see_ objects, I have got something which my neighbor has not." Wittgenstein challenges this by asking, "In what sense have you _got_ what you are talking about . . .? Do you possess it? You do not even _see_ it" (1953, §398). And of course the problem over 'having' is compounded by obscurities about what you have. Here again we should follow Wittgenstein. Suppose the mind-philosopher insists that

> he sees a private picture before him . . . [T]hat means that you can describe it . . . more closely. If you admit that you haven't any notion what kind of thing . . . he has before him . . . [i]sn't it as if I were to say . . .: "He _has_ something. But I don't know whether it _is_ money, or debts, or an empty till"? (§294).

This last is a fine example of unadorned nonsense, inasmuch as we cannot even begin to request details regarding whatever the person 'has', and specifics on the type of 'having', so long as our alternatives are not narrowed further than "money, debts, or an empty till". For example, the question "Where does he keep what he has?" will be totally out of order if we are dealing with someone's indebtedness or bankruptcy. Of course these objections will not be enough to convince partisans of mind and mental contents that they should give up their notion of 'having'. Most surviving theories concern what is 'in' our mind.

5. <u>Maybe we have the contents of our minds by perceiving them.</u> A most venerable theory, alluded to by Wittgenstein, represents us as bystanders or spectators of our thoughts and other psychical belongings. Against this Ryle complains,

> Observing is a task which can be of some arduousness, and we can be more or less successful in it and more or less good at it. But none of these ways of characterizing the exercises of one's powers of observation can be applied to the having of . . . sensations . . . We can make mistakes of observation, but it is nonsense to speak of either making or avoiding mistakes in sensation (1949, pp. 204 f.).

Our alleged perceptual contact with the denizens of our consciousness will have to be very unlike standard gazing, listening, touching, sniffing, and delecting. Two or more onlookers may gawk at the same parade; however, as Ryle says,

> the cobbler cannot [be said to] witness the tweaks that I feel when the shoe pinches . . . [Tweaks] are not the sort of things of which it makes sense to say that they are witnessed or unwitnessed at all, even by me. In the sense in which a person may be said to have . . . a robin under observation, it would be nonsense to say that he has a twinge under observation (p. 205).

A further Rylean point is that we can describe how we use microscopes and other instruments to examine bacteria. Yet it is unintelligible to suppose we employ such devices to scrutinize our feelings of chill. Nor can we speak of interferences such as fog or background noise disturbing my observation of my nausea. Similarly, Ryle notes, to ask whether someone's "inspection of a tickle had been hampered, close or casual, and whether he could have discerned more of it, if he had tried", is on a par with asking "how the first letter in 'London' is spelled" (p. 207). Words, but not letters or paragraphs, can be spelled or misspelled. Only garden-variety objects and events, but not the putative items occupying our mind, can be perceived or misperceived.

Ryle is particularly disturbed by the axiomatic-sounding doctrine that each of us is unique percipient of our mental contents. Ryle argues,

> it was wrong . . . to contrast the common objects of anyone's observation, like robins . . . with the supposed peculiar objects of my privileged observation, namely my sensations, since sensations are not objects of observation at all . . . [T]he cobbler cannot feel the shoe pinching me . . . but . . . not because he is excluded from a peep-show open only to me, but because it would make no sense to say that he was in my pain (pp. 207 f.).

Since we cannot under any imaginable conditions meaningfully assert that the bootmaker is in my pain, we should stop regretting that he is unable to perceive my pain by somehow being in it. He does not miss an opportunity reserved for me alone. It is unintelligible to describe anyone, including myself, as having perceptual contact with my pain.

The arguments from nonsense that I have reviewed so far will be insufficient to de-program most votaries of the doctrine that each person is the exclusive owner of a mind and its contents. We must burrow deeper.

6. <u>Necessarily private 'having'</u>. No other form of ownership seems like this. Ordinarily, when an individual or a group is the sole proprietor of something, there are other options. A pasture that in fact belongs to just one cattle-breeder could be purchased by someone else; it could be jointly owned by several partners; it might be collectivized; the government might confiscate it; conceivably, it might be unowned, if nobody has staked it out. All these ownership situations depend upon the existence of social practices--buying, transfer, dividing up, leasing,

foreclosing, dispossessing, laying claim. Our everyday concept of proprietorship is inseparable from this cluster of standardized activities. However, the mind-philosopher's doctrine that we own our itches, moods, and deliberations will not fit into this familiar scheme of things. "Bill and Jane are co-proprietors of one backache" sounds demented; so does talk of auctioning off a surge of pride, homesteading it, expropriating it, or illegally trespassing on it. In what sense, then, do we *have* minds and their contents?

Some ownership theorists will be untroubled. They will keep on asserting, in Wittgenstein's phraseology, "only I have got THIS". Wittgenstein's retort pulls together most of the examples I've been toying with. He suggests, "If as a matter of logic you exclude other people's having something, it loses its sense to say that you have it" (1953, §398). Until theorists devise a more cogent account of their unprecedented form of possessing, debate should be adjourned.

But some mind-philosophers will insist, "Another person can't have my pains" (§253). Wittgenstein is ready with a further challenge. He asks, "Which are *my* pains? What counts as a criterion" for identifying them as mine? (§253) The possessive pronoun sounds as incongruous here as our commonplace vocabulary of ownership. Wittgenstein explains using a new model of downright nonsense: "When I say 'I am in pain', I do not point to a person who is in pain, since . . . I have no idea *who* is. I don't name any person. Just as I don't name anyone when I *groan* with pain" (§404). An inarticulate groan is not composed of parts of speech--for instance, pronouns and other referring expressions. Thus it is plainly unintelligible to say that in groaning I name or refer to myself.

How is apparently referential talk of "my pains" analogous? I believe that the phenomena of misnaming and faulty reference offer a clue. Suppose a racketeer is browbeaten by the authorities. To avoid prosecution, he agrees to name his cohorts, and officials on their payoff list. He might make errors, and either deliberately or unwittingly denounce some people who are actually not affiliated with his organization, or bribed by it. This illustrates how ordinary reference can go awry. I think Wittgenstein would use this case to inquire whether mistakes of this or any other type can occur when we discuss our pains, or say "I am in pain." For instance, could the speaker be right that pain is present, but incorrectly designate himself as its owner when it actually belongs to someone else? We seem to be speaking nonsense again. But some mind-philosophers will blithely reformulate their doctrine.

7. <u>Theories of private reference and private language</u>. If we are going to pursue this turn in the debate over what it is to have mental contents, we must temporarily withdraw our objection against perceptual terminology. Our principal target now will be a doctrine I call "epistemological solipsism". Its main tenet is that when you truthfully report your aches, emotions, desires, and so on, you are using terms such as 'ache' to stamp mental items that are somehow accessible to you alone. I cannot get at what you call an ache, and so on this view I cannot possibly know anything of its nature. I cannot be at all sure that you have any mental contents at all. Possibly each of us refers to something radically different, or to nothing at all, when we utter the word 'ache'.

Wittgenstein dramatizes epistemological solipsism by supposing he records

> the recurrence of a certain sensation . . . I associate it with the sign 'E' and write this sign in a calendar for every day on which I have the sensation . . . I write the sign down, and at the same time I concentrate my attention on the sensation--and . . . impress on myself the connexion between the sign and the sensation . . . I remember the connexion <u>right</u> in the future (1953, §258).

How cogent is this scenario? The everyday physical objects and events on which we "concentrate [our] attention" either remain stable or else undergo changes while we are keeping tabs on them. If one observer fails to detect alterations, another may spot them. But only I can ever focus on my E-sensations. So it appears to make little sense if we draw our usual distinction here--between Es that <u>are</u> steady, and those that seem to be steady, in my judgment, though they really change. For the same reason, it sounds dubious to say that I only imagine that E altered. We cannot meaningfully describe the objects of private reference in the terms that comfortably fit the ordinary things we refer to. Hence it is unclear what inner reference is all about. Wittgenstein seems to be hinting at this kind of camouflaged nonsense when he urges us to "get rid of the idea of the private object in this way: assume that it constantly changes, but that you do not notice the change because your memory constantly deceives you" (p. 207). We can also assume that numerically different though qualitatively indistinguishable private objects constantly replace the one you called 'E', but that you are not attentive enough to detect these substitutions. In the case of standard items that we refer to, you can investigate whether they undergo alterations, and whether they have been replaced by a clever duplicate. Inquiries of this type appear not to be meaningful vis-à-vis objects of private reference. Consequently, insofar as the epistemological solipsist argues that we know nothing of other people's mental life because we lack access to whatever they have baptized 'E', his position is threatened. Of course he can revise his doctrine; but Wittgenstein has back-up arguments to reveal nonsense in the most plausible variant of epistemological solipsism.

8. <u>Do we follow private rules of reference?</u> I believe privacy theorists will want to refine their idea that when I mentally paste the label 'E' onto "a certain sensation", this guarantees that I shall "remember the connexion <u>right</u> in the future". Probably they will translate their doctrine into 'rule' terminology, and say, "I make it a rule for myself that I shall henceforth reserve the sign 'E' for sensations like this one."

Nonsense may be lurking just below the surface here. My ordinary rule-governed behavior is often faulty without my realizing it. However, we cannot meaningfully speak of my "unnoticed deviation from my E-rule". I might sometimes change my mind about whether I should rank a current or bygone sensation as an E. But in these circumstances, there could be no reason either for or against saying that my latest opinion is more--or less--in harmony with my E-rule than was my earlier opinion. Hence Wittgenstein declares that "in the present case I have no criterion of correctness . . . [W]hatever is going to seem right to me is right. And that only means that here we can't talk of 'right'." Our allegedly private rules for naming mental contents are only "impressions of rules" (1953, §§258 f.)--which are not genuine rules any more than a re-enactment of a famous murder trial is itself a murder trial, famous or otherwise. Epistemological solipsists have not made sense of their claim that we follow private rules of reference.

Surprisingly many post-Wittgensteinian philosophers of mind have rejected this argument from nonsense. For example, A. J. Ayer imagines a Robinson Crusoe who has lived entirely alone since birth on his island. Crusoe has made up "words to describe the flora and fauna", along with various 'E'-like "words to describe his sensations". Ayer is convinced that Crusoe may refer incorrectly as well as correctly with both sets of expressions. All that matters for Ayer is Crusoe's

> remembering what objects [his words] are meant to stand for . . . Undoubtedly, he may make mistakes. He may think that a bird which he sees flying past is a bird of the same type as one which he had previously named, when in fact it is of a sufficiently different [type] for him to have given it a different name if he had observed it more closely. Similarly, he may think that a sensation is the same as others which he has identified, when in fact, in the relevant aspects [sic], it is not . . . In the case of the bird, there is a slightly greater chance of his detecting his mistake since the identical bird may reappear: but even so he has to rely on his memory . . . that it is the identical bird. In the case of the sensation, he has only his memory as a means of deciding whether his identification is correct or not (1954, p. 45).

How plausible is Ayer's analogy between naming or misnaming birds, and classifying or misclassifying one's mental contents? Naturally I will continue to suppress my earlier objections against perceptual terminology here. So I will not complain that we utterly lack inner equivalents of 'seeing a bird fly past', 'observing it more closely', and 'subsequently taking another look at the same individual fowl'. Leaving that to one side, I wonder if Ayer has any backing for his anti-Wittgensteinian thesis that Crusoe "may make mistakes" in chronicling his itches, chills, and hunger-pangs. All I come across is the general--and apparently question-begging--statement that Crusoe "may think that a sensation is the same as others . . . when in fact . . . it is not". Ayer neglects to reveal what it might be like for such a mixup to occur.

On the other hand, a few trifling modifications of the background story make indisputable sense of the claim that Crusoe has placed a bird in the wrong pigeonhole. For instance, a pelican glides overhead, but Crusoe believes and writes that it is a seagull. Now a secret onlooker might have registered Crusoe's breach of his taxonomic rule. There could be photographic proof, acceptable even to Crusoe, that he has misdescribed the bird. Furthermore, witnesses and evidence would provide essential support for any claims he makes regarding the accuracy of his present description, and for his confidence that he remembers the features of those birds that he has previously classified as pelicans and seagulls. In the context of Crudoe's amateur ornithology, we can say what we mean by 'misidentifying' and 'correctly identifying', 'misremembering' and 'correctly recalling'.

The situation alters radically when we turn back to Crusoe's sensations. What could possibly confirm, and in particular what unfavorable testimony, counterevidence, and so on might override, Crusoe's description of his present inner goings-on, or his alleged "memory" of sensations that he has assigned to the E-basket? When we speculate whether "his identification is correct" and his recall of his past sensations is trustworthy, "correct" and "trustworthy" do not stand opposed to any defects. However confident he is in his latest judgments, there is no proof that Crusoe's earlier, contrary beliefs about the same sensations were erroneous. Ayer has not distinguished between ways of describing sensations that "seem right" or wrong to Crusoe, and ways that are in fact right or wrong. So far, then, we are still unable to give a cogent interpretation of epistemological solipsism--particularly of the doctrine that each person follows his (or her) private rules of reference in cataloguing his sensations. The relationship between people and the supposed contents of their mind remains a mystery.

We should not dismiss the private-rule theory, however, without reviewing a somewhat different elaboration of it by H.-N. Castañeda. His diary-keeper is Privatus, inventor of a one-man language, Privatish. Unfortunately, in fleshing out his example, Castañeda seems to take for granted most of the assumptions that Wittgenstein found intolerably puzzling. For instance, Castañeda simply announces that "ordinary pains and after-images are private in [two] senses": (i) their "existence is entailed by the speaker's belief" that they exist; and (ii) their "possession of some characteristic $\underline{A}$ is . . . [similarly] determinable by the speaker $\overline{a}$lone" (1964, pp. 92, 90). In short, whatever any person believes about his or her sensations will be decisive. As for Privatus, and I suppose the rest of us, Castañeda asserts that the lucky man is blessed with "enough private objects which manifest sufficient regularities" (p. 101). Better yet, Privatus "can avail himself of the [private] objects of his experience" (p. 103)--that is, he can "resort to" them (p. 99). Finally, Castañeda says we may

> assume . . . that Privatus is for the most part consistent in his use of Privatish, that his use of signs possesses "enough regularity", and that he holds certain true beliefs about his private objects, which beliefs are the counterparts of the judgments agreed on in the case of a public language (p. 98).

Castañeda does not explain how we "avail" ourselves of, or "resort to", the items that fill our inner sanctum. But he implicitly models these operations on our sensory dealings with the world around us. He thinks material objects are "known by perception, pains . . . by feeling, or introspection" (p. 94). Privatus, for his part, "apprehends" both "private and public" items (p. 99).

We should be especially concerned with Privatus's "true beliefs about his private objects". From what does Castañeda distinguish them? Does he provide room for genuinely mistaken beliefs "about . . . private objects", for example? Castañeda sounds reassuring. He insists that Privatus has "some false beliefs . . . about certain facts (or propositions) formulable in the purely private part of Privatish" (p. 103). So we look forward to clarification of statements such as Ayer's to the effect that Crusoe "may think that a sensation is the same as others . . . when in fact . . . it is not".

Interestingly enough, Castañeda diverges from Ayer on this point, and denies the possibility of such mistakes. Castañeda says, "'I believed falsely at [time] t that I was in pain at t' . . . expresses a conceptual contradiction" (p. 93). For Castañeda, it is "logically true" that "if X feels a pain Y at t, and at t he is capable of thinking that he has a pain at t, and is attending to . . . his mental goings-on . . . then at t X knows that he has Y" (p. 92). Accordingly, Privatus's "false beliefs" will not be on a par with his "true beliefs about his private objects". Castañeda's logic does not allow any person X to believe erroneously that he "has" private object Y. Therefore Privatus's "false beliefs" will have to be about other "facts" or "propositions" than what private objects he is currently apprehending.

With some disappointment we learn from Castañeda that Privatus can make "linguistic errors"--notably slips of the tongue--only when he reports his mental state. Castañeda has a public-language analogue of such a mistake: an English person who refers to "'that red . . . I mean, brown chair'"--a case where mis-speaking is followed by "linguistic self-correction" (p. 99). I gather that Privatus would err similarly if he believed that his current sensation is an E, but while nonchalantly describing it, he uttered the word 'D' instead of 'E'.

Have we satisfactorily pinned down Privatus's "false beliefs . . . about certain facts (or propositions) formulable in the purely private part" of his language? Take the English speaker first: if he does not correct himself, then perhaps he falsely believes he said what he intended to say; of course if he corrects himself, he has no false belief at all in the circumstances. The same for Privatus: he may erroneously believe that he has called his sensation an 'E'.

None of this sounds germane to Wittgenstein's argument that it is unintelligible to talk of someone following private rules of reference. Wittgenstein challenged the defender of private rules to elaborate his notion that each of us correctly labels our mental contents, thereby displaying our accurate memory that we have referred to previous contents of this sort as Es. It seemed incumbent upon the private-rule theorist to tell us what he means by success-terms such as 'correct' and 'accurate'. Specifically, what corresponding failures does he think we avoid when our sensation-reports are correct and our memories accurate? Plainly Wittgenstein is inquiring about possible cognitive failures, such as my falsely believing that my sensation is vertigo, though it is really a cramp--or mistakenly recalling that discomfort of this type is what I have regularly labeled 'vertigo'. But Castañeda has not even attempted to set forth cases of people misclassifying or misremembering their sensations. Instead he has depicted a somewhat trivial non-cognitive breakdown: Privatus utters a different word from the one he intended. He may or may not also fail to notice his linguistic lapse. We are no closer to making sense of the baffling relationship between people and the mental contents they are said to "have". The initially appealing doctrine that I bestow names on the items that drift past my consciousness, and afterwards conform to my naming rules, has brought no illumination. Nevertheless epistemological solipsists and others will try one last variant of it.

9. Do you, and you alone, simply know what your sensations are? For decades philosophers of mind have lamented that we are barred from knowing another person's toothache or anger--at least in the peculiar way that he knows it. When John Wisdom repeatedly deployed this formula in his highly imaginative writings on the 'other minds' problem, Austin took him to task. Austin pointed out that "'knowing his sensations' . . . presumably means . . . 'knowing what he is [feeling]'". Austin then argued that it is "a grammatical mistake" to interpret this "what" as if it were a "relative" phrase; actually, "'what' . . . in 'know what you feel' is an interrogative . . . 'I know what he is feeling' is [sic] not 'There is an x which both I know and he is feeling' but 'I know the answer to the question "What is he feeling?"'" (1946, p. 143). Ryle's warning is even blunter: we cannot intelligibly "speak of knowing, or not knowing, this clap of thunder or that twinge of pain", since "these are accusatives of the wrong types to follow the verb 'to know'" (1949, p. 161).

The grammar lesson appears to have sunk in. But many thinkers are disinclined to share Austin's and Ryle's caution with the phrase 'to know that'. Thus we constantly read about how each person knows, in some virtually foolproof manner, that he or she feels pain or whatever. There is some disagreement on whether people with the linguistic or cognitive capacity to describe their sensations could fail to know that they are undergoing pain. In Section 8 we saw that Ayer believed this could occur, while Castañeda strongly dissented. A more recent work by Ayer elaborates and refines his position. Ayer concedes to Wittgenstein "that we seldom, if ever . . . use such sentences as 'he knows that he is in pain' or 'I know that I am thinking about a philosophical problem' . . . [P]refixing . . . 'I know that' or 'he knows that' makes . . . otherwise . . . respectable sentences appear somewhat ridiculous" (1959, p. 59). But Ayer rejects the Wittgensteinian diagnosis "that the claim to knowledge is inapplicable in these cases"; instead he considers it "superfluous", for if someone "is in pain we take it for granted that he knows it" (p. 60). Unlike Castañeda, however, Ayer is reluctant to explain our supposed self-knowledge in perceptual terms. What then does it amount to? Ayer's

> answer . . . is that knowing what one's thoughts and feelings are, as distinct from merely having them . . . consist[s] in being able to give a true report of them . . . if required . . . For the claim to knowledge to be justified it is sufficient that [the report] should be true. And this helps us to explain why expressions like 'I know that I am in pain' . . . sound so odd . . . It is . . . that if someone <u>says</u> truly that he is in pain . . . it follows that he knows it.
>
> . . . Our knowledge of our thoughts and feelings accrues to us automatically in the sense that having them puts us in a position and gives us the authority to report them. All that is then required is that the reports be true (pp. 63 f.).

Notice that Ayer's formula does not imply the truth of every sincere report of one's sensations. His doctrine is rather that <u>if</u> the report is true, then one knows it is. In the earlier essay, we recall, he declared that Crusoe "may think that a sensation is the same as others which he has identified, when . . . it is not". But now he is unsure. How could a "statement [that] refers to our present thoughts or feelings" turn out false, he asks; "What would such a situation be like?" Still he refuses "to say dogmatically that it is impossible" (pp. 70 f.). Actually he must suppose that we can erroneously report "our present

19

thoughts and feelings"; otherwise he will have to explain what he contrasts with knowing--which for him is truly reporting--our thoughts and feelings.

More on that problem shortly. At the moment I prefer to inquire why Ayer assumes that a true report suffices for knowledge in this case. His rationale reads,

> If . . . one were challenged to give a list of things that one knew, I think it would be quite proper to give such replies as 'I know that I am thinking about a philosophical problem', or . . . 'I know that I am in pain' . . . A proof that they are legitimate examples [of knowledge] is that the information [that] they convey can be made the subject of a lie . . . But to lie is . . . to make a statement that one knows to be false; and this implies denying what one knows to be true (p. 60).

The 'challenge' argument is of course question-begging. The 'lie' gambit depends on a dubious premise: that when you lie you must know, rather than correctly believe, the statement you make is untrue. Knowledge sounds like too strong a requirement for lying. And Ayer seems to have no other reasons for his outlook.

Perhaps other theorists fill this gap. Bruce Aune, like Castañeda, supposes it is logically true that if you have the linguistic or cognitive wherewithal to delineate your sensations, and you are introspectively alert, then you will know what sensations are afflicting you. In fact, Aune holds that "a condition of having the concept of pain is that one can, with perfect confidence, say or think 'I'm in pain' and be right"--which for Aune is the same as knowing one is on pain (1961, pp. 56 f.). As to what opposites we rule out when we credit someone with this knowledge, Aune says,

> The contradictory of "He knows that p" is . . . "He doesn't know, or is ignorant of the fact, that p". Now . . . a sufficient condition of being ignorant of a given fact is that one lack the conceptual resources necessary for the description . . . of that fact . . . [A] man who lacks the concept of jealousy . . . when he is jealous . . .

> doesn't know that he is, [and thus] it is
> <u>meaningful</u> (though not true) to say that he
> <u>does</u> know . . .
>
> . . . It is only a <u>contingent</u> fact about
> a person that he has [the] concept [of pain]
> . . . Of course, when it is well known
> that a person has this concept, it is gene-
> rally pointless to <u>say</u> that he knows he is
> in pain, but . . . [that] comes from saying
> something . . . too obviously true . . .
> [C]ircumstances can always be dreamed up in
> which <u>any</u> <u>assertion</u> <u>whatever</u> is utterly
> pointless (e.g., saying "It is raining" to
> someone . . . trapped in a downpour) (p. 58;
> see Aune's 1967, pp. 86-100).

With considerably less ado over contrasts and logical truths, John Searle hands down the same verdict. Searle proclaims, "It's obviously true that when I have a pain, I know that I have it . . . and it is odd to announce such things under normal circumstances . . . because they are too obvious" (1969, p. 141). According to Searle, "only if the situation is aberrant . . . is it appropriate to <u>say</u> these things" (p. 143). Searle is equally brisk with "negations and opposites", such as "He does not know whether he has a pain": Searle finds "nothing nonsensical about them"; in standard conditions "they are just false"--which makes the corresponding knowledge-claim true (p. 145).

Have Aune and Searle done better than Ayer and Castañeda in clarifying the doctrine that you know what your sensations are? I wonder if any of them appreciate the Wittgensteinian and Rylean charges of incoherence. Forget Aune's and Ayer's equation of correct reporting with knowing of one's sensation. Do not worry if Aune and Searle appear to take for granted what they should demonstrate--<u>viz</u>., how "obviously true" it is that when you are <u>in</u> pain you know you are. My objections are more comprehensive. I believe these commentators may not realize that many different obscurities about having and cognizing sensations have to be confronted.

To begin with, Ayer, Castañeda, Aune, Searle, and others talk as if they need only set forth <u>one</u> alternative to knowledge of our own sensations. Ayer nominated Crusoe's "mistakes". Castañeda imagined that

Privatus was plagued by slips of the tongue. Aune's protagonist lacked "conceptual resources". But Wittgenstein's intelligibility requirement is much broader. He suggests that often "'I know . . .' may mean 'I do not doubt'"; and he quickly adds, "One says 'I know' where one can also say 'I believe' or 'I suspect'; where one can find out" (1953, p. 221). He asks rhetorically, "Can one say: 'Where there is no doubt there is no knowledge either'?" (1969, §121). He connects both doubting and knowing with reasons. He suggests that we "need grounds for doubt", and that "one says 'I know' when one is ready to give compelling grounds"; moreover, if a person's "grounds . . . are no surer than his assertion, then he cannot say that he knows" (§§122, 243).

At least Aune bothers to take issue with the 'finding out' and 'doubt' requirements. Unfortunately he seems to think Wittgensteinians are claiming that to feel a sensation is to be aware of the sensation, and that such awareness is "inseparable" from finding out that one has the sensation. Aune quite rightly distinguishes between "what one is allegedly aware of"—backache, for example—and "what one might find out, namely the truth of some proposition". Having made this distinction, Aune wonders, "Why should the two be inseparable? Why should it be impossible to feel pain and yet not know, and so later come to find out, that pain is what one feels?" (1967, p. 94). He leaves it on this abstract level, perhaps missing Wittgenstein's point: what would 'finding out' look like in this sort of case? Are there methods of investigation, technical equipment, clues, false leads? Could you try but fail to learn whether or not you are in agony? The only sort of finding out that Aune allows is when a conceptually impoverished sufferer manages by some miracle to acquire the idea of pain, thereby discovering the truth "that pain is what [he] feels". This is not enough—it does not span the range of familiar cases where the explorer or inquirer already can specify what he is attempting to establish, and has methods of finding out.

Aune offers a counter-example to the doctrine "that knowing implies the possibility of doubt" instead of knowledge. Aune imagines a person who

> did not know that one plus one equals two, [and thus] probably . . . did not know what addition is, or . . . what is meant by

> 'one', 'two', or 'equals' . . . [The] person could not possibly doubt whether one plus one equals two, since to doubt this would require the exercise of these primitive arithmetical concepts. If it were true, however, that knowing implies the possibility of doubt, we would then have to conclude that "One plus one equals two" states something that could not . . . be known—which is absurd, considering the normal usage of the word "know" (pp. 95 f.).

Clearly the Wittgensteinian answer would be that it is not at all obviously meaningful to say we know that one plus one equals two. What would it be like <u>not</u> to know this, while understanding the arithmetical formula—or to prove it, or merely suspect that one plus one equals two, or have a stubborn but so far unfounded hunch . . .? So Aune's parallel case does not settle the question whether we can intelligibly speak of knowing what our mental state is. Moreover, Wittgenstein himself gives non-mentalistic cases which sound as bizarre as the claim to have knowledge of one's sensations. Here are some of his best: When your hand is in normal, healthy condition, and your view of it is unimpeded, you declare, "I know this is a hand". "I guess", "I'm pretty sure", and "I wonder if . . ." would be no less baffling. Again, suppose you say you are quite certain—or have some fairly convincing evidence—that your name is such-and-such, that you have resided at . . . for many years, or that the color plainly visible before you is called 'red' in your native language. Finally, a more philosophical example: You say you know that there is a material world—or anyway it seems to you as if physical objects exist, but perhaps you are deluded (1969, §§32, 461, 491, 515, 527, 624, 35). Thus it is not only when we announce our sensations that 'know' and other terms normally linked with 'know' seem out of place. And mere counter-assertions, such as Searle's claim, "It's . . . obvious that I do not remember [i.e., know] my own name" (1969, p. 141), are insufficient to allay our Wittgensteinian misgivings.

    10. <u>Residues of almost pure nonsense</u>. I have mainly dealt with attempts to rehabilitate or at least defensively fortify the general theory of mind which Ryle, Wittgenstein, and their allies have bombarded. As we noted earlier, all factions agree that human beings are 'mindful'—that they sometimes suffer, think,

rejoice, worry, and decide on a course of action. The dispute is over how we should analyze or depict these familiar goings-on. Wittgenstein's and Ryle's comparatively novel contention is that some of the most ingenious and appealing theories will turn out to be unintelligible, hence neither true nor even false. I illustrated their hunch with a less provocative case. Then, beginning in Section 4 of this chapter, I canvassed an array of doctrines which purport to explain our mental life in terms of our having a mind, and also having the events or quasi-objects that seem to waltz through our mind. It sounded initially plausible, for instance, to model 'having a mind' on the unmysterious authority relationship between a social group and its leader--say, a tribe and its chieftain. But undeniable nonsense emerged as soon as we introduced other socio-political terms, and started asking for the kind of details that you would expect if our having a mind is at all like a tribe's having a ruler. There should be a plain answer to such questions as 'How did this individual get to be chief?'; yet any reply you make to counterpart queries about someone's mind will sound deranged.

    The situation is no less confusing with various updated theories of what it is to have aches, thoughts, moods, cravings, or intentions. Whenever we requested a few rudimentary specifics, along the very lines suggested by the terminology of a standard doctrine, we encountered arbitrariness or inexcusable vagueness. You can truly, and thus meaningfully, say a great variety of things when you deal with ordinary circumstances involving ownership, perception, reference, linguistic rule-following, or knowledge. Not so if you dare question theorists who proclaim one or another doctrine associated with epistemological solipsism: 'This sensation is exclusively <u>mine</u>--no one else can possibly have it'; 'Another person cannot <u>feel</u> my earache'; 'You cannot be sure what I <u>refer to</u> as "dizziness"'; 'I remember to abide by my <u>rule</u>, and consistently label sensations of just <u>this</u> kind "nausea"'; and (from Castañeda, 1964, pp. 92 f.), "Nobody else knows . . . that $\underline{X}$ has [pain] $\underline{Y}$ at [time] $\underline{t}$, <u>in the same way</u> that $\underline{X}$ knows that he has $\underline{Y}$ at $\underline{t}$". Suppose you inquire further about this "way" of acquiring knowledge of one's own sensations. Can you skip such a procedure, as a dieter might omit to weigh himself one day. He has put on weight but does not know it. Why can't you have pain without knowing it? Does this "way" of knowing ever yield false verdicts, as other methods sometimes do? What you are asking is just how one gets this type of knowledge—a reasonable enough demand when less arcane forms of knowledge are at issue. But what are you told? "The . . . answer to 'How do you know [of your pain]? is . . . 'By having the pain' or 'By attending to [your] feelings'"; more generally: "One knows . . . of his own pains by merely having them" (Castañeda, 1964, pp. 94, 93). The reply is particularly unhelpful inasmuch as originally we hoped to explain having sensations in terms of knowing about them. At all events, the doctrine of 'knowing by having' leads nowhere.

Of course a die-hard believer in this or any of the other theories I poke fun at may take the easy way out. All he need say is this: The form of ownership, perception, reference, rule-following, knowledge—or 'having'—that he is concerned with bears no resemblance to gross, everyday ownership, perception, and so on; the form he has discovered is special, sui generis; and therefore we should not expect to discuss meaningfully this unique type of ownership or whatever in terms appropriate for its garden-variety counterparts. So be it. However, a fairly serious disadvantage of this move is that we now cannot pretend to have any inkling what the mind-theorist wants us to believe. All we rustics have to go on is our understanding of those everyday kinds of ownership, perception, and the like which we have run into. If we are forbidden to say any of the very different things appropriate to these phenomena, the mind-doctrines lose meaning. Until their champions reformulate them, in terminology that connects with the rest of our language, we should not fritter away time quarreling over them. Nevertheless we should acknowledge the profound appeal of such theories of mind. Wittgenstein might say that they are "statements one would like to make here, but cannot make significantly" (1969, §76). But as long as we cannot elucidate them, or construct other nonsense-free analyses of what it is to have a mental life, I believe we should content ourselves with the provisionally brute fact that human beings suffer, think, rejoice, rage, plan their actions, and so forth.

In the next chapters, I shall continue to assess what seem to me quite fascinating views of mind, beginning with the widely popular and hotly disputed claims that minds, and particularly mental goings-on, must be non-physical. Normally this claim is an ingredient of epistemological solipsism or at least

generally Cartesian theories. But it is not shown to
be unintelligible by the Wittgensteinian and Rylean
criticisms we have made against those doctrines.

CHAPTER TWO

COULD MENTAL STATES BE NON-PHYSICAL?

Scientists and philosophers have wondered for centuries: How could a mere flesh-and-blood man or woman, a physical creature, be capable of sensation, of thinking, of deciding what to do? Plato, Descartes, and their many followers up to the present day are of course sure that we are equipped with an incorporeal mind, which is the locus for some or all of these highjinks. Sir Karl Popper and the neurologist Sir John Eccles in their 1977 book defend a straightforwardly dualistic account of interaction between our brain and our "self-conscious mind". Other contemporaries reach the same conclusion. For reasons not unlike Descartes', Jerome Shaffer contends that a person is "a non-physical entity" which is "a subject of mental events"; in fact Shaffer believes that "to talk of a body's having mental events is self-contradictory" (1966, pp. 59-63).

Psychological goings-on do seem radically different in kind from anything bodily--even from those neural processes we know to be intimately associated with conscious experience. The physiologist Sir Charles Sherrington writes of

> mental events which seem to lie beyond any physiology of the brain . . . A pencil of light from the sun enters the eye and is focused . . . on the retina. It gives rise to a change which . . . travels to the nerve-layer at the top of the brain. The whole chain of these events . . . is physical. Each step is an electrical reaction. But now there succeeds a change wholly unlike any which led up to it, and wholly inexplicable by us. A visual scene presents itself to the mind: I *see* the dome of the sky and the sun in it, and a hundred other things (1950, p. 3).

The leading experimentalist in parapsychology has taken a yet bolder position. J. B. Rhine believed that his careful studies of telepathy, clairvoyance, precognition, and psychokinesis "require the rejection of the conception of man as a wholly physical system"; Rhine said "physical explanation" of these baffling phenomena "seems to be clearly excluded", and we must countenance "properties and operations that are part of the personal living system although they are non-physical in . . . character" (1960, pp. 76 ff.).

Legions of materialistically inclined thinkers disagree that mental happenings of any sort are incorporeal. Yet since Greek times the partisans of matter have shown little curiosity about what Platonists and Cartesians, as well as scientific fellow-travelers such as Sherrington, Rhine, and Eccles, could mean when they characterize the mental as non-physical. An example is U. T. Place, whose lucid restatement of the materialistic view is most often debated today. Place says the alternative to materialism is "a dualistic position in which sensations and mental images form a separate category of processes over and above the physical . . . processes with which they are . . . correlated" (1956, p. 278). His comrade in arms, J. J. C. Smart, frankly declares, "I am concerned to deny that in the world there are non-physical entities" (1963, p. 652). David Armstrong, the most thorough-going proponent of a materialistic psychology, remarks that whether or not "disembodied existence is empirically possible . . . [it] seems to be a perfectly intelligible supposition . . . [and] therefore . . . it is a criticism of any theory of mind if it is unable to allow the logical possibility of disembodied existence" (1968, p. 19). Jenny Teichman reasons along similar lines. She contends that "a Materialist must accept . . . a distinction . . . between that which is material and that which is non-material . . . [He] can presumably <u>understand</u> such a statement as 'The mind is not a material thing' . . . [Otherwise] how would he be able to deny it, and argue against it?" (1974, p. 7). Teichman goes on to assert, "The world is full of . . . ordinary non-material things"; she says rainbows, holes, surfaces, corners, facial expressions, magnetism, electricity, "beams of light, and the sky, are all non-material" (p. 8). But she concedes that this is hardly the "sort of immateriality" dualists attribute to mind.

What "sort of immateriality" are dualists concerned with? The question has been virtually ignored. In some of his early work, the "eliminative" materialist Richard Rorty seems unaware of any difficulties. He announces that our term "'immaterial' gets its sense from its connection with 'mental'"; Rorty then explains that the dualistic notion of "'immaterial substance' would never have become current if Descartes had not been able to use <u>cogitationes</u> as an illustration of what he intended" by 'immaterial' (1970, p. 402). A similarly unhesitant claim has been made more recently by Yuval Lurie; he assures us that

> a notable use of the term 'inner' . . . is . . . to describe certain (mental) states and [to set] them apart from physical states. Sometimes . . . we substitute . . . 'inner' for 'mental' . . . for example [when we] say of a person that he is in a state of <u>inner</u> conflict . . . The context makes it quite clear that 'inner' <u>means</u> 'non-physical' . . . [M]ental states that are said [in this use] to be 'inner' are thereby said to be . . . non-physical . . . By describing the state . . . as 'inner conflict' we . . . see to it that no mistake in meaning occurs: [we indicate] that we do not . . . refer to a physical sort of conflict (1979, pp. 242 f.).

Subsequently Lurie adds, "It is a contradiction in terms to say that someone is in a state of physical inner exhaustion. For 'inner exhaustion' means a mental, non-physical exhaustion" (p. 245). What interests me here is Lurie's assumption that sometimes 'inner' means 'mental', and that on those occasions 'inner' is equivalent to 'non-physical'. This entails that 'mental' is sometimes a synonym for 'non-physical'. Rorty's thesis appears to be more general: that it is <u>always</u> "part of the sense of 'mental' that being mental is incompatible with being physical" (1970, p. 402). More of that later. I should mention one philosopher who displays some curiosity about what dualists are saying. Alan Sussman's worries over immateriality derive from concern with scientific method. He wonders, "Could psychology, and allied fields, ever need to posit nonmaterial entities in order to explain human behavior? What kind of evidence could lead to such a conclusion? . . . [M]ore broadly . . .: could science vindicate dualism? How?" (1981, p. 96). Ultimately Sussman concludes that

> our notions of explanation are drawn in physical terms. To make nonmatter explanatory, we would probably turn it into something that may as well be matter . . .

> . . . Methods of inquiry that rest on the assumption of materialism cannot be expected to vindicate dualism . . .
>
> . . . Science as we know it cannot vindicate dualism and . . . we have no idea of what could or what it would mean to do so (pp. 110 f.).

I'll have to take Sussman's word on science and whether we can imagine its practitioners agreeing "to posit nonmaterial entities in order to explain" our capers. The question that I think Sussman, and especially the others, neglect is not so much what it could mean for accredited researchers to <u>decide</u> that mental events are incorporeal. I believe we should ask the logically prior question: What would the official psychologists be deciding is the case? In short: What would it be like if episodes or states of pain and thinking were non-physical? Sussman hints that this might well be worth asking. Everyone else gives the impression of understanding clearly enough what 'non-physical' and its cognates mean in the dualism-materialism fracas.

My hunch is that all these otherwise astute reasoners may be victims of a grammatical illusion which is encouraged by our procedures in English and consanguineous languages for modifying adjectives, adverbs, and nouns. Our rules of syntax allow us to combine negative prefixes--'non-', 'un-', 'in-', 'im-', and for present purposes irrelevant ones such as 'ir-', 'mis-', 'dis-', and 'de-' --with a vast range of expressions. Custom and euphony set further, and I suppose quite arbitrary, limits on which prefixes we may attach to a given term. 'Imphysical' would be ill-formed, and 'uncorporeal' sounds slightly odd to me. But the compound expressions that intrigue me-- 'immaterial', 'non-physical', and their synonyms-- violate no such restrictions of phonetics or grammar; they belong to the vocabulary of English.

This may be what fosters the illusion I referred to. Generally, the unprefixed terms of our vocabulary are meaningful, as well as grammatically and phonetically acceptable. It is also generally the case that when negative prefixing of these terms is allowed, the modified terms we get are meaningful too. An example, which I shall supplement in good time with countless others, is that it makes sense to describe furniture as painted--and also as unpainted.

Well, then, are the category terms 'physical', 'material', 'corporeal', and 'bodily' meaningful? Surprisingly, there is heated disagreement on how these terms may be defined, if at all (see Sussman, 1981, for some difficulties). But we seem to have a number of rough-and-ready criteria of corporeality. For instance, physical objects and events occupy space; no more than one of a given type can entirely fill a region of space at the same moment; they are publicly observable, and measurable; they may enter into causal relations, and in principle we should be able to discover specifically how one affects another. More important than homespun characterizations of this sort, we can provide uncontroversial examples which even die-hard dualists will accept. Trees and rocks are material objects; forest-fires and rock-slides are physical events. When we put forward such illustrations, we leave it altogether open whether a person, a mind, or an episode of rejoicing is physical or not.

Since we can make clear what we understand by 'physical', aren't we entitled to assume that we understand 'non-physical' and its equivalents too? Specifically, don't they mean the opposite of 'physical'? Can't we just say that an object or event is non-physical if it is the way things are that happen <u>not</u> to be physical? I wonder. 'Non-physical' has the same grammatical form as other negatively prefixed terms that are meaningful, and it is legitimately derived from a meaningful adjective. But this hardly suffices to prove that we understand what 'non-physical' means. As for the alleged 'opposite' of 'physical', what is it? What characteristics does an object or an event have when it is not physical? At a minimum, dualists and those materialists who say dualism is an "alternative"--who "deny that . . . there are non-physical entities", "allow the logical possibility of disembodied existence", and "<u>understand such a statement as 'The mind is not a material thing'</u>" --should be able to furnish us examples of the "sort of immateriality" they are discussing. However, these examples should not pre-determine the outcome of debate between theorists who believe and theorists who doubt that mental goings-on are incorporeal. Therefore neither Descartes nor Rorty should be permitted "to use <u>cogitationes</u> as an illustration of what [Descartes] intended" by 'non-physical'. A remark of Wittgenstein's may reinforce this latter point.

Having denied that thinking is "an incorporeal process which lends . . . sense" to overt speech, Wittgenstein muses, "How 'not an incorporeal process'? Am I acquainted with incorporeal processes, then, only thinking is not one of them?" (1953, §339). If the experts concur that only mental things are eligible for non-physical status--an opinion once defended by Rorty (1970, pp. 402, 412) and tentatively held by Sussman (1981, pp. 101 ff.)--then we should ask why this is so, or at least what it is about some particular mental item that earmarks it as incorporeal.

These demands are pretty moderate, and in fact we have no trouble meeting them if we turn to everyday terms with negative prefixes. Here are only a few random examples of adjectives modified by 'non-' and 'im-'. Non-prescription remedies are drugs that you are legally permitted to buy over the counter at a pharmacy. Aspirin is the most popular such medication. Non-profit corporations, such as the Public Broadcasting System, are set up to earn just enough money to meet their operating expenses and to fund new undertakings. Non-academic employment is any job except college-level teaching. University administrators, farm-hands, business executives, plumbers, social workers, and salespeople all have non-academic occupations. Non-alcoholic as well as alcoholic beverages are sold in most bars. Perrier water is becoming a fashionable non-alcoholic drink. For variety, an immobile object is something that stands still. Ordinary dwellings, as opposed to house trailers and mobile homes, are stock examples. An impious person is someone who mocks religion, lightheartedly breaking taboos and scoffing at dogma. An impartial hearing, before a court or some other forum, is a hearing that is neutral between the contending parties. It gives each side a full opportunity to speak, and treats each one equally. You display impatience if you start grumbling because you must wait--for example, to get a table at a busy restaurant. We could multiply illustrations: non-aligned nations, non-aggression treaties, non-communist governments, non-partisan editorials, non-discriminatory hiring policies, non-unionized industries, non-strikers, non-negotiable demands, non-denominational schools, non-smokers, non-taxable income, non-ferrous metals, non-fat milk, non-toxic crayons; immeasurable distances, impassable mountain ranges, impenetrable armor plating, immodest behavior, imprudent spending, implausible alibis.

This hodge-podge of paradigms should be enough to remind us that there are plenty of meaningful English expressions with negative prefixes. It should also highlight a peculiarity of 'non-physical' and its equivalents. For every case I gave, we could put together a reasonably clear general definition, in positive terms, or at least produce down-to-earth, easily understood specimens of what we mean by 'non-prescription', 'immobile', and their clan. I take it for granted that we can reach a consensus on a vast array of terms as to their positive character. As for the dualistic view, we are only trying to figure out what its adherents are asserting. For this purpose, we hardly need a universal litmus test that will establish the polarity of any relevant English term.

'Non-physical' and its gang stand out because they seem irreducibly negative. With my rustic examples, we <u>can</u> be slothful, of course, and call upon further negative terms. We can say that non-prescription remedies are drugs you may purchase <u>without</u> a doctor's written authorization, and that <u>immobile</u> objects are those that do <u>not</u> move. But we are never compelled to follow this lazy procedure. Instead of saying that a non-alcoholic refreshment contains <u>no</u> alcohol, we can list its ingredients: the minerals, flavoring, or sweetener it <u>does</u> contain. The situation is radically different when metaphysicians and psychologists attempt to explain the sense in which mental happenings are non-bodily. Genuinely positive information seems to elude us.

To document this complaint, I shall only review some of the best-known attempts of dualists. For instance, St. Augustine, following Plato's hints and anticipating Descartes, wrote that "the soul has [<u>no</u>] quantity and so to say, local extension . . . [B]ecause it is <u>not</u> a body . . . it <u>lacks</u> the space by which bodies are measured" (in Flew, 1964, p. 98; emphasis added). This account of immateriality as non-spatiality ought to compound our puzzlement. If a mind, and the episodes taking place 'in' it, are of no size, occupy no volume of space, and presumably have no spatial position, then what do they do? What alternatives are there to having an address--to hanging out somewhere in the physical universe, filling up a small portion of the cosmos? We should be equally perplexed by Descartes' logically subsidiary contention that minds and mental occurrences are not divisible. So be it. But if we cannot segment them into spatial parts, what can we do with them? What other options are left for non-physical things?

   I would raise similar objections, alongside the complaints of nonsense that I made in Sections 4 through 10 of Chapter One, if you characterized the immaterial mind and its denizens as observable by you alone--which sounds like '<u>not</u> publicly observable'. If you insisted that you <u>were</u> furnishing a positive account of the mental, I would ask what sort of private scrutiny you were alluding to. Do you feel your aches in the way you feel the keys in your back pocket --with your fingertips? You surely don't hear, smell, taste, or see your aches! The supposedly incorporeal episodes of thinking, planning, or wishing are even more of a mystery: no standard type of sensory observation is even a candidate for the job of putting you in exclusive contact with these occurrences. What would it mean to say you keep tabs on your thinking by watching it or overhearing it? So this special form of self-observation not only turns out to be inexplicably different from the public gawking and snooping we are familiar with, but also in some unspecified manner makes no use of our sensory apparatus.

   More problems spring up if you describe a mind and especially the incorporeal happenings in it as <u>known</u> exclusively and infallibly to its owner. What <u>sort</u> of knowledge, awareness, or consciousness is this? We just agreed that dualists have furnished us too few positive details regarding the way each individual supposedly observes his or her aches and thoughts. Consequently we are in no position to assume that this special knowledge is attained through any observational procedure. How then does a person acquire knowledge of non-physical items and events within himself or herself? If you try to avoid difficulty by labeling this knowledge 'direct' or 'immediate', I wager that these positive-sounding portrayals ultimately turn out to be stand-ins for 'non-inferential'. If so, my question will be, How <u>do</u> you gain this kind of knowledge, if not by some accredited form of reasoning? The champion of immateriality will probably declare that his knowledge of his discomforts and decisions is <u>not</u> based upon evidence or anything else: that he does <u>not</u> have to back up his introspective reports with documentation or eyewitness and expert testimony, nor does he follow any method of 'finding out' what his incorporeal states are. Epistemological accounts of the non-physical, using the vocabulary of perception and cognition, seem only to substitute other negative terms for the ones that originally baffled us.

Do we progress any further if we specify that each person has 'privileged access' to, or 'necessarily private ownership' of, his non-physical states of mind? This ought to provoke new requests for particulars: What sort of 'access' is this? How do you 'get at' your immaterial sensations and thoughts? That is, how do you approach and claim ownership of such items? When we fail to elicit intelligible answers to that line of inquiry, I expect we will be told that 'privileged' and 'private' simply mean '<u>not</u> available to anyone else', and 'not transferable to, or capable of being shared with, others'. But how much does it enlighten us to hear that this is <u>unlike</u> all orthodox types of proprietorship? that it <u>is</u> unique because it involves no purchasing, stealing, confiscation, forfeiture, collectivization; no possibility of immaterial pains and thoughts being owned?

As a last resort, friends of incorporeality might suggest that each of us has a distinctive authority to describe our current aches, beliefs, desires, and similar non-physical states. Although this implies that <u>nobody else's</u> report of your mental condition overrides your sincere avowal, we can go beyond such a negative account. On the plus side, we can suggest an interesting parallelism between your first-person disclosure and the verdict of top-level referees or judges in sporting contests and legal proceedings. Your word has a similar type of finality.

Does this sufficiently elucidate what 'non-physical' and affiliated terms mean? I doubt it. For we have no reason to move from the premise that each of us has authority to specify some of our mental states, to the conclusion that all or any of them are or is non-physical. What seems to be missing is a link between the finality of some first-person, present-tense psychological utterances and the alleged non-bodily character of mental events. Why should my psychological state be non-physical, merely because my candid, instantaneous description of it carries the day? It is significant that when I report my bodily states--processes occuring in my cerebral cortex, or the motions of my limbs--my word is not decisive, at least if I delineate these events in physical terms. However, some materialists would reply that all I have to do is report these very same physical events in our familiar mentalistic vocabulary. I would then be describing events that <u>are</u> physical, although I would not be describing them <u>as</u> physical brain events or limb movements. I would be saying what mental events they are--episodes of suffering, rejoicing, pondering-- and my characterization of them would be unimpeachable. The upshot is that instead of proving my mental states to be incorporeal, the doctrine of first-person authority is consistent with a materialistic view of them. Conversely, if it were somehow a fact that mental events are incorporeal, that would be no reason for us to expect first-person descriptions of them to be final. So the rather positive and promising claim that our candid disclosures of our mental states are normally honored is little help to us in understanding the dualistic notion of immateriality.

Along somewhat different lines, it has been suggested to me (by William Rowe) that mental events and objects are immaterial by the following positive criterion. From the fact that they occur or exist at time <u>t</u>, it follows logically that someone is having an experience at <u>t</u>. On the other hand, from the fact that a material event or object occurs at <u>t</u>, it does not follow logically that anyone is having an experience at <u>t</u>. My reply is that although the criterion of immateriality for mental goings-on is positive enough, it begs the question against materialists. Materialists would agree, to begin with, that from the fact that a mental event (an episode of pain or joy) occurs, we can deductively infer that someone experiences it (experiences pain or joy). But why should this be taken as proof that the mental event is non-physical? The materialist wants a chance to argue that this mental occurrence is physical as well as mental. Finally, a materialist ought to argue that from the fact that a material event occurs at <u>t</u>, it does <u>not</u> <u>follow</u> <u>logically</u> that anyone has an experience. However, it is logically possible that the material event in question <u>is</u> the very same event as someone's experiencing pain or joy. More of that in Chapter Three.

Later in this chapter I shall evaluate another attempt to say what it would be for psychological occurrences to be non-physical. At this point we should briefly consider a quite different strategy. Followers of Plato must be champing at the bit to challenge my skepticism toward incorporeality. I think they would ask in dismay, Are not numbers and other abstract entities--classes, properties, propositions--all perfectly acceptable exemplars? If they are, how can you be unsure what dualists are asserting when they say a mental event is non-physical? At least they must be likening it to numbers and their kin.

My skepticism lingers. I do concede without hesitation that numbers, whatever they are, do not belong in the categories of physical object or physical event. In fact they are totally uneventful. If some authority in mathematics ruled that numbers are nevertheless objects of some kind, I would probably knuckle under. But I would insist that they are clearly not <u>particular</u> objects, as individual people, animals, houses, and mountains are. Moreover, a mind <u>is</u> supposed to be a particular--a definite arena where particular episodes of pain or thinking unfold, and relatively enduring states, such as grudges and ambitions, tend to lurk. Because numbers are so different from both minds and mental goings-on as conceived by dualists, I am unconvinced that the comparison gets us anywhere. Perhaps in some sense numbers and mental items are neither of them physical; but the reasons why each is not must be incommensurable. So even if Platonists succeed in explaining what they mean when they declare numbers to be non-physical, that will scarcely illuminate the "sort of immateriality" that might characterize mental things.

If my counter-argument sounds schematic, we can easily flesh it out by recalling disparities between numbers and psychological phenomena. For instance, mental events take place at various times, and may go on for long or short intervals. Numbers do not begin or cease to exist at one or another moment; it makes no sense to say that they start, continue, or stop existing on any date. As we noticed three paragraphs ago, mental events such as suffering or thinking cannot simply occur--on their own, so to speak. There must be a person who is afflicted with discomfort or absorbed in thought. By contrast, numbers cannot possibly be anyone's--or nobody's, as an iceberg at the North Pole might be nobody's property. Obviously a soccer player who wears a sweatshirt with '8' inscribed on it does not own the number eight; the number itself is not hers or his; she is just player number eight. Furthermore, itching, aching, and other so-called bodily sensations appear to be located in parts of our anatomy. Areas of our skin itch; aches seem to be located in our ears, heads, muscles, or joints. But what could it mean if we said that a number was in some part of our body, or anywhere else? Again, mental goings-on change; pains become more or less acute; however, it is nonsensical to say numbers grow, shrink, or undergo any other type of alteration. Given these radical dissimilarities, we should not digress to investigate why Platonists believe numbers are incorporeal; clues about the incorporeality of mind are more likely to be found elsewhere.

The 1970 essay by Richard Rorty that I quoted already takes the most direct approach I know of in the recent literature. Rorty of course believes that the terms 'non-physical' and 'immaterial' have meaning. Earlier I quoted his statement that "'immaterial' gets its sense from its connection with 'mental'". He also says that "'immaterial' and 'nonphysical' [sic] . . . have sense only if the mental is given as an instance of them"; what is more, our positive, unprefixed terms "'material' and 'physical' would be vacuous . . . without the contrast with 'mental'" (1970, p. 402). This latter "contrast" thesis of Rorty's appears to derive from a more sweeping, implicit assumption about how language-users make category words intelligible. Rorty seems to believe we can only give a category word like "'physical' a sense by contrasting it with something else" (p. 412).

The assumption is dubious, but let's grant it. Why then must the "something else" we oppose to 'physical' be 'mental', with the result that by virtue of what our terms mean, anything mental has got to be non-physical, and non-mental things have to be physical? On this point Rorty is explicit. According to him, our categories, mental and physical, "are supposed [by ordinary language-users] to form an exhaustive and mutually exclusive division of the universe" (p. 402). Rorty is not alone in believing this. Sussman, in an article I referred to several pages ago, more cautiously accepts a variant of Rorty's premise. Sussman writes, "so far, the common assumption seems to be that only minds are nonmaterial"; in fact, "mental phenomena may be the historical source of any notion of anything nonmaterial, and . . . the only thing anyone ever managed to talk about . . . when speaking of the nonmaterial" (1981, pp. 101, 103). I think, however, that neither Rorty's nor Sussman's premises are justified. Platonists say that classes, properties, propositions, and numbers are not material, and also that these abstract entities are not mental--creations or denizens of our minds. This clashes with Rorty's statement that mental and physical are "exhaustive", and with all three of Sussman's exegetical speculations. Nevertheless, I won't bicker. Instead I'll go along with Rorty's view that we conceive of everything as either physical or mental.

What puzzles me is Rorty's claim that people customarily think this "division of the universe" is "mutually exclusive". What argument does he offer in support of his belief in "the incompatibility of the mental and the physical" (1970, p. 422), as ordinarily conceived? The stakes are high. If Rorty is correct, then so long as we hold onto our standard notions of the mental and the physical, we cannot consistently assert, the way most materialists do, that each mental event is or at least could be some physical event or other. That is why Rorty's "eliminative" brand of materialism simply does away with our mentalistic vocabulary. Rorty thinks that if we describe any occurrence as psychological in character, or as a specific mental event such as deliberating, we imply that it is non-physical. The eliminative solution is to deprive us of the terminology we need so to classify an event. We would have only the option of saying what physical features it has, and all describable events would be physical. An objector might remind Rorty of his statement, quoted above, that our term "'physical' would be vacuous . . . without the contrast with 'mental'", but I cannot worry about such minor problems.

I would rather discuss Rorty's contention that 'mental' and 'bodily' are polar concepts, and that we must elucidate our puzzling negative term 'non-physical' by reference to mental goings-on. This view is consistent with his broader thesis about the way category terms acquire meaning through pairwise antagonism. But I cannot discern much of a rationale for his underlying thesis or his account of 'mental' and 'physical'. Mostly I encounter <u>ex cathedra</u> pronouncements, as when Rorty declares "thoughts and sensations" to be "paradigm cases of the nonphysical" (p. 420). Should we acquiesce, or should we insubordinately ask what exactly is non-physical about "thoughts and sensations"? What is Rorty telling us when he thus categorizes them?

Perhaps we will find out of we examine the reasoning in a crucial passage of Rorty's essay. I number his statements for subsequent discussion. He says,

> if [1] we have a contrast between two categories X and Y, which [2] are supposed to form an exhaustive and [3] mutually exclusive division of the universe, [4] we cannot mean by 'X' something that might turn out to be either X or Y. [5] We cannot define 'mental' as something that might turn out to be either mental or physical, because [6] we cannot define any term as something that might turn out to refer to what is denoted by a contrary term. [7] It is part of the sense of 'mental' that being mental is incompatible with being physical, and [8] no explication of this sense [that] denies this incompatibility can be satisfactory (p. 402).

Assertions 1, 2, and 3 have a familiar ring. We have implicitly cast doubt on the specific claim that when our X and Y happen to be the categories 'mental' and 'physical', X and Y must be both exhaustive and mutually exclusive. As remarked, a Platonic realist about abstract entities understands the terms 'mental' and 'physical', yet has interesting if not conclusive reasons for denying that his entities fall into either basket. So Rorty's premise 2 is questionable. How about 3? My objection is similar: Plenty of non-eliminative materialists understand our terms 'mental' and 'physical' but hardly concur with Rorty that a mental event is by definition unsuited to be called 'physical'. Rorty's assumption 3 begs the issue against these materialists, who should be allowed to argue--without immediately seeming to contradict themselves--that every psychological occurrence is also bodily.

Imagine nevertheless that 1, 2, and 3 are somehow true. We are still not compelled to accept 4 and 5. In any case both are ambiguous. A trivially true but irrelevant reading of 4 and 5 is that our category term 'X' ('mental') is not equivalent in meaning to the expression 'something that might turn out to be either X (mental) or Y (physical)'. No sensible materialist would say that 'mental' means 'something that might turn out to be either mental or physical'-- though most believe that mental events probably will turn out to be physical. Anyway there are more perspicuous readings of Rorty's statements 4 and 5, namely 4* and 5*: 'We cannot define "X" in such a manner that something that qualifies as X (mental) might at the same time qualify as either X (mental) or Y (physical)--with the consequence that it might be Y (physical) as well as X (mental)'. Like Rorty's laconic statement 3, my reconstructions 4* and 5* are objectionable because they unfairly rule out, by linguistic fiat, the possibility that non-eliminative materialists are right when they say mental events are bodily too.

Rorty's 6 sounds equivalent to my reconstruction 4*, and must be rejected for the same flaw. His 7 seems to give a justification for my 5*, but ought to be turned down for once again begging questions against non-eliminative materialists. After all, what we are debating is, inter alia, whether "being mental is incompatible with being physical". As for Rorty's 8, we have already developed independent reasons not to endorse it. Nearly one-third of the way through this chapter, I concocted an imperfect but "satisfactory" enough statement of what is involved in "being physical". Nearly two-thirds of the way through, after I attacked some ultimately negative characterizations of the mental--as non-spatial, indivisible, publicly unobservable, known without observation or evidence-- I mentioned first-person authority. Although it is no "explication" of "the sense of 'mental'", this crude mark helps us identify some psychological goings-on. Another serviceable mark I have not yet discussed is intentionality--the characteristic 'aboutness' of thinking and all other psychological occurrences and states, which include cognition. We shall see in the next chapter that if some materialists are right, it will turn out that many corporeal happenings are also 'about' one thing or another; these corporeal events will be the ones that materialists identify with our thinking. But more of that shortly. What counts here is that we can put together a rough "explication" of "being physical" and "being mental" which ignores their supposed incompatibility. The doctrine of non-eliminative materialism I have been alluding to goes further and flatly "denies this incompatibility". Rorty's arguments do not seem to rebut such a doctrine. In fact I should acknowledge that Rorty himself, in his exciting recent book (1980, part I), vigorously attacks the "incompatibility" thesis and many of the arguments for it which I have been examining on their merits here. At any rate, no antithesis between mental and physical seems to be warranted. So we can stand by our earlier misgivings: compared with our occasionally stop-gap but tolerably cogent elucidations

of everyday negative terms such as 'non-violent' and
'impolite', the adjectives 'non-physical' and 'immaterial' are extremely resistant to analysis. We
have yet to learn what it could mean to say that minds
and the happenings they shelter are non-physical.

But suppose I am altogether wrong. Assume we do
understand the adjective 'non-physical' and its synonyms. Then recall the difficulty that Plato, Descartes, and their modern-day sympathizers have with the
idea that an entirely material organism should feel,
think, or decide. Surely something else must be
added? Well, then, bring on an immaterial mind, and
stock it with non-physical happenings <u>ad gustam</u>.
Here I borrow heavily from Richard Taylor (1983,
pp. 27-32), and ask, How do these incorporeal additions
enable the creature to feel, think, and decide? Alternatively, how does an immaterial mind do these things
on behalf of the creature? You assume a mere flesh-and-blood human cannot do this, but a non-physical
mind can. No bodily or cerebral event will qualify
as feeling or thinking, but a non-physical one will
make the grade. Why? What is different about minds
and incorporeal goings-on, and how does this difference
engender our mental life? This is as obscure as the
meaning of our key term 'non-physical'.

Remember Sherrington's talk of mental events
which "seem to lie beyond any physiology of the brain".
His example is the "visual scene" he experiences, and
he believes such phenomena are "wholly inexplicable"
by physical science. Rhine too believes that paranormal occurrences such as telepathy elude "physical
explanation". Perhaps Sherrington and Rhine are correct; but can they tell us how an incorporeal mind
or happening manages to produce--or to constitute--a
"visual scene", or to facilitate telepathic communication?

You might defensively reply that the principal
function of immaterial minds and events--their job or
<u>raison</u> <u>d'être</u>--is to produce sensation, thought, perhaps telepathy. All right; but how? No champion of
the non-physical has explained what it is about an
immaterial mind or happening that makes it better able
than a finely tuned organism to carry out this task.
Hence even if it were intelligible, and true, to characterize minds and the events they shelter as non-physical, we would be no closer to understanding how
mental life is possible. But I have mainly tried,

and consistently failed, to make sense of the dualist's negative claim that psychological goings-on are non-physical.

Is dualism out of the running? Yes, at least until someone makes it sound more coherent. May we also conclude that some version of materialism must be true? Not until it has passed the same tests that dualism flunked. As I mentioned during my introductory remarks, some thinkers profess to find extant formulations of it as unintelligible as I have found the major tenet of dualism. Our task in the next chapter will be to evaluate this and other related matters. For now I only want to stress that although dualism is in deep trouble, there is still indispensable, challenging work to be done on materialistic alternatives.

CHAPTER THREE

COULD MENTAL EVENTS BE PHYSICAL?

   We attempted and repeatedly failed to make sense of theories that rank mental happenings and states as non-physical. So perhaps we should be willing to consider alternative schemes. For example, can we propound an intelligible--and maybe even convincing--materialistic account of psychological goings-on? I believe we stand a better chance of developing new perspectives if we do not immediately encumber ourselves with ready-made jargon and theses. Instead we might dwell briefly on some undeniably relevant yet surprisingly recalcitrant facts.

   Many physical circumstances, and particularly certain conditions of our bodies, have a lot to do with our mental states and tendencies. Ancient physicians, as well as plain folk, realized that when a person sustains head injuries, contracts a raging fever, stays out too long under hot sunlight, or ingests some drugs or fermented liquors, very often his or her thinking, mood, and behavior change dramatically. Recent neurophysiologists have pinpointed some of the really important material conditions that have a bearing upon our memories, skills, beliefs, emotions, desires, dreams, and so forth. Clearly the events in our central nervous system play a vital and ubiquitous part in our normal and our aberrant psychological capers.

   But how should we analyze these humdrum and arcane facts? I hope that my aversive therapy in the foregoing chapters made us at least temporarily disinclined to see various bodily and neural events as mere outward correlates of the supposedly <u>bona fide</u> immaterial happenings within. However, I suspect that few uncommitted inquirers will be comfortable saying that any one of the physical events to which I alluded <u>is</u> an episode of lumbago pain, a state of euphoria, or whatever. As we noted at the beginning of Chapter Two, there seems to be a fundamental disparity between the richness, color, depth, and turbulence of our conscious experience, on one side, and the drab unidimensionality of electro-chemical impulses among our neurons, and our peripheral bodily movements, on the other side.

   Yet perhaps we can avoid saying <u>either</u> that some

mental occurrence is one of these physical events, or that it is incorporeal. For instance, why not say that the mental and physical events in question are causally related? Then we could rank each mental episode as either a consequence or else a cause of happenings in our brain and elsewhere in our body. The disparity between mental and physical would thus be no greater than that between cause and effect.

    The suggestion is promising but specious. If you nominate a mental event as either a cause or an effect of some physical event, and you refuse to identify the mental happening with any physical counterpart, then you are forced to deny that the mental happening itself is physical. This hardly needs illustration; but for completeness I shall offer an example. First we will backtrack slightly. Imagine that you carry a huge load of groceries from the supermarket to your apartment. As soon as you put down the grocery sacks, you are afflicted with lumbago pain for several minutes. You lie down as quickly as possible, and prudently remain quiet for a while after the discomfort subsides. Now that the story has ended happily, we ask how your transitory bout of pain is related to contemporaneous physical goings-on. You quite rightly deny that the pain-episode could be your homeward struggle with the provisions; and you again rightly cast the pain as either an immediate or a somewhat delayed effect of your toting. This brings us to the neural disturbance that roughly coincided with your suffering. We suppose you still find this event too unlike your discomfort to be identical with it. Since you believe these happenings are causally linked, we inquire further. Is your bout of pain a result of the neural activity? If so, the pain-event must be distinct-- separable from the neuron-firings that allegedly produced it. However, you want it to be a physical event. But which physical happening or state is it? Your large-scale, overt behavior that occurs while you suffer? Presumably your wincing and groaning are also insufficiently like your discomfort to be identified with it; you will probably say that it causally engenders them. Thus we continue wondering which physical event your pain-episode can be. We have not yet considered the possibility that instead of resulting from neural processes, it makes them occur. Unfortunately this proposal does not help. If your pain is a cause of your neuron firings, and if your pain must be a physical event too, the only event within your body that we might look at is the injury you got from

lifting too many groceries. Maybe some vertebrae were
compressed. Again this corporeal event does not sufficiently resemble your discomfort, and seems to be a
very important cause of it. We keep searching vainly
for a physical happening or condition to equate with
your discomfort. Nothing seems to qualify. So if we
stick with the idea that your pain either results from
or brings about each physical event in the series, we
will be driven to the apparently meaningless conclusion
that your pain is non-physical.

   At this juncture, we ought to re-evaluate our
belief that mental events are causally linked, but not
identical, with bodily and neural goings-on. Specifically, we should try doing without the requirement
that whenever a mental and a physical event are one and
the same, they must somehow mirror each other. No
such requirement holds for a number of widely accepted
identities. The boiling of our breakfast coffee seems
very different from the agitation of countless H_2O and
other molecules. The former involves heat and noise,
rich aroma and hues. We cannot intelligibly ascribe
these characteristics to a molecule or its motion.
Yet we hardly balk at the idea that boiling is one and
the same event as molecular agitation. Why then should
we not equate our various psychological attitudes and
capers with appropriate bodily states and occurrences?
As we remarked above, modern research in neurophysiology has made brain events seem the most eligible
candidates. So we might as well begin by assessing
their chances.

   A short genealogy may help us understand the central issues. Since the late 1950s, Herbert Feigl,
U. T. Place, J. J. C. Smart, and their adherents have
made use of recent neuroscience to revitalize a doctrine that has turned up in various guises from the
time of Democritus onwards. Plato demolished a primitive version of it in his <u>Phaedo</u> (§96). But Feigl,
Place, Smart, and their sympathizers have done more
than clothe the doctrine in the stylish and imposing
white smock of laboratory experimentation. They have
also fleshed it out, adding thorough analyses of its
key notions, and providing argumentation for its main
tenets.

   I believe these pro-materialist philosophers have
two overriding worries. They are queasy about posit-
ing an occult domain of mind, alongside the physical
universe; and they have a distaste for the sort of
theories that I labeled "epistemological solipsism"

(see sections 4 through 10 of Chapter One). Broadly speaking, the strategy of these materialists is to argue that we need not countenance immaterial entities or happenings, and mysterious, private modes of naming or knowing them. We can dispense with all that if mental events are simply identical with brain events. This mental-neural identity doctrine is independent of my claims in Chapters Two and One, respectively, that the non-physicalist theory of mind and epistemological solipsism are both examples of disguised nonsense. But if I am right, and if a mental-neural identity doctrine is too, we will be able to say positively that mental goings-on are physical, and may be studied in the same objective, unproblematic way that white-garbed experimenters study a brain.

Before I face any of the interesting problems that beset mental-neural identity claims, I should illustrate some differences among their proponents. First, with regard to some kinds of mental occurrence, Place and Smart have no ontological or epistemological worries. They believe that a behavioristic account of these phenomena will be adequate. Place remarks,

> In the case of cognitive concepts like 'knowing', 'believing', 'understanding,' 'remembering', and volitional concepts like 'wanting' and 'intending' . . . an analysis in terms of dispositions to behave is fundamentally sound. On the other hand, there would seem to be an intractable residue of concepts clustering around the notions of consciousness, experience, sensation and mental imagery, where some sort of inner process story is unavoidable (1956, p. 276; see Smart, 1959).

The problem is to show that a neurological "inner process story" is plausible.

Feigl's approach is somewhat different. He admits that behavior is important in cases like those mentioned by Place. But apparently Feigl believes that these—indeed, all psychological states—include what he calls a "raw feel". He says,

> If I report moods, feelings, emotions, sentiments, thoughts, images, dreams, etc., that I experience, I am not referring to my behavior . . . I am referring to those

states or processes of my direct experience
which I live through (enjoy or suffer), to
the 'raw feels' of my awareness (1960, p.
34; emphasis his).

The most thorough ideologue of identity, D. M.
Armstrong, makes it unnecessary for us to segregate
"raw feels", or the "intractible residue" which pre-
occupies Place and Smart, and treat other mental
events as behavioral dispositions. Armstrong prefers
a unified, across-the-board neurological story. He
explains,

> Against Place and Smart . . . I . . . defend
> a Central-state account of <u>all</u> the mental
> concepts. We do naturally distinguish be-
> tween the thought . . . and its expression
> in words or action, between the emotion and
> its expression in action . . . [We have] the
> picture of an inner state bringing about
> outward behavior. Surely some strong rea-
> son . . . must be advanced if this pic-
> ture is to be rejected? In default of such
> a reason it should be accepted . . .
>
> Smart . . . now accepts a Central-state
> account of all . . . mental concepts . . .
>
> . . . The concept of a mental state is
> primarily . . . of <u>a state of the person
> apt for bringing about a certain sort of
> behavior</u> (1968, pp. 80 ff.).

Like Place's and Smart's materialistic theories, Armstrong's is put forward as a contingent truth. Empirical scientific discoveries, reinforced by considerations
of theoretical economy, will make particular states of
our central nervous system appear the most "apt" to
produce this or that "sort of behavior". Thus Armstrong expects that neurophysiology will yield a more
convincing "inner process story" of our whole mental
life than strict behaviorism--or dualism, to be sure.

The ontological and epistemological dividends of
this would be impressive. Those mental occurrences
and conditions that we subjectively experience as episodes of aching, itching, pondering, doubting, exult-
ing, fuming, deliberating, and so on, would all be
physical events, namely, electro-chemical processes
within our brain and its appendages. Instead of

remaining eternally private, and cordoned off from experimental study, our so-called mind would be no more elusive, in principle, than other material phenomena.

What prevents an occurrence or state from being both mental and corporeal? Specifically, what stands in the way of our identifying all psychological events, or at least episodes of sensation, with brain processes?

Disavowing any pretence of completeness, I suggest that for illustrative purposes we glance at a trio of alleged mental-neural discrepancies which come up regularly in this debate. Ironically, in each case a materialistic identity claim appears to generate nonsense.

The most straightforward *prima facie* dissimilarity is that every neural happening takes place in a fairly definite and limited region of our anatomy. But with regard to many prominent psychological occurrences and states—my trying to recall a dinner guest's name, or deciding what clothes to pack for a trip—it sounds very peculiar to assign them any precise habitat. Some mental goings-on do seem to afflict regions of our body—earaches, itching, feelings of congestion in our sinuses or stiffness of our joints. But brain processes seemingly cannot take place in our ears, skin, sinuses, or joints. Moreover, it seems unintelligible to complain that your central nervous system aches, itches, feels congested or stiff.

Before we evaluate this contention, we should look at the other two, since all of them overlap to an extent. In fact, the next objection to mental-neural identity that I shall take up derives from something we struggled with in sections 5 through 10 of Chapter One, and pinned down more in Chapter Two. I am alluding to our special right or authority to say what some of our current psychological states are—and if they are of the ordinary locatable kind, to say where they are. As we remarked, it makes no sense for me to ask if you were in a good position to spot and recognize your feelings of chill, if you are an expert in these matters, if you have a lot or only a little evidence, whether you are merely guessing or have made certain that chills are what you experience. Nor could you meaningfully explain *how* you know, or why you say that you feel frozen. On the other side, you cannot get away with unsupported, authoritative statements about your current brain processes. We _can_ ask you to substantiate your reports of happenings in your nervous system, and your estimate of their precise locale. It is both meaningful and appropriate for you to back up your brain-process reports with an account of your credentials, your methods of inquiry, your observational findings and theoretical assumptions.

This second disparity connects with a third. With regard to _many_ of your current psychological states, your unsupported word is final as to their nature, their anatomical position (if any), and also what they are 'about', if they are object-directed psychological states. If you bear a grudge, it is for you to say against whom, and why. If you are indignant, you do not have to investigate or gather data before you confidently tell us what situation irks you and why you are outraged by it. This characteristic of "aboutness", intentionality, or referring to something seems to be unique to psychological phenomena--under which I include linguistic and other purposive behavior. Curiously, those mental goings-on that have the best territorial claim are _not_ directed at anytime. It is nonsensical to say, '_My_ elbow hurts that I played too much tennis', 'My earache is about the recent election'; but this need not detain us. My point is that believing, hoping, fretting, envying, wanting, deciding, trying, purposive doing, and countless other mental events are focused on something. By contrast, physical events and items, as well as locatable bodily sensations, cannot meaningfully be said to be about anything. I should also mention a further peculiarity of the objects that mental happenings and states may be about. You can expect, and fear, a stock market collapse next month although in fact no crash subsequently occurs. But I am unsure what sense it would make if we supposed that physical events or items are related in any way to such unreal or non-existent things as the crash you anticipate. If all this sounds too complicated, perhaps the following illustration by Richard Taylor will clarify things. Taylor asks us to

> suppose I have . . . the desire to be in some foreign land . . . or thoughts of the Homeric gods. It seems at least odd to assert that my body, or some part of it [such as my nervous system], wishes that it were elsewhere, or has thoughts of the

> gods. How indeed can any purely physical state of any purely physical object ever be a state that is _for_ something, or _of_ something, in the way that my desires and thoughts are . . .? And how . . . could a purely physical state be in this sense _for_ or _of_ something that is not real? (1983, pp. 11 f.; see pp. 25 f.).

How genuine and significant are the alleged differences in locatability, first-person authority, and intentionality between neural and mental events? Are they enough to refute identity claims?

Here is Thomas Nagel's response to the locatability problem. Nagel would redescribe both the mental and the neural sides of our equation. He proposes

> to identify a person's having [a] sensation with his body's being in a physical state . . . The psychological term of the identity must be the person's having a pain in his shin rather than the pain itself, because although . . . pains exist and people have them . . . this describes [sic] a condition of one entity, the person, rather than a relation between two entities, a person and a pain. For pains to exist _is_ for people to have them . . .
>
> I deviate from Smart in making the physical side of the identity a condition of the body rather than . . . of the brain . . . I do not mean to imply that the presence of a particular sensation need depend on the condition of any part of one's body outside of the brain. Making the physical term of the identity a bodily rather than a brain state merely implies that the brain is _in_ a body (1965, pp. 216 f.).

Nagel uses this view of what states are identical with each other to deal with the location difficulty. He concedes,

> Brain processes are . . . in the brain, . . . a pain may be . . . in the shin and a thought has no location at all. But . . . [the events of] my _having_ a certain sensation or thought and my _body's being_ in a certain

> physical state . . . will both be going on
> in the same place--namely, wherever I (and
> my body) happen to be . . . [My body is] in
> that state which may be specified as 'having
> the relevant processes going on in its brain'.
> <u>That</u> state . . . has been located as pre-
> cisely as it can be when we have been told
> the precise location of . . . my body. The
> same is true of my having a sensation . . .
> [E]ven if a pain is located in my right shin,
> I am having that pain in my office . . .
> The location of bodily sensations . . . is
> . . . one feature of a psychological attri-
> bute . . . [of] the <u>whole</u> person (p. 218;
> emphasis his).

I agree wholeheartedly with Nagel that mental events such as undergoing discomfort and engaging in thought involve a "<u>whole</u> person", not just pains, shins, thoughts, and brains. In previous chapters I have also highlighted events, such as "the person's having a pain in his shin", and expressed diffidence toward the so-called "pain itself"--and especially toward the idea that there is a "having" relationship "between two entities, a person and a pain". Nagel is definitely on the right track. Suffering involves a complete human being. However, this needs elaboration.

My immediate misgivings concern the whereabouts of the physical event that Nagel equates with "a person's having a pain in his shin". Nagel says this physical event is "a condition of the body rather than . . . of the brain". But how does a body get into the picture? It has "the relevant processes going on in its brain". Moreover, Nagel believes he has thereby situated the physical event "as precisely as it can be". I am skeptical. Here is a parallel case that seems to refute Nagel. Recently Sugar Ray Leonard and Roberto Duran fought for the welterweight boxing title. Where, precisely? Following Nagel, I might talk about the city of Montreal 'having the championship bout go on in its Olympic stadium'. And since the opponents exchanged no punches outside of the roped boxing ring, I could speak of the stadium in turn as 'having the fight go on in its ring'. But do we want to agree with Nagel that these circumlocutions only narrow down the event to the city of Montreal? Nagel remarks that an episode of pain does not "depend on the condition of any part of one's body outside the brain". Certainly the Leonard-Duran match did not depend on the condition of any part of Montreal outside of the boxing ring. As long as both pugilists and the referee do their job for fifteen rounds within the roped enclosure, there is a title bout, whatever happens elsewhere in the stadium and city. If we are after precision, we must say the combat occupied only the ring. By analogy, the "condition" that Nagel would stretch out to cover the body does not take up any more space than a nervous system. Therefore, on Nagel's analysis, the mental event of someone's having a pain in his shin does not coincide spatially with the physical event of someone's body "having the relevant process go on in its brain".

I said earlier that Nagel was moving in the right direction when he refused to let a pain-episode fill up less room than the whole person does. The same is true, in my opinion, when he attempts to expand the matching physical event beyond the confines of a person's brain. But I think I can develop his identity claim more plausibly. To start with, what might it mean to say that the mental event of someone's having pain occupies as much territory as the person does? My explanation is that not only the person's bruised shin, but the whole individual, enters the picture. I grimace, curse, gnash my teeth, limp, rub liniment over the bruised area, and wind a support bandage around my lower leg. My shin cannot do these things. More important, such carryings-on by the complete person are inseparable from the mental event of his having pain. And of course his whole body figures in them; consequently they and the mental episode of having a pain both extend equally far afield. Their frontiers are the body's. Yet the event we are demarcating is mental. If we adopt this conception of having pain, we must abandon the dichotomy that all Cartesians and some materialists set up, in Armstrong's phrase, "between the thought . . . [or pain] and its expression in words or action". The pain event is not somewhere else, lurking behind its behavior "expression".

This brings me to the other side of Nagel's identity, and suggests a motive for his attempt to puff up brain events. In my diagnosis, Nagel's mistake was in thinking that only one physical event is available to be identified with a pain episode, namely, the victim's brain process. Nagel may have sensed that he needed more on the physical side; but instead of enlisting other corporeal events, he tried to stretch out brain processes so that they would seem to occupy as much terrain as the whole person's display of agony. So our revisionist task is childishly easy. All we have to say is that a mental episode of pain, and the corporeal cum neural event which is identical with it, both take up the space filled by the sufferer's body. The model for our identity claim should not be the narrow event of Leonard slugging it out with Duran, which was spatially limited to the ring. Instead we might consider the more comprehensive event of these two adversaries meeting before an excited audience of fifty thousand ringside spectators and several million closed-circuit television-watchers throughout North America. That event took no more time than the slugfest in the ring, but more individuals participated in it, mostly by cheering and wagering, and it spread unevenly--like a scattered cloud formation--over a larger space. If I may push this model one step further, I would compare what happened inside the ring and what happens in our nervous system when we experience pain. The fisticuffs inside the ring were part of the wider collective get-together and media event. Similarly, the brain process is one of the crucial goings-on that, along with bodily behavior, constitute a pain-episode.

   This distinction between sub-events, or components, and the broader happening that they make up, does not only help us smooth over the 'different location' problem. The distinction comes in handy when we turn to the 'first-person authority' and 'intentionality' puzzles.

   Nagel and most other materialists seem to believe they must equate a mental state or happening only with what I call its neural sub-event. All of these thinkers wish to describe both neural and mental events in the same terms. Here unanimity ends. Few materialists buy the Wittgensteinian argument I discussed in Chaper One, that it makes no sense to suppose we have perceptual or any other kind of knowledge, evidence, or methods or inquiring about our sensations and thoughts. Consequently most of these thinkers will say that both your brain processes and your mental goings-on may be objects of knowledge, conjecture, or total ignorance for you. Another group will say that only knowledge, but none of the other usual alternatives, are possible in regard to your own sensations, thoughts, and their kin. Nagel's reasoning seems to me a good example of this latter approach. Having previously reminded us of "Leibniz's law, which requires that if two things are identical they have all their non-intensional [sic] and non-modal properties in common" (1965, p. 216), Nagel explains,

> If state x is identical with state y it does not follow by Leibniz's law that if I know I am in state x then I know I am in state y, since the . . . [properties we are dealing with, namely being known to be in mental state x, and being known to be in mental state y, are both] intensional. Therefore neither does it follow from 'If I am in [mental] state x then I know I am in state x' that if I am in [brain] state y I know I am in state y (p. 219).

We can solve the first-person authority problem without exploring the nature of intensional and modal properties. I am particularly interested in straightening things out for those few materialists who consider it nonsensical to claim knowledge of your own mental state of feeling chilled, for example. Clearly it is meaningful to say you know or guess or haven't the least idea about your current brain state. How then could these be one and the same? A simple answer is that they are not the same, and that your brain process is only part of the bodily goings-on that constitute your mental state of feeling chilled. After all, it sometimes makes no sense to say of a totality what can be meaningfully said of its individual components—and vice versa. A tennis-player may be the doubles partner of another teammate; but he or she cannot be intelligibly described as the team's partner, for it can't have or lack one. The same with events. We can't say that a New Year's Eve celebration was off-key, on-key, or sung at all. Yet an important part of the celebration may have been the singing of "Auld Lang Syne", and it might have been either on or off key. Conversely, to be sure, the celebration may have depleted the host's liquor supply, but what could it mean if we said that our singing used up the liquor supply? At any rate, my suggestion is that it makes sense to say a person knows, guesses, errs, has evidence, and so on about his brain processes, although it is unintelligible to say this regarding the overall bodily state of the person, which includes his brain processes.

So far I have relied on far-fetched analogies. But maybe there are clear examples of this sort in the physical world. A Wittgensteinian case like those I noted at the end of section 9, Chapter One, might go as follows. Normally it will be incomprehensible if I say I know, believe, suspect, or have just discovered that my body is in a sitting position. Yet I might know or be quite ignorant about what my tendons, ligaments, and bones are doing, even though the global event here--my limbs being arranged in a certain manner--seems to consist entirely of those muscular and skeletal sub-events. Normally it makes no sense to ask me how I know, or what reasons I have for believing that I am seated; but I might give plausible, detailed replies if you inquire about the mini-events that constitute my being seated. By parity of reasoning, then, it might be unintelligible to say of the large-scale event that is my feeling chilled, that I know, guess, or find out about it; yet I might know, conjecture, and gather evidence about the various brain states, muscular happenings, and so on that are the ingredients of my feeling chilled. On this view, there is a discrepancy between my mental state of feeling chilled and the accompanying brain state--but not between my mental state and the complete physical state that is to be identified with my feeling chilled.

If you are reluctant to say it is meaningless for someone to claim knowledge of his or her sensations and thoughts, you can take another approach. You can underscore the seemingly vast difference between our quasi-infallible cognizance of our thoughts and sensations, and our ignorance of our brain processes. How then could they be identical? My solution is even simpler here. You deny the identity of mental with neural happenings alone; but you point out that we often have knowledge of a global occurrence--an explosion, a burglary--though we can only guess what specifically transpired.

My part-whole treatment of neural processes and mental states will also help materialists who would rather speak of linguistic conventions than of knowledge. The conventionalist might argue that most linguistic groups simply follow a tacit rule. Their rule is that you should only ascribe sensations, thoughts, and the like to another speaker when you believe roughly the following: If she (or he) had occasion to talk unguardedly of her current mental state, she would describe it the way you do; and however she described it, her say-so would prevail. A conventionalist might add that as a matter of fact most groups allow each person ultimate authority to proclaim his overall state of mind, which happens to be a bodily and neural state; nevertheless he is not thereby entitled to determine any of the neural and other physical minutiae of his condition.

A part-whole analysis of the related 'intentionality' problem works just as effectively--and flexibly. Most materialists of course argue that it makes sense, and is true, to say that our brain processes are directed toward the very items that our thoughts, emotions, desires, and decisions are about. These mental-neural identity theorists dazzle us with the latest electronic gadgets: chess-playing machines, computers that respond to and produce ordinary speech sounds, problem-solving devices, robots carrying out the duties of assembly-line workers, even physically unrealizable Turing machines (see Putnam, 1960 and 1967). J. J. C. Smart's method is representative. He evokes "a fully automatic aeroplane with goal-seeking navigating equipment built into it", and assures us that its "goal . . . is to reach the North Pole" (1964, p. 147). I am somewhat cowed by this, since I would like to give the impression that naturally I am conversant with computer technology, artificial-intelligence research, information theory, and whatever else we require to discuss our mental life. At the risk of exposing my naïvete, however, I might ask if it is perhaps the human designers and operators of Smart's flying machine, not the aeroplane itself or its navigational apparatus, that have a goal. In other words, it is not clear that we have to say of the aircraft or its automatic steering device that it--and by analogy a brain--can have intentional objects. If we report that the person who adjusted the directional equipment and launched the aircraft wants it to reach the North Pole, do we need to say more or less the same thing over again regarding the plane?

At any rate my analysis does not force you to say that either navigating devices or brains and brain processes are about existent or non-existent objects. Complete flesh-and-blood people, not their brains, are in object-directed states. For any of the reasons we considered above, you may say that each individual's sincere declaration is enough to specify what he or she is ruminating, rejoicing, or deliberating about. But his other verbal and non-verbal antics will provide confirmation, and sometimes counter-evidence, regarding whatever he has nominated as the object of his cognitive, affective, or conative state. People tend to run away from things they dread, approach things they like, and blush when something occurs that embarrasses them. Their brains cannot run away, draw nearer, or turn pink. Obviously if our central nervous system stopped functioning, or if it were not in the right state, we would be unable to announce the objects of our thinking, emotions, and desires; our object-directed behavior would cease. But it certainly does not follow that our brain or brain state has an object. If you believe this does follow, you must be reasoning invalidly. In particular, if you argue that since the whole mental state has an object, its neural component must have one too, you commit a fallacy of division. If you reason that because my speech behavior has an object--insofar as I tell you what I believe or fear--and my non-verbal capers seem to have one also, therefore my brain state is 'about' something too, you are committing a part-part fallacy. You must be assuming that what is true of some component events has to be true of other component happenings.

However that may be, we have come to terms with three prominent, interrelated difficulties of materialism. In each case, we sustained the objection that there is a sharp disparity between some mental event and the brain processes that most identity theorists equate with the mental event. Mental and neural goings-on are not similarly located, known, or directed toward things. But this refutes only mind-brain materialism, not the broader contention that mental events are physical, and in part neural. We found no clear differences of spatial position, of first-person authority, or of intentionality, between mental events which involve a full-fledged human being, and the complex bodily and neural events that we propose to identify with mental goings-on.

I am sure that objectors will wonder, Is the component analysis I advocate precise enough to supplant the more scientific-sounding mind-brain identity theory? They will insist that I produce an axiomatic, definitional account of what it is for one event to be part of a larger event. Perhaps they will demand that I say what events are, and delineate all their species: states, changes, non-changes, processes, terminations, what have you. Well, I have not done any of that undoubtedly valuable work, and do not plan to. I could temporarily put off the day of reckoning, and wave in the direction of journal articles (1971, 1973a, 1973b,

1974, 1975, 1978a, 1978b, 1980, 1980), and a book (1977), where I have struggled with particular conundrums about the nature and individuation of events and their sub-events. But ultimately the champion of axioms and logically necessary and sufficient conditions will be dissatisfied.

So I may as well confess straightaway my belief that we understand eventhood and componency adequately enough in a case-by-case manner. Have we not already produced many illustrations of both? I suppose I could rehearse various distinctions that were germane to those dialectical contexts. But for purposes of this chapter, I hope just one additional comment will do.

Of presently competing theories of mind, "whole person" materialism appears to be the most viable. The dualistic doctrines I looked at in Chapters One and Two seem to be out of the running. Yet as we have seen throughout this chapter, you can hold on to a surprising number of those quaint views; for instance, you can accept "whole person" materialism and still follow tradition in claiming knowledge of your sensations. We have actually done justice to a fundamental insight of mind-brain identity theorists. We have reserved a place of honor for brain processes, merely denying that they are the only corporeal goings-on that constitute our states of mind. Although we have declined to follow Armstrong in identifying a mental event with "a state of the person apt for bringing about a certain sort of behavior", we leave plenty of room for causal transactions. We can safely assume that the various physical sub-events that make up an episode of feeling chilled, of thinking, or of disappointment affect each other. Neural happenings will cause our muscles to contract, which will alter the positions of our limbs; and in turn feedback impulses will flow back to our brain. Evidently there can be no causal interactions between our overall state of mind and these sub-events, which compose it; but is that a great loss?

Actually I should record one further overall gain. I believe the holistic type of materialism I have sketched in this chapter is a congenial and in no way burdensome working hypothesis to have backstage when you face the issues that occupy the rest of this book. My next chapter, for example, will focus on Freud's revolutionary theories of the person; and even though I shall not reconstruct his explicitly materialistic ontology, or his arguments for it, I would say that he is theorizing about complete human beings, not just their nervous systems. Subsequent chapters are also concerned with the control that persons--not Cartesian spirits or human brains--exercise over their actions, and how various circumstances either diminish or augment their power to act. We can reasonably assume that these self-directing persons are 100% physical. After all, how could an incorporeal thing--whatever it might be like--do better at running its affairs than a complex material organism, which deliberates, plans, and forms relationships with other people?

CHAPTER FOUR

FREUDIAN MODELS OF MENTAL LIFE

Freud's theories of the person are diametrically opposed to traditional Cartesianism in at least two very significant ways. He is a fervent materialist, of course, who attempted, in his early <u>Project for a Scientific Psychology</u> and elsewhere, to formulate quite detailed accounts of mental phenomena, using only neurological and other physicalistic terms. He resigned himself to using familiar psychological terms for entirely pragmatic reasons: because neurophysiology was not sufficiently advanced. Yet he assumed that someday we would "replace the psychological terms by physiological or chemical ones".* Freud's thinking contrasts even more sharply with the outlook of both Descartes and the vast majority of Freud's fellow materialists. Mind-body dualists and nearly all their opponents have equated mentality and consciousness. Following Descartes' famous argument, mind is <u>res cogitans</u>, and what goes on in your mind is pre-eminently what you--perhaps alone--somehow manage to perceive, become aware of, or infallibly know. I articulated and attacked these doctrines in previous chapters, and joined materialists in arguing that mental states, hence conscious states, may well be physical too; for example, partly made up of brain-processes. Now Freud challenges not only the dualist's assumption that mental events are non-physical, but, more audaciously, our almost unexamined belief that they are conscious. This is salutary, for mind-brain identity proponents, and also "whole person" materialists such as myself, usually focus their attention on episodes or states of pain, careful thought, vehement emotion, or momentous decision-making. Obviously the person will in some

---

*Most quotations in this chapter are from Freud's writings, usually as translated in Strachey (1953-74). I quote Freud abundantly because he is such an enthralling stylist, and because I want readers to judge for themselves what his words mean. In a previous look at these topics (see Wollheim, 1974, pp. 147-71), I gave volume and page numbers, and Strachey's dating of the publication, each time I cited Freud. Here I shall do so--by Strachey volume, page, and date, unless otherwise noted--only when I foresee exegetical controversies.

sense be aware of such mental goings-on. However, why must we take it for granted that every psychological state belongs to this 'conscious' family? Maybe, as Freud boldly proclaimed, there are other, more fruitful ways of representing our mental life. Even if we run into profound difficulties, including nonsense, these alternatives are clearly worth pursuing.

1. <u>The general pattern of Freud's theorizing</u>. Before we start, you may wonder if it is fair, much less philosophically rewarding, for us to subject Freud's so-called metapsychological doctrines to close scrutiny. Many commentators would endorse P. H. Nowell-Smith's remark that the "cash value" of psychoanalytical theory is "that certain types of behavior can be predicted and, above all, cured" (in Brodbeck, 1968, p. 715). Freud's experience as a neurologist, then as a clinician, must have slanted his metapsychology. But we should recall some things he wrote to his early intellectual mentor and friend Wilhelm Fliess. As a youth, Freud says, he wanted "philosophical knowledge", and later, "by going over from medicine to psychology . . . I am in the process of attaining it"; nevertheless, he adds, "I have become a therapist against my will" (letter 44, in Kris, 1954). Subsequently Freud explains to Fliess,

> I am plagued with two ambitions: to see how the theory of mental functioning takes shape if quantitative considerations, a sort of economics of nerve-force, are introduced into it; and secondly to extract from psychopathology . . . clear assumptions about normal mental processes (letter 113).

Perhaps Freud's work with patients has this relevance. If you deal regularly with the sorts of troubled people that Freud encountered in his practice, you might justifiably feel tempted to imagine something like a conflict of the individual with himself or herself. You might then envisage a clash of forces within the person, as Freud so often does. You might conjecture about the warring elements inside of us, and the dynamic forms their struggles could take. At any rate, many of Freud's outstanding speculations display this overall pattern. They may generate problems not altogether unlike those that beset Cartesian dualism, but I suspect that they stand a better chance of being made intelligible, even plausible.

I realize that the doctrinal thickets I want to explore have been staked out already by a legion of Freud commentators. But few of the skeptics have bothered to argue their case in detail. Those who have done so have not fully appreciated how reasonable it was for Freud to divide the self into contending factions, and how instructive his difficulties are for philosophy of mind and action.

Before I elaborate those themes, I should outline for non-Freudians what I consider to be Freud's most interesting theories of the person. He is best remembered, of course, for his tripartite divisions of the self into unconscious, preconscious, and conscious "systems", from roughly 1900 until 1923, and into id, ego, and superego thereafter. But his accounts of our mental processes made use of countless other items within us. In conformity with tradition, he assumed that "ideas" populate our minds and their compartments. By the slippery term "idea" he seemed to mean images, concepts, propositions, and thoughts. In addition, Freud always supposed that our mental machinery runs on some kind of "energy", which resembles but is not a species of electrical current. In the guise of emotive "affect" and conative pushiness, this psychic energy adheres to some of our ideas. However, from the time he began such theorizing, Freud conceded that "we have no means of measuring" psychic current. And in a posthumously published monograph he declares that "in mental life some kind of energy is at work", though we will not "come nearer to a knowledge of it by analogies with other forms of energy".

Freud also consistently gave top billing to our drives, impulses, or "instincts" (<u>Triebe</u>), which he regarded as somehow derived from psychic energy. This creates a minor puzzle. For while Freud recognizes just one kind of psychic energy, from relatively early in his theorizing he makes it a methodological principle that "instincts occur in pairs of opposites" (XI, p. 44, 1910a). To the end he believed that only by the "concurrent or opposing action" of instincts "can we explain the rich multiplicity of the phenomena of life" (XXIII, p. 243, 1937c). In this sense, <u>not</u> in the Cartesian mind-<u>versus</u>-matter sense, Freud's explanatory schemes are dualistic. One competing instinct he regularly calls "libido", and says that it propels us toward erotic endeavors. At first its rival is the "ego-instinct" of self-preservation (XI, p. 214, 1910i). From 1920 on, the destructive instinct, directed at oneself and others, becomes the antagonist of libido.

Since I mentioned the ego instinct, I should post a warning. Freud's conception of the ego (das Ich) was unsettled prior to 1923. Frequently he seems to mean by "ego" the whole person (III, p. 54, 1894a; XVIII, p. 11, 1920g). Other passages, occasionally in the same works, suggest that the ego is only part of us, and that Freud is contrasting the ego with parts that we are not conscious of (III, p. 48, 1894a; XVIII, p. 19, 1920g). At times Freud makes the ego a delegate within us of conventional morality, and has it keep shameful thoughts away from our "consciousness" (V, p. 526, 1900a). On this view, we would not be fully conscious of everything our ego does. Particularly when it censors thoughts, we are not better apprised of its activity than we are of whatever it manages to exclude from our consciousness (see section 6). Yet another characterization of ego appears in Freud's 1895 Project. There ego is nothing but a subsystem of "neurones", whose job it is to maximize "discharge" of psychic energy from our whole homeostatic mental apparatus.

2. A distinction between strictly physical and broadly anthropomorphic models. Since we are taking a census of the items Freud invokes to explain conflict behavior, we should notice that he portrays their relationships in correspondingly varied terms. Because of his commitment to materialism, you would expect him to describe psychological phenomena in the language we reserve for inanimate objects and events. Thus Freud's topographical account of the person makes "reference . . . to regions in the mental apparatus, wherever they may be situated in the body". We also remember his mechanistic imagery of tensions and tugs. For instance, he says "the repressed [idea or thought] exercises a continuous pressure in the direction of consciousness, so that this pressure must be balanced by an unceasing counter-pressure". Equally familiar is Freud's hydraulic talk of flow and "blockages". We hear of libidinal instincts pouring through "channels". If libido is dammed up, after leaving its "reservoir", it "may . . . move on a backward course . . . along infantile lines". Freud occasionally draws upon crystallography, and imagines the fusion of repressed, hysterogenic memories around a "nucleus". When we dream, our childhood experiences may operate as a "nucleus of crystallization attracting the material

of the dream thoughts to itself". Sometimes resorting to botany, Freud compares a repressed idea with a fungus that "proliferates in the dark". A recurring zoological simile is that libido goes out to objects, and then returns, much like the pseudopods of an amoeba. From pathology Freud takes the notion of "strangulated affects", along with the comparison between a repressed memory-idea and a wound that contains some irritating "foreign body". Toxicology also enriches Freud's theorizing. He supposes that libidinal currents, or "sexual substances", become poisonous if they do not escape from our mental apparatus.

Freud's anthropomorphic models come from several domains of social life. When we perform an "erroneous action", Freud says that "control over the body" passes from one's ego, and its "will", to an opposing "counter-will". Freud regularly speaks of "two thought-constructing agencies" within us, "of which the second enjoys the privilege of having free access to consciousness for its products". Other political and social arrangements besides "privilege" and "free access" enliven the relationship between parts of the self. There are upheavals too. Freud explains that the

> soul . . . is a hierarchy of superordinated and subordinated agents, a labyrinth of impulses striving independently of one another towards action . . .

> . . . Psychoanalysis . . . can say to the ego: ". . . a part of the activity of your own mind has been withdrawn from your knowledge and from the command of your will . . . [S]exual instincts . . . have rebelled . . . to rid themselves of . . . oppression; they have extorted their rights in a manner that you cannot sanction".

Freud describes the psychoanalyst's task in similar language: "the physician . . . works hand in hand with one part of the pathologically divided personality, against the other partner in the conflict"; his or her goal is to "give . . . back command over the id" to the neurotic's ego. Freud brings in more political terminology when he says that neurotic symptoms themselves, as well as dreams and slips of the tongue, are like negotiated "compromises" between our unruly impulses and our moralistic inclinations.

Social life provides Freud with yet another model when he calls his theories "economic". He deploys financial imagery at least twice, likening an instinct to a "capitalist", who loans us energy for our undertakings (VII, p. 87, 1905e; XV, p. 226, 1916-17). Now and then he describes an individual, or his ego, as acting on "economic" grounds when they maximize pleasure (XVIII, p. 7, 1920g). But, as in the letter to Fliess that I quoted earlier, Freud's term "economic" usually has to do with the "strength" or "pressure" exerted by psychic or neural forces (I, p. 283, 1950a; XIV, p. 181, 1915e; XIX, p. 152, 1924b).

More intimate relationships have a place in Freud's doctrines. He says that a person becomes narcissistic when his or her ego "offers itself . . . as a libidinal object to the id, and aims at attaching the id's libido to itself". In melancholia, however, "the ego . . . feels itself hated . . . by the superego, instead of loved". Finally we should note a model that appeared already in Plato's Republic. Freud's variant is that the ego "in its relation to the id is like a man on horseback, who has to hold in check the superior strength of the horse". Again, as we found in most of Freud's analogies with person-to-person dealings, and with inanimate phenomena, the underlying pattern is discord, tension.

I trust that my hurried conspectus of Freud's schemes for explaining conflict behavior has exhibited their great diversity, sophistication, and attractiveness. Before I start evaluating them, I anticipate a complaint similar to the one I rehearsed early in the previous section. I believe some Freudians would grumble that the doctrines I want to pore over really are nothing but metaphors, hardly meant to have any literal application, and therefore immune to philosophical prosecution. Freud himself cautions, "What is psychical is . . . so unique . . . that no one comparison can reflect its nature". But far from being a prohibition, this is an encouragement to consider seriously as many images as possible. For Freud continues, "The [therapeutic] work of psychoanalysis suggests analogies with chemical analysis, but just as much with the incursions of a surgeon or the manipulations of an orthopedist or the influence of an educator" (XVII, p. 161, 1919a). In regard to one of his favorite topographical cum social models, Freud assures us that his "crude hypotheses [about] the two chambers, the doorkeeper on the threshold between them, and consciousness as a spectator at the end of the second room, must indicate an extensive approximation to the actual reality" (XVI, p. 296, 1916-17). In any event, I insist that if a metaphor is to be at all enlightening, we should be able to locate some points of contact between it and what it is intended to explain. But I want to put off such methodological issues until we consider some of the reasons a theorist might have to divide up the soul, on the model either of contrary inanimate forces, or of interpersonal wrangling.

3. <u>Evidence of strife within the person</u>. Freud reports that when he began working in psychiatric hospitals and in his own practice, he was not "pledged to any . . . psychological system"; rather, he "proceeded to adjust [his] views until they seemed adapted for giving an account of . . . the facts [that] had been observed". Some of the behavior he witnessed especially demanded an explanation in terms of inner discord. A good example is Freud's quite early theoretical response to the syndrome then called "hysteria". He speculates,

> if I find someone in a state which bears all the signs of a painful affect--weeping, screaming and raging--the conclusion seems probable that a mental process is going on in him of which those physical phenomena are the appropriate expression . . . The problem would at once arise of how it is that a hysterical patient is overcome by an affect about whose cause he asserts that he knows nothing . . . He is behaving as though he <u>does</u> know about it.

At the time Freud was convinced that hysterical afflictions of this type result mainly from a "summation of traumas"--as a rule, sexual experiences. When patients began treatment, they seemed to have forgotten these traumas. But when they were helped to recall the incidents, their hysterical disorders vanished. Freud is driven toward a partitioning theory. He believes that

> everything points to one solution: the patient is in a special state of mind in which all his impressions or his recollections . . . are no longer held together by an associative chian . . . [and thus] it is possible for a recollection to express its

> affect by means of somatic phenomena without
> the group of the other mental processes,
> the ego, knowing about it or being able to
> intervene to prevent it.

Further evidence comes from work on hysterically blind patients. Freud asserts,

> Excitations of the [supposedly] blind eye
> may . . . produce affects . . . though they
> do not become conscious. Thus hysterically
> blind people are only blind as far as con-
> sciousness is concerned; in their uncon-
> scious they see . . . [O]bservations such
> as this compel us to distinguish between
> conscious and unconscious mental processes.

In the same essay, and repeatedly elsewhere, Freud says that other experiments with hypnotism also prove that unconscious mental activity takes place in us. He declares that a post-hypnotic suggestion must be "present in the mind", since a person to whom it was given will obey it while candidly disclaiming knowledge of its origin. We will say more of Freud's notion of "presence" later (section 10).

For now we should remark that in Freud's view dreaming appeared to call for a 'divided soul' theory. He staunchly held that "there must be a force here which is seeking to express something, and another which is striving to prevent the expression". One of his last discussions turns upon the memory we display in dreams of incidents we cannot recall when awake. Surely these recollections have been "present" all along, but inaccessible? (XXIII, pp. 160 f., 1940a).

One typical phase of psychoanalytical treatment itself also struck Freud as requiring an 'inner strife' explanation. Sincere patients who are progressing steadily all at once come to a halt. Abruptly they find themselves unable to bring forth dreams and asso- ciations; or on the other hand they become too oblig- ing, and produce whatever material their analyst seems to expect. According to Freud, such "resistance" be- havior proves that some internal impediment is at work. He argues, "The existence of this force could be assumed with certainty, since one became aware of an effort corresponding to it if, in opposition to it, one tried to introduce the unconscious memories into the patient's consciousness". Later Freud amplifies:

"There can be no question but that . . . resistance emanates from the ego". In fact, "no stronger impression arises from the resistances during the work of analysis than of there being a force which is defending itself by every possible means against recovery and which is absolutely resolved to hold onto illness and suffering".

A final source of conflict theories we might call 'respect for the ordinary language of psychotics'. Freud conjectures about paranoid individuals, who stubbornly insist that they are being observed and criticized, and constantly 'hear' voices commenting unfavorably upon their deeds and attitudes. Freud wonders, "How would it be if these insane people were right, if in each of us there is present an agency [viz., the superego] which observes and threatens to punish", and which they have "mistakenly displaced into external reality?" (XXII, p. 59, 1933a; see XIV, p. 95, 1914c). In his very last résumé of psychoanalytical doctrine, Freud similarly finds it significant that victims of hallucinatory confusion, when they recover, will often say that throughout their most disturbed periods, "in some corner of their mind . . . there was a normal person hidden, who . . . watched the hubbub of illness go past him".

Two distinguished recent commentators on Freud believe that there is also a close match between Freud's tripartite conception and the way sane people think and speak of themselves. Jerome Bruner says that the id-ego-superego story exemplifies "the dramatic technique of decomposition, the play whose actors are parts of a single life", and its "imagery . . . has an immediate resonance with the dialectic of experience" (1968, p. 710). Richard Wollheim is more explicit; he says Freud's theory "provides a model of the mind and its working . . . [that] coincides with, or reproduces, the kind of picture or representation . . . we consciously or unconsciously make to ourselves of our mental processes" (1971, p. 234). I will add that Freud's doctrines should be especially welcomed by his stodgier materialist comrades-in-arms, even "whole person" materialists such as myself, because our visions of mental life are so comparatively sanguine and simplistic.

Yet I have misgivings. I believe that Freud's consistently non-anthropomorphic theories make sense, in the straightforward way that Cartesian views did

not when I examined them earlier. Despite that solid
advantage, these non-anthropomorphic schemes consistently fail to elucidate those aspects of mental life
that most baffle us. I shall not take up the much-belabored question of whether Freud's physicalistic
theories of mind qualify as 'scientific'. As for his
animistic accounts, I concur with Bruner and Wollheim
that these generate illumination--no doubt because we
already have a practical and theoretical understanding
of social transactions, and Freud miniaturizes such
events inside us. But I think a careful assessment
will show these doctrines to be instructively unintelligible, and thus on a par with much less refined old-style dualism. If I am right about this, it is a moot
question whether Freud's 'society' models are scientific. In any case, I begin the critical phase of my
discussion with a strictly neurological theory of
Freud's to which I have referred more than once.

4. A mental apparatus and its sub-systems of
"neurones". Freud's homeostatic model, as we would
call it nowadays, seems to me a marvel of relative
cogency together with explanatory emptiness. It
seems to be taking shape in his earliest metapsychological essays. He elaborates it with a treasury of
details in his Project of 1895 (I, pp. 295-387,
1950a), and its silhouette hovers behind many of his
subsequent writings. Freud envisages a "mental apparatus" composed of three kinds of "neurones", classed
according to how "permeable" they are to currents of
psychic energy, called "Quantity" or "Q". The system
of least permeable neurones Freud labels "the ego".
As I noted at the end of section 1, this "ego" system
operates to maximize "discharge" of Q from the whole
apparatus--hence my comparison with present-day homeostatic devices. More philosophically intriguing is
Freud's name for the most permeable system, which receives "stimuli" from our "external" surroundings. This
neurone system he baptizes "consciousness". If you
wonder what it has to do with the phenomena that plain
folk call by this name, my hunch is this: whenever
these "consciousness" neurones transmit Q, notably
upon receipt of external stimuli, we will be conscious;
that is, at least we will be awake, and probably we
will be conscious of one thing or another.

This is a coherent empirical hypothesis. It
makes sense. I can easily imagine that whenever some
particular neurones buzz with Q, we are conscious.
Or perhaps no brain activity of the right sort

coincides with our moments of lucidity and contact with our environs. My complaint about Freud's neurological model is that it furnishes us no clues regarding those aspects of our consciousness that are most puzzling to curious laypeople and to practicing therapists. In Bruner's and Wollheim's terminology, the Freudian neural apparatus has no "resonance with . . . experience"; it lacks kinship with our "picture . . . of our mental processes". You would not expect anyone to say, 'Aha, so consciousness is the passage of Q energy through this group of neurones!'

One shortcoming of Freud's neural theory is obvious: it leaves out, and thus fails to elucidate, peculiarities of consciousness like those we dealt with in the foregoing chapter. Our ultra-permeable neurones have a definite spatial habitat, and the same goes for any currents of Q that shoot through them. Not so with consciousness. We have ordinary knowledge of neural events within us--knowledge acquired through perceptual snooping and grounded in evidence as well as previously accepted theory. We have a mysteriously different kind of authority to say that we are conscious, and that our conscious state is one of doubt, belief, or what-have-you, on such-and-such a topic. This last-mentioned 'aboutness', or intentionality, is a central feature of most states of consciousness; however, it is unclear whether we can meaningfully say that the Q-transmissions of a neurone system are on a topic, or about anything. Now it would be unfair of me to criticize Freud because he did not go into these and similar philosophical niceties which were barely discussed in his time, least of all by psychologists. My gripe is not against Freud. I doubt that anyone could develop a neurone theory, limited to brain events, so that it became a theory of consciousness. I would expect any such theory to fail more or less the way mind-brain identity doctrines seemed to in my third chapter, and I would prescribe analogous remedies.

I shall not go over those points again; but I might as well add that difficulties just like those we had with Freud's neurological account of consciousness are bound to emerge elsewhere. Here is one last example. Freud says of our homeostatic neurone system that it is governed by "the principle of constancy or or stability", which he later re-names "the pleasure principle". Obviously Freud does not mean that neurones follow principles, or that they are unprincipled either. He must be claiming only that the apparatus, or a part of it, usually operates in a stabilizing manner--and maximum amounts of Q leave the apparatus. But what does this outcome have to do with pleasure? Well, Freud equates pleasure (in German, Lust) with discharge of Q, and the buildup of Q he describes as "unpleasure" (Unlust). Again it is clear he does not mean that we enjoy the release of Q from our mental apparatus, or that our "ego" or "consciousness" neurone systems do. Freud is simply conjecturing about what quasi-electrical events take place in our brains when we are pleased or distressed.

His conjecture is meaningful, and may in fact be true--or false. Yet it cannot be the whole story of our joys and sufferings. Freud's and anyone else's neurological account will have the serious deficiencies that we just saw in his companion theory of consciousness. Moreover, it does not enlighten us about the important relationships, causal or otherwise, between our states of pleasure or displeasure and our beliefs, our purposes--including the unconscious ones so astutely discerned by Freud--as well as social convention and conditioning. I believe that any materialist who intends to produce a better theory than old-fashioned dualism will have to say something about those factors of our mental life.

I have no transcendental proof of this, and I certainly cannot set forth the requirements I think should be met by a philosophical theory of mind. But I believe I ought to illustrate how you risk incoherence if you try to enrich a neurological story with notions from the sphere of interpersonal behavior.

5. A mixed account of hysterical symptoms. Perhaps because he sensed that theories of the kind we have been examining leave out something vital, Freud often added anthropomorphic embellishments. Slightly before he wrote the Project, Freud was busy attempting to understand hysteria. I have already referred to a pair of his doctrines: that a form of psychic energy, emotional affect, clings to some of our memory ideas; and that this is the result of a series of traumatic incidents, usually during our childhood and sexual in character. Freud also believed that if this load of affect is not discharged, or "abreacted", through our overt actions, including our emotional outbursts and our conscious recall of the incidents, then we are in for trouble.

What sort? When affect builds up inside of us, what happens to it and to us? As Freud develops his central theme of repression, and how repression causes hysterical and other troubles, his account begins to sound animistic. He says the affect-laden memory is "objectionable"; the person's "ego . . . decides on the repudiation of the . . . idea"; in somewhat different terms, one patient herself "repressed her erotic idea from consciousness and transformed the amount of its affect into physical sensations of pain" (II, pp. 123 and 164, 1895d). Yet plainly Freud wanted to stay as much as possible within the bounds of a neurological or at least mechanistic explanation. Here is a typical result, from a landmark case study written a decade after the <u>Project</u>. Freud imagines that the potential victim of hysteria has

> contrary thoughts . . . paired off in such a way that <u>the one thought is excessively intensely</u> [sic] <u>conscious while its counterpart is repressed and unconscious</u>. This . . . is an effect . . . of repression. For repression is often achieved by means of an excessive reinforcement of the thought contrary to the one which is to be repressed . . . [T]he thought which asserts itself . . . in consciousness . . . I call a <u>reactive thought</u>. The two thoughts . . . act towards each other much like the two needles of an astatic galvanometer. The reactive thought keeps the objectionable one under repression by means of a certain surplus of intensity; but for that reason it itself is 'damped' and proof against conscious efforts of thought (VII, p. 55, 1905e; see II, p. 12, 1893a).

Any theorist would be tempted to weave notions of personal agency and interpersonal conflict into the electromagnetic tapestry. <u>If</u> you restrict yourself to the terminology of psychical mechanics, all you can report is one entity bouncing another away from part of the mental apparatus that is inexplicably named "consciousness". You will be unable to express the fact that the "reactive" entity is protecting the <u>person's</u> own <u>moral</u> beliefs, while the entity that it pushes under is "erotic", and for that reason subject to "repudiation". You cannot go on to describe the person's hysterical symptom as a "mnemic symbol" of the ancient trauma (II, p. 90, 1895d). And how would you articulate the hypothesis that it is less unpleasant for the victim to have hysterical symptoms than to clamp down altogether on his or her nasty idea? Besides, the patient as well as theory-builders might derive some gain if we blend in anthropomorphic elements. After listening to some of Freud's mixed accounts of their predicament, hysterics might claim enhanced self-understanding, and feel they are beginning to put things together. A purely electromagnetic explanation is unlikely to produce this kind of "resonance" for victims.

So much for incentives to humanize our story. Why are concepts from personal and social life at odds with an otherwise mechanistic theory? In line with the view of philosophically significant nonsense that I sketched in Chapter One, my guess is as follows. Suppose you introduce terms such as "objectionable", "repudiation", and "transform"--this latter verb being used as it would be in the sentence, 'Mary transformed the flour sack into a blouse'. In contexts where it is indisputably meaningful to deploy these terms, it also makes sense to say other things. For instance, you can say why various people find X-rated movies objectionable, what a candidate for office intended to achieve by repudiating his or her party's program, and how Mary went about transforming the flour sack. However, it is blatant nonsense to speak about any kind of electronic device, or any part of such a device--for that matter, any brain or neurone system--in these terms. You might have complex reasons for objecting to X-rated films. Perhaps you have evidence that many rapists seem to have been inspired by such films. Maybe you have a gut reaction against the genre, but no particular reasons for your negative attitude. Or possibly you consider it unobjectionable. However, what could you possibly mean if you discussed an electrical apparatus or a brain in this manner? At least on the genesis of hysteria, Freud himself admits,

> I cannot . . . give any hint of how a conversion [of affect into symptoms] . . . is brought about. It is obviously not carried out in the same way as an intentional and voluntary action. It is a process which occurs under the pressure of the motive of defense in someone whose organization . . . has a proclivity in that direction (II, p. 166, 1895d).

I shall not try to understand how an electrical or neural process could result from "pressure of the motive of defense". My suspicion at this stage is that our animistic terminology, rather than our blending of it with neurological or electromagnetic schemes of explanation, must be to blame for nonsense here. We can test this by working through a relatively minor yet exemplary 100% anthropomorphic theory: Freud's altogether fascinating account of what it is to dream. A question will focus some of my misgivings.

6. <u>Is our ego awake or asleep when we dream?</u>
This should be a dilemma for any Freudian account of dreaming, whether one means by "ego" the whole person who dreams, or only part of him or her. I see no way around it, as long as we explain his dreaming by reference to what various agencies do within him, or what he does to them. A casual reader of Freud's pellucid prose may not be jolted by some of his lapses of cogency on this topic. So here are samples, numbered to facilitate discussion.

> (i) The wish to sleep (which the conscious ego is concentrated upon . . .) must . . . be . . . one of the motives for the formation of dreams (IV, p. 234, 1900a).
>
> (ii) Dreams are given their shape by the operation of two psychical forces . . . [O]ne of these forces constructs the wish which is expressed by the dream, while the other exercises a censorship upon the dream-wish and . . . brings about a distortion of the expression of the wish (<u>Ibid.</u>, p. 144).
>
> (iii) Criticism . . . involved. . . exclusion from consciousness. The critical agency [has] . . . a closer relation to consciousness than the agency criticized . . . [and also] directs our waking life and determines our voluntary, conscious actions (V, p. 540, 1900a).
>
> (iv) The ego . . . goes to sleep at night, even though then it exercises the censorship on dreams (XIX, p. 17, 1923b).
>
> (v) The critically disapproving agency does not entirely cease to function during sleep (XVIII, p. 268, 1923a).

(vi) A dream may be described as . . . fantasy working on behalf of the maintenance of sleep . . . It is . . . a matter of indifference to the sleeping ego what may be dreamt . . . so long as the dream performs its task (XIX, p. 126, 1925i).

(vii) Between the two agencies . . . a censorship . . . only allows what is agreeable to it to pass through to consciousness . . . [R]epressed material must submit to . . . alterations which mitigate its offensive features . . .

. . . The formation of obscure dreams occurs <u>as though</u> one person who was dependent upon a second person had to make a remark which was bound to be disagreeable in the [latter's] ears . . . [O]n the basis of this simile . . . we have arrived at the concepts of dream, distortion and censorship (V, p. 676, 1901a).

(viii) While this second agency, in which we recognize our normal ego, is concentrated on the wish to sleep, it appears to be compelled by the psycho-physiological conditions of sleep to relax the energy with which . . . [it holds] down the repressed material during the day . . . The danger of sleep being disturbed by [the repressed material] . . . must . . . be guarded against by the ego . . . [E]ven during sleep a certain amount of free attention is on duty to guard against sensory stimuli, and . . . this guard may sometimes consider waking more advisable than a continuation of sleep (<u>Ibid.</u>, p. 679; see XXII, p. 16, 1933a).

(ix) Our ego . . . gives credence to the dream images, as though what it wanted to say was: "Yes, yes! You're quite right, but let me go on sleeping!" The low estimate which we form of dreams when we are awake . . . is probably the judgment passed by our sleeping ego . . .

. . . Anxiety dreams . . . can no longer [prevent] . . . an interruption of sleep but . . . [bring] sleep to an end. In doing

> so it [sic] is merely behaving like a con-
> scientious night watchman . . . suppressing
> disturbances so that the townsmen may not
> be waked up . . . [He] awakens them, if
> the causes seem to him serious and of a
> kind he cannot cope with alone (V, p. 680,
> 1901a; see XXII, p. 17, 1933a).

These statements and the overall account of dreaming to which they belong are initially plausible. But I believe that if we press for additional information about the characters in this story, and their multifarious activities, we are sure to elicit plain nonsense—a sign that the story was covert nonsense to begin with. I shall not worry that at some junctures Freud's narrative seems to have the distinct flaw of implying a vicious regress. In quotation ix, for example, our ego is pictured as not only sleeping, but apparently dreaming too—hardly an auspicious way to explain *our* dreaming.

I-ix represent a dramatic conflict. The main antagonists are the unnamed "agency" working on behalf of our illicit wishes and "repressed material"; and our ego, which keeps the material away from our "consciousness" and prevents its discharge through "voluntary, conscious action". Like a symptom, a dream is a "compromise" between the opposed "psychical forces" (see XXII, p. 15, 1933a). And since this compromise leads to relative calm within us, sleep is made easier.

Obviously Freud means that *we* slumber, but how about our ego? Well, the agency that "constructs the wish which is expressed by the dream" is on the alert, ready to send forbidden material to consciousness. If there is going to be any struggle, or negotiated compromise, our ego must be reasonably awake. On the other hand, would it not sound incongruous if Freud said that our ego is fully vigilant as we snooze? After all, we tehd to consider our ego the real us; and if we sleep when we dream, our ego should too.

If my reconstruction is near the mark, we can see why Freud inconsistently portrays our ego as wishing to sleep, definitely "sleeping", wanting to "go on sleeping" (i, vi, ix), and yet exercising "censorship", imposing "alterations" on the repressed material, doing guard duty (ii, vii, viii), and even simultaneously going to sleep and censoring our dreams (iv).

No wonder that he often tries to slip between the horns of this dilemma with a drowsy ego (i, viii). Evidently that is no solution. The nearer our ego comes to being asleep, the less it can act as inquisitor and sentinel.

So far we have only illustrated how Freud's 'interpersonal action' model for dreaming and similar mental states may be self-contradictory. Next I shall try to elicit particulars about the identity and consciousness of his dramatis personae. The upshot is likely to be unmistakable nonsense.

7. 'Who?' questions. At this point I shall occasionally branch out from the numbered anthropomorphic statements of Freud's about dreaming. Now it seems to me that when we hear stories of this type about people, rather than about denizens of a person's mind, we legitimately seek to learn more. Hence my inquiries regarding the personified ego. Consider its "wish to sleep" (i, viii). For whose sleep does it yearn? Does it want me to sleep, or only itself? What relationship is there anyway between its repose and mine? Can I doze off while it remains on the qui vive? In this case there are other identification problems. For instance, whose "free attention is on duty" (viii)? Whose "waking" may the "guard" think "more advisable than a continuation of sleep" (viii)? Mine? Surely not his own! As for the somnolent "townsmen", we should raise further questions. Given Freud's general view of human motivation, can we suppose that any "watchman" is "conscientious" enough to care what happens to his fellow citizens? Why does he call them from their beds to help him quell "disturbances"? Does he otherwise risk harm? Any reply we make to such questions will sound capricious—or deranged. Yet if we were discussing ordinary sentries and villages, we could find answers.

The puzzle is not isolated. Recall Freud's treatment of our instincts or drives. Freud says "these processes strive toward gaining pleasure; psychical activity draws back from any event which might arouse unpleasure" (XII, p. 219, 1911b). But whose enjoyment do they "strive" for? Why mine? Surely it is unintelligible to suppose they enjoy escaping from my homeostatic mental apparatus.

Our bewilderment should become fairly general

when we remember Freud's functional characterization of the ego. He always assigns it "the task of self-preservation", which it carries out "by learning to bring about changes in the external world to its advantage (through activity)" (XXIII, pp. 145 f.). Again we ought to inquire: Which "self" does my ego have the duty of preserving? How is its continued existence related to mine? Granted that it is unconcerned to promote my interests, what exactly do we mean by "its own advantage"? Freud's notion of this prominent actor within us, the ego, now seem quite elusive.

Nor do we find it easier to characterize other performers in his troupe. Our superego must "impose" our "ego ideal" upon our ego (XIX, pp. 34-39, 1923b). Speaking more broadly, our superego has the "functions of self-observation, of conscience and of maintaining the ideal" (XXII, p. 66, 1933a). By analogy with similar descriptions of people, we should find out what goals an "ego ideal" or superego can set for a mini-person, why it bothers to do so, and how it goes about its work. In fact, whom does my superego watch when it engages in "self-observation"--me, my ego, itself? Once more, things you can say about interpersonal goings-on seem to make no sense when the protagonists are inside your mental apparatus.

8. _A counter-argument_. Kathleen Wilkes has recently challenged this kind of reasoning, which I have been calling an "argument from nonsense". In her formulation, the "charge" is

> that only a person, not any part of him, can literally "repress", "censor" . . . and the like. Just as a man, and not his hand, signs a cheque, so a human being, and not a part of his brain, is the one who can perform such actions as "displacing" or "suppressing" emotions. Crediting the ego or superego with such functions is a solecism, a use of anthropomorphic metaphor (1975, p. 133).

Against this, she wants to "defend the allegedly anthropomorphic characterizations" of "hypothesized structures in the brain--such as the ego or id . . . or information retrieval mechanisms", "claiming that [these characterizations] are not metaphorical but literal"; for instance, "describing a cerebroceptive mechanism as . . . 'suppressing id-impulses' can be a literal and accurate description of what goes on, and is not illegitimate but irreducible anthropomorphization" (p. 132).

In support of her claim, Wilkes has a string of examples:

> a washing machine . . . cleans dishes by soaking, soaping, rinsing, and drying them. So also does a human being not possessing such a machine. Thus, a machine does something which humans also do (washes dishes), and, at one general level of description, "in the same way" as a human, namely by soaking, soaping, rinsing, and drying them . . . ["Same way"] must be tied to a specified level of generality in the task description. The point remains, however, that humans and simple machines undeniably share some abilities. A more sophisticated kind of machine plays chess . . . [and] has the capacity to learn from its mistakes, to anticipate and guess the moves of its opponents, to select . . . strategies . . .; it plans, adapts, and follows through strategies, tries to win and can lose . . . [T]he human chess player does also; researchers . . . would . . . say that the computer carries out many of these sub-tasks (at some fairly detailed level of description) "in the same way" as the human . . . [I]t is literally true to say of a machine programmed to φ that it φs: there is no need and no justification for insulating the verb in raised eyebrow quotes, saying that it "φs" (p. 134).

Finally she pictures a "highly sophisticated computer" which

> cleans shoes, plays chess, does the accounts, minds the children . . . and similar tasks . . . [W]e would be justified in saying that it did something intelligently, or perhaps stupidly . . . [I]t might be said to act over-hastily, without thinking hard enough. Such attributions--adverbial comments on the manner of performance--would not be anthropomorphic. We can make <u>literal</u>

> attributions of many psychological states to it . . . [C]ertain predicates hitherto restricted to humans . . . may be true of sophisticated computers also.
>
> . . . The ego . . . is no more "human" than our advanced robot--indeed, far less . . . [since] it shares far fewer predicates with us than does the robot. The id and superego are even more restricted in scope . . . Yet they are capable of some highly complex tasks . . . The inference . . . is . . . that . . . such predications [are] completely <u>literal</u> (p. 135).

Wilkes repeatedly underscores literalness. Apparently, then, she believes that theorists such as Freud are not merely using "anthropomorphic metaphor". At any rate, she does say it "is not illegitimate but irreducible anthropomorphization" to describe something inside us (or our brain) as "suppressing id-impulses". This implies that such descriptions <u>are</u> anthropomorphic--literally and not metaphorically. Yet when she introduces her "sophisticated" (but I hope not jaded) robot, she declares that her comments on its "manner of performance" are "not . . . anthropomorphic" after all. So we have a choice. We can interpret Wilkes's counter-argument as <u>either</u> an attempt to legitimate anthropomorphization, <u>or</u> an attempt to prove that we are not really anthropomorphizing, not even metaphorically, when we say of an ego, a neurone system, or a machine that it represses, censors, retrives information, washes the dishes, plans and follows a strategy, wins, loses--and thereby acts intelligently, stupidly, or over-hastily.

For my purposes, it scarcely matters how you read Wilkes, or how you define anthropomorphization. I believe Wilkes might agree with me on the essential point. We do speak quite "literally" of secret policemen repressing dissidents; of bureaucrats censoring the newspapers; of historians retrieving documents; of Girl Scouts washing their mess gear; of a chessmaster devising and sticking to his plan, triumphing, conceding defeat--and doing so astutely, unwisely, or prematurely. If any descriptions are anthropomorphic, these are. Presumably if we go on and give "literal" reports, using the same verbs and adverbs, of what an ego, a neurone system, or a machine is up to, these verbs and adverbs retain the same "literal" meaning.

Whether or not you choose to say that our descriptions of ego, neurone, or machine behavior are anthropomorphic, you have to admit that they put the antics of policemen, bureaucrats, historians, Girl Scouts, chessmasters, egos, neurones, and machines into the same respective categories. We are ascribing the same behavior to a human agent and to his or her counterpart.

Apparently Wilkes is untroubled by the discrepancy that has interested me since Chapter One: We can say many _other_ things of the human agent that we cannot intelligibly say of his or her counterpart. My reviews of the Freudian scenario for hysterical symptoms and dreams had enough examples. Why does our ego find certain ideas "objectionable", and therefore repress them? A human censor might either take pride in his work, or simply do it because the job offers high pay and retirement benefits; but how could an ego or a mechanical device be thus motivated? Do Wilkes's computers play chess for the prize money or renown they will get, or only because the game fascinates them? Are they squeamish about cheating in order to win? Are they sore losers? Do they slip into despondency when they are behind? Do they go out of their way to humiliate opponents? I gather that Wilkes has no more inclination than I do to answer these otherwise appropriate questions. I am strongly inclined to reason that since you can answer inquiries of this type when you relate the carryings-on of paradigmatic agents--human beings--your verbs and adverbs must not mean what they do in those cases. Wilkes's counter-argument is largely negative: such characterizations "are _not_ metaphorical"; "there is no need and no justification for insulating the verb in raised eyebrow quotes"; "the ego . . . is no more 'human' than our advanced robot". We are never told what the verbs and adverbs do or could mean. Hence my conclusion that as things stand, these delightful animistic stories of our mental life are incoherent.

To corroborate and amplify my misgivings toward animism, I shall devote the final two sections of this chapter to puzzles about the Freudian notions of consciousness and the unconscious. My immediate question will be this:

9. <u>Can there be multiple centers of consciousness within us?</u> We have accumulated riddles about consciousness. In this chapter alone, we noticed

(section 4) that Freud called a system of permeable neurones "consciousness", and we considered the honorific title unwarranted. We struggled to make sense of Freud's doctrine that in hysteria, your "charged" memory of a traumatic event gets pushed away from your consciousness (section 5). When we examined Freud's anthropomorphic model of dreaming (section 6), we saw no way to avoid saying that our ego is, or is not, endowed with waking consciousness while we dream. From our attempts to learn more about the agencies within us whose struggles create or disguise our dreams, and produce neurotic symptoms (section 7), we can derive another untoward result: We must distinguish our own consciousness from that of our alert or drowsy ego. For doesn't our ego consciously repress ideas? And how can it do so without being conscious of those that are dangerously erotic? Since our consciousness fails to register the harmful ideas and our ego's repressive behavior, it follows that there are two separate arenas of consciousness within us: our ego's and our own. This may not be an unintelligible doctrine. Let's test it.

Freud briefly took over a 'multiple centers' view from Charcot, and beginning in 1892 wrote of an hysteric's "second consciousness" (I, p. 153, 1940d; II, p. 15, 1893a; III, p. 39, 1893h). Later Freud objected to this view on methodological grounds. He vigorously rejected the argument that "instead of subscribing to the hypothesis of unconscious ideas of which we know nothing, we had better assume that consciousness can be split up, so that certain ideas or other psychical acts may constitute a consciousness apart" (XII, p. 263, 1912g). He condemned this proposal as

> a gratuitous assumption, based on abuse of the word "conscious". We have no right to extend the meaning of this word . . . to . . . include a [second] consciousness of which the owner himself is not aware. If philosophers find difficulty in accepting . . . unconscious ideas . . . an unconscious consciousness seems to me even more objectionable. The cases described as splitting of consciousness . . . might better be denoted as shifting of consciousness between two different psychical complexes which become conscious and unconscious in alternation (Ibid., see XIV, p. 170, 1915e;

XX, p. 3, 1925d).

Perhaps; but Freud's theories hardly conform to this rule. Turn back to his statements about dreaming that I quoted in section 6. Statements i-v and vii-ix all record activities that demand conscious mini-agents--at least two opponents, really--of whose machinations the dreamer himself is ignorant. Here and elsewhere, animistic theories inevitably saddle us with one or more "consciousness of which its owner himself is not aware".

Are there good reasons that Freud should allow but one consciousness per individual? He remarks that "the assumption of consciousness" in a person other than onself "rests upon an inference and cannot share the direct certainty we have of our own consciousness" (XIV, p. 169, 1915e). For the sake of argument, I must withdraw all the accusations of nonsense that I made in Chapters One (sections 4-10), Two, and Three against this notion of "direct certainty". I shall not balk at Freud's inferential account of our knowledge of other minds. Then I will ask whether it is any more dubious to suppose that other centers of consciousness exist within me, than to suppose that consciousness exists within another person.

My non-Freudian reply is that the cases are radically different. It makes sense to describe various procedures for identifying other people, deciding whether they are awake, and determining what they feel, think, fear, want, or intend to be doing. I can perceptually discriminate the body of another person. I can watch his facial expression and his gestures, both of which often convey his moods, wishes, and intentions. Above all, he can verbally disclose his mental state; he can tell us--candidly, or perhaps exaggerating, understating, or distorting--whatever he believes, feels, and wants. We can meaningfully explain how we draw an "inference" of this type, how it may go wrong, how we double-check, and how we rectify our mistakes. If you feel comfortable with jargon, you can say that this is part of our language game of inferring another person's consciousness.

If there were other centers of consciousness within me besides my own consciousness, they could not possibly have a role in these proceedings, these "inference" language games. My ego, id, superego, neurone systems, and so on have a kind of body, I suppose, but it is nonsense to speak of their faces and limbs, their facial expressions and their gestures: their grins, frowns, blushes, shrugs. They have no voices, and consequently it is unintelligible to describe them as telling me their state of mind--or keeping it secret from me. When my psychoanalyst learns about the agencies he thinks I shelter, he or she cannot dispense with my consciousness. He must listen to <u>me</u> report or misreport my dreams, and free-associate about them. So we have an additional reason against postulating egos and similar agencies within us: they must have their own consciousness, and we can make no sense of that implication.

In fact I believe there are deeply interesting general difficulties of a similar kind about consciousness and the unconscious. I think a key question is this:

10. <u>What is it for an idea to be 'in' our consciousness or unconscious?</u> The doctrines I want to examine here seem largely animistic, and they are to some degree analogues or extensions of the standard philosophical theories of mind that we examined in previous chapters. For instance, the simplest account Freud gives is perceptual. He likens the presence of an idea before our consciousness to our "perception of the outside world through the sense organs" (XIV, p. 171, 1915e). I shall not go over the ground we covered in sections 4 and 5 of Chapter One. But I will admit some parallelism between our awareness of what happens inside our bodies--digestion or indigestion, for example--and our tactile, auditory, and other methods of perceiving the extra-somatic world. We can meaningfully speak of unawareness, inaccuracy, and downright error in both cases. Not so with our ideas. What would it be like to misperceive or to overlook an idea? Until such details are explained, I will shelve this Freudian account of our having an idea before consciousness.

Freud also proposes what I would call an 'attention' theory. He writes,

> Becoming conscious is connected with the application of . . . attention . . . which, as it seems, is only available in a specific quantity, and this may have been diverted from the train of thought in question on to some other purpose . . . If . . . we come

> upon an idea which will not bear criticism,
> we break off: We drop the cathexis of at-
> tention . . . [But] the train of thought
> . . . can continue to spin itself out with-
> out attention being turned to it again,
> unless . . . it reaches a specially high
> degree of intensity which forces attention
> to it (V, pp. 593 f., 1900a).

This doctrine is vulnerable to 'Who?' questions and also the charge of multiplying centers of consciousness within each person. For instance, who directs attention to the ideas and trains of thought that run through our mind? Do we focus and shift our attention, or does a mini-agency have this job? Is the aiming done consciously by us or the agency? Who continues thinking our unattended train of thought? Is it perhaps not entertained by any agency--including ourselves--when our attention leaves it? Yet how could it reach "a specially high degree of intensity" while there is no one attending to it whom it bothers intensely? If we were talking literally of people and any of the countless things they attend to--expectant mothers and their labor pains, machinists and their lathes--questions of this form would be answerable. Here all replies sound bizarre.

I would derive a third and last theory of ideas-in-consciousness from an attempt of Freud's to characterize "preconscious" ideas. According to Freud, their peculiarity is that they are

> brought into consciousness with word presentations . . .
>
> These word presentations are residues of memories: they were at one time perceptions . . . [O]nly something which has been a <u>Cs.</u> [conscious] perception can become conscious, and . . . anything arising from within (apart from feelings) that seeks to become conscious must try to transform itself into external perceptions: this becomes possible by means of memory traces . . .
>
> The part played by word presentations now becomes perfectly clear. By their interposition internal thought-processes are made into perceptions . . . When a hypercathexis [intensification, excitation] of

> the process of thinking takes place, thoughts
> are <u>actually</u> perceived--as if they came
> from without--and are consequently held to
> be true (XIX, pp. 20-23, 1923b; see XIV,
> p. 201, 1915e).

Again we will elicit nonsense if we try to identify the actors, and decide whether their consciousness is distinct from that of the person in whom these high-jinks take place. Even if it made sense to say "thoughts are . . . perceived", I would doubt, as a matter of humble fact, that such thoughts "are . . . held to be true".

We have not attained such clarity about ideas and thoughts that are in our consciousness. So, although Freud's notion of unconscious mental events is quite daring and original, we should expect to have analogous difficulties with it. We should be particularly hesitant to say, without preliminary questioning, that certain ideas and instincts are "before" or "in" our unconscious.

We should start with Freud's explanations. Mostly he seems to rebut objections of principle against his notion of the unconscious. He seldom attempts to spell out what it means to assert that there are ideas and various other mental goings-on in our minds that we are not aware of. The nearest he comes to furnishing a positive argument for his assumption is when he discusses one of Bernheim's experiments with hypnosis. Freud reports that the hypnotized subject

> was ordered to execute a certain action at
> a . . . fixed moment after his awakening
> . . . He awakes . . . [with] no recollec-
> tion of his hypnotic state, and yet at the
> pre-arranged moment there rushes into his
> mind the impulse to do such and such a thing,
> and he does it consciously, though not know-
> ing why. It seems impossible to give any
> other description of the phenomenon than to
> say that the order had been present in the
> mind of the person in a condition of latency,
> or had been present unconsciously, until
> the given moment came (XII, p. 261, 1912g).

Freud also proposes a more "dynamic view of the phenomenon":

> this idea became <u>active</u> . . . The real
> stimulus to the action being the order . . .
> it is hard not to concede that the idea of
> the physician's order became active too.
> Yet this idea did not reveal itself to con-
> sciousness . . . it remained unconscious, an
> so it was <u>active</u> and <u>unconscious</u> at the same
> time (<u>Ibid</u>.; see XXIII, p. 285, 1940b).

What does Freud's preferred "description", and especially his "dynamic view", amount to here? Could Freud mean that the <u>subject</u> of this experiment was thinking of Bernheim's order in between times? No, because Freud says the man was unaware that he had received it until a corresponding "impulse" flooded his consciousness. Is Freud claiming that part of the subject's mind--for instance, the receptacle for unconscious ideas--was pondering Bernheim's command? If so, Freud would have to deal with awkward 'Who?' questions, and also postulate another center of awareness within the subject. We already noticed this kind of difficulty in Freud's 'attention' theory of conscious ideas, when he said that a "train of thought . . . can continue to spin itself out without attention being turned to it". Our puzzlement should not diminish because now we are talking about unconscious ideas. What could we mean if we supposed that they unfold or persist, although neither the person in whom they occur, nor any agency within him--his id, his unconscious, his repressive ego--takes note of them? Surely the unconscious idea resulting from the hypnotist's order did not contemplate itself!

Defenders of Freud may retort that neither the subject nor any part of him must dwell upon the hypnotically induced idea: It is simply laid up within his psyche, but outside the range of his consciousness "until the given moment". I would ask for clarification of the spatial metaphor "outside", and probably I would be told that it means simply "not apprehended by the conscious mind" (XIV, p. 161, 1915e). Freudians might attempt to enrich this 'warehouse' theory by adding that the hypnotist's command has left a "permanent trace" in our unconscious (see XIX, p. 230, 1925a). But I would remain perplexed, for three reasons:

(i) Like the Cartesian account of the mental as non-physical, which I examined a couple of chapters ago, the warehouse theory of unconscious ideas sounds too irreducibly negative; all the more so because we found ourselves unable to articulate what it is for ideas to be present to our consciousness.

(ii) The "permanent trace" proviso helps very little; certainly it is not sufficient to distinguish between our unconscious and conscious ideas. Why should not both sorts of ideas leave a mark on our unconscious?

(iii) A negative characterization of unconscious ideas, with or without a "permanent trace" clause, lends no support to Freud's imaginative "dynamic" view that certain ideas may be "active and unconscious at the same time". Why should an idea that does "not reveal itself to consciousness" be active? Scars, bruises, and similar traces often have no effect on us.

So much for the attempt to illustrate how hypnotically induced ideas are in our unconscious. I am equally unimpressed by Freud's appeal to our capacity for calling up ideas we have not been conscious of in quite a while. He argues, "When all our latent memories are taken into consideration, it becomes totally incomprehensible how the existence of the unconscious can be denied" (XIV, p. 167, 1915e). No doubt human powers of recollection are mystifying, and we need some explanation of them. But will we do anything more than compound our bafflement if we account for these powers by means of an unintelligible "active" theory, or an intolerably vague 'storage' doctrine?

Freudians may protest, 'How else can we explain our abilities and sometimes peculiar inabilities to remember, our post-hypnotic behavior, as well as our dreams, free associations, parapraxes, and neurotic symptoms? Must we not assume the presence of more ideas in us than we are conscious of?' Yet this 'How else?' begs the very question we have just been debating: what it means to say that unconscious ideas are present in us. Besides, nonsense explains nothing.

Generally, we have noticed that both Freud's mechanistic and his anthropomorphic stories of our mental life require the existence of things within us that we do not detect: streams of energy, high-voltage ideas, pressing instincts, battling agencies. In order to explain people's conflict behavior as a clash of inanimate forces, or of contentious actors within the mental arena, Freud must find room for more than what appears in our stream of consciousness. However, he fails to elucidate what it is for mental goings-on to be in our consciousness or elsewhere--presumably in our unconscious. Since all of his explanatory schemes depend on this distinction, they would be premature even if they were both relevant and coherent. But in spite of these problems, I remain convinced that Freud's models of the mind, its component forces and their interplay, are highly original and suggestive. They encourage us to take unorthodox and fruitful perspectives toward aberrant as well as 'normal' human conduct. The difficulties we have uncovered should challenge us to repair Freud's theories and to explore alternatives that are as bold and wide-ranging. In particular, as we shall be reminded in the next chapter, any post-Freudian theory of what goes on in a person must come to terms with the provocative data that he brought to our attention, and his ingenious attempts to account for them.

CHAPTER FIVE

THE PROBLEM OF 'ALIEN DESIRES'

We have seen repeatedly that no theorist of mind would disagree on a number of salient, plain facts. Here is a sampling. Human beings enjoy a rich inner life. For instance, they are conscious most of the time. Often they think, worry, decide, dream, and seem to be troubled in the ways that Freud noticed. By the same token, no theorist would dispute that people sometimes exercise more, or less, control over what they do. Occasionally various circumstances force them to act, or render them powerless to do something. At other moments they seize the initiative, and it is up to them which among several courses of action they pursue.

We also remarked that there is an undeniable connection between these two clusters of plain fact. A creature, or a robot, that has no mental life--no awareness of what it is doing, or of what it could do, and no favorable or unfavorable attitudes on the subject--can hardly be said to exercise or to lose control over its behavior. An apartment door might be forced open, but we cannot intelligibly report that it was forced open against its will--or that it sprang open voluntarily, or was glad to oblige. Speaking positively, part of what makes our behavior voluntary, or unwilling, as the case may be, is our consciousness of what we are doing and could be doing, as well as our corresponding pro- or con-attitude. The same goes for power to act and powerlessness. Under present conditions, it depends upon me whether I remain seated or stand. It is not up to me whether I jump up and touch the ceiling, which is out of my reach. My power in the first case, and lack of it in the second, obviously have something to do with the fact that if I resolve to stay seated or to get up, I will act accordingly, while my decision to touch the ceiling will have no such result. By contrast, an unstable explosive might blow up or it might not; there may be no way to predict. However, the outcome does not depend upon the explosive in the way my standing or sitting depends upon me; for it is nonsense to assert that the explosive decides, or cannot decide, whether it should detonate.

Once we forge beyond such truisms, and particularly when we try to analyze free action, power to act in alternative ways, and the role of our mental states in both, we get bogged down in seemingly endless controversy. I hope to make some headway by concentrating on a rather limited but very obdurate puzzle: what might be called the enigma of 'alien desires'.

1. *Acting freely and doing what you want.* As we noted, only when a person wants to perform an action of kind $\underline{A}$, and does so, can we say that he acted freely. We could not characterize him as doing an $\underline{A}$-type action unwillingly--for example, under coercion--unless we assumed that he is somehow against doing it. To illustrate, imagine a zombie. It is conscious but bereft of pro- and con-attitudes, even toward being bossed around. How could it be said to act unfreely, or freely? How would you go about forcing it to do your bidding if it were not reluctant?

Thus in circumstances where you do $\underline{A}$, your wanting to seems to be a logically necessary condition for your doing $\underline{A}$ freely, and your wanting not to seems equally indispensable for your doing $\underline{A}$ unfreely. Are these conative states sufficient as well? Apparently not. At least two prima facie solid counter-examples deserve careful scrutiny. The first one I shall look at connects with the Freudian theories I examined in the preceding chapter. Despite their imperfections, these daring conjectures must be taken very seriously by philosophers of mind and action.

Freud's view seems to imply that when people do what they have a repressed, unconscious urge to do, their freedom is diminished. But should it not be enhanced when they do what they want? Or must we distinguish between our own desires and those that assail us from our id or unconscious? Freud says a neurotic may have "ideas and impulses" that "give the patient himself the impression of being powerful guests from an alien world" (Strachey, 1953-74, XVI, p. 378). Yet he also asserts that the "core of our being . . . is formed by the obscure id" (XXII, p. 197). So it is unclear whether we can separate the person from his wayward inclinations.

The other counter-example I plan to worry about also touches our "core". Our socialization decisively shapes our personality, including our basic desires. Often the result seems to be a serious loss of freedom. I shall use a familiar but politically charged illustration from two social psychologists, Daryl and Sandra

Bem. They ask us to imagine that miraculously "sex discrimination were to end tomorrow" in contemporary American society. Nevertheless, they believe, women would not rapidly gain a proportionate share of political and corporate offices, professional training and employment, or simply control over their own individual lives. Why not? Bem and Bem's account underscores the effect of social conditioning upon a female's key attitudes. They write,

> job discrimination . . . does impede women who choose to become lawyers or managers or physicians. But it does not, by itself, help us to understand why so many women 'choose' to be secretaries and nurses rather than executives and physicians; why only 3 percent of ninth-grade girls as compared to 25 percent of the boys 'choose' careers in science or engineering; or why 63 percent of America's married women 'choose' not to work at all. It certainly doesn't explain those young women whose vision of the future includes only marriage, children, and living happily ever after; . . . who almost never 'choose' to pursue a career. Discrimination frustrates choices already made. Something more pernicious perverts the motivation to choose (1975, p. 201).

The Bems' percentages may be outdated, but the pattern endures. What interested me is Bem and Bem's inverted-commas notion of choosing and acting upon one's choice. The women in question are doing what they want; and if instead their goals were similar to those of men, they would not be held back merely because they are female. Why isn't this enough for freedom? How does their conditioning "pervert . . . the motivation to choose", with the result that many females who opt for subordinate and dependent roles, notably "marriage, children, and living happily ever after", are not acting as voluntarily, are not as free to act differently, as they appear to be? In what sense are these women's socially induced desires for auxiliary status 'alien' desires? I shall try to elucidate this species of diminished freedom, and also the kind resulting from neurosis, by looking first at some easier cases. For brevity, I shall mainly discuss the conative attitudes we get from socialization and neurosis; but a thorough-going inquiry into this subject would have to take account of the relevant beliefs on which our attitudes are based, such as women's underestimation of their talents.

2. <u>Coercion</u>. Most probably we think of someone who acts on alien desires as being somehow coerced, or anyway in the same predicament as a coerced individual. But what do we mean when we say that people are forced or compelled to do something they do not want to do? Here are two representative accounts, by eminent contemporary philosophers:

> If a hurricane wind blows you twenty yards across a street, you cannot be said to have crossed the street voluntarily, since you were compelled to do it and given no choice (Feinberg, 1970, pp. 274f.).

> We act under <u>compulsion</u>, in the literal sense . . . <u>when we are literally being physically restrained from without in implementing the desires which we have upon reacting to the total stimulus situation</u> . . . <u>and are physically made to perform a different act instead</u> (Grünbaum, 1971, pp. 303 f.; emphasis his).

The "hurricane wind" satisfies both formulations. I gather that it is supposed to lift you off your feet and deposit you on the far side of the road. Your desire, which you have "upon reacting to the total stimulus situation", is to remain on this side, and to continue your stroll without interference.

Undoubtedly these accounts of being forced to act are on the right track. But I discern two noteworthy hitches in them so far. To begin with, if you are "physically restrained" in this manner by wind currents, we do <u>not</u> have a case of your acting, but of something happening to you. Being swept twenty yards across a street is not the same as performing any sort of action. Therefore in the circumstances it is false to assert that you are "compelled to do" something, or that you "are physically made to perform a different act" from the one you desired. Which act, precisely? No act seems to have been reported. So accounts like these appear to rule out, rather than to elucidate, acting under compulsion.

The second hitch has to do with the inescapable notion of choice. Is it true that when you are forced to do something, you are "given no choice"? Consider the hostages of a terrorist, their agonized relatives, and the embarrassed authorities. Some of these individuals might simply be overcome by panic. Their behavior would resemble an episode of shivering, stuttering, or uncontrollable weeping. These are not forms of action, any more than being propelled by a hurricane wind is a form of action. So if the hostages and some of the others become frightened out of their wits, they are not doing anything in compliance with the terrorist's demands. The significant point is that insofar as they _are_ complying, knuckling under to actual or threatened violence, they seem to be doing what they have chosen to do. In general terms, I assume they have chosen to do whatever appears most likely to minimize death and suffering. In their justifiably agitated state of mind, compliance may seem a less risky alternative than defiance.

The second author I quoted displays some awareness of the mismatch between such paradigms of constrained action and his "literal" definition. But he takes the heroic course of denying that these _are_ examples of coerced action. He argues, "When a bankteller [sic] hands over cash during a robbery upon feeling the revolver pressing against his ribs, he is _not acting under compulsion_ in my literal sense . . . [He] is doing what he genuinely wants to do _under the given conditions_" (Ibid., p. 304; first emphasis added). In response, I feel like asking, If this individual's behavior and circumstances do not illustrate "acting under compulsion", what could? A die-hard might hold fast to the proposed "literal" definition, and tell us that we would have a _bona fide_ instance of constrained action if the cash were "physically" wrenched from the teller's clutches. But then we confront the first hitch again: when currency is torn from your grasp, that is not an action of yours, and consequently there is no action you are compelled to perform. So far we have failed to explicate coercion and its link with choice. However, a general theory of free and unfree action has been available, and increasingly popular, since the early 1970s; perhaps it will do the job.

3. _A hierarchical analysis of acting under compulsion_. Our aim is to understand how some of our conative attitudes, which have their source in neurosis and in socialization, may deprive us of freedom. If we can articulate the sense in which a coerced individual wants and also does not want to do what he is

forced to do, perhaps we will have a model for these trickier situations. The analysis I am going to explore now seems promising because it distinguishes "orders" of desire, choice, and kindred types of conative attitude.

The earliest explicitly hierarchical account that I have seen in print is Gerald Dworkin's (1970). He realizes that only actions can be compelled, not things that happen to you, such as being lifted up by the wind, or having money ripped from your grasp. Thus Dworkin's main example features the prey of a highwayman timorously surrendering his billfold. Uninspired behavior, no doubt, but nonetheless an action. The holdup victim also exercises choice. He deliberately turns over his money to the armed robber, hoping thereby to save his skin. Dworkin also has an account of the victim's not wanting to do so. This is where the analysis becomes hierarchical. Dworkin postulates a further level of choice and desire, explaining, "What [the victim] doesn't want to do when faced with the highwayman is to hand money over in these circumstances, for these reasons" (1970, p. 372). You could say that Dworkin's levels of conation are semantical or logical. On the ground floor, his protagonist wants to abandon his money so as to stay alive. But he has a contrary attitude, on a higher plane, toward the prudential motive of his action. In effect, he condemns his operative desire. In Dworkin's words, people

> resent acting for certain reasons; they would not choose to be motivated in certain ways. They mind acting simply in order . . . to avoid unpleasant consequences . . .
>
> [P]art of the human personality . . . takes up an "attitude" toward the reasons, desires and motives which determine . . . conduct . . .
>
> [We] consider ourselves compelled because we find it painful to act for these reasons (pp. 377 ff.; see Dworkin, 1976, p. 25).

Dworkin proceeds to define the overall notion of "acting freely" in similar terms. He says that "$\underline{A}$ [the person] does $\underline{X}$ freely if, and only if, $\underline{A}$ does $\underline{X}$ for reasons which he doesn't mind acting from" (1970, p. 381; cp. Dworkin, 1976, pp. 24 ff.).

Before we decide whether this is a satisfactory approach to the kind of wanting and not wanting that seems to be involved in coercive situations, we should acknowledge some refinements that Harry Frankfurt has added to the hierarchical theory, most of them subsequently adopted by Dworkin (1976, pp. 24 f.). For one thing, Frankfurt attributes great ontological significance to the distinction between various strata of desire within us. He says, "one essential difference between persons and other creatures" is that persons "are able to form what I shall call 'second-order desires'" (1971, p. 6). Actually he goes on to separate two kinds of second-order desire: our desire merely to <u>have</u>, or experience, a certain type of ground-floor desire; and our desire that it should "be the desire that moves [us] effectively to act" (1971, p. 10). The latter sort of elevated desire is what interests Frankfurt, and he dubs it a "second-order volition". In effect, it marks off persons from "other creatures". Frankfurt explains, "It is having second-order volitions, and not having second-order desires generally, that I regard as essential to being a person" (<u>ibid</u>; see also Charles Taylor, 1976, pp. 281 ff.). Certain individuals whom Frankfurt brands "wantons" fall short of personhood on this criterion. They "are not persons because, whether or not they have desires of the second order, they have no second-order volitions"; specifically, "a wanton does not care about his will . . . [H]e does not care which of his first-order inclinations is the strongest" (1971, p. 6).

How does this hierarchical theory of motivation bear on constraint? Frankfurt's view is that offers as well as threats may be coercive. His upstairs-downstairs account of both reads,

> an offer is coercive . . . when the person is moved into compliance by a desire . . . which he would overcome if he could . . . a desire by which he does not want to be driven . . .
>
> [A] person's autonomy may be violated by a threat in the same way . . .
>
> In submitting to a threat, a person invariably does something which he does not really want to do (1972, pp. 80 f.).

On this analysis, a coerced individual's second-order volition is at odds with his operative desire. But in a more recent account of these matters, Frankfurt seems to acknowledge another possibility. This is when "the alternatives [a person] confronted comprised a set from which he did not want to have to choose", but he "preferred without reservation the one he pursued"; moreover, "he endorses the desire that moves him to act", so that it is "in accordance with a second-order volition" (1975, pp. 14 ff.). Frankfurt only declares that such a person "did not act altogether willingly" (p. 14). Yet I believe some examples of being forced to act display this pattern, although they violate Frankfurt's requirement that a coerced individual must be "moved into compliance by . . . a desire by which he does not want to be driven". So perhaps compulsion does not have to involve conflict between levels of desire.

    This brings me to my principal misgiving toward both Dworkin's and Frankfurt's double-decker analysis of constrained action: Do any cases like theirs satisfy their general stipulation that when you give in to a coercive offer or threat, you have a second-order desire not to be thus motivated? The only cases I know of occur when we carry prudence to cowardly extremes, find ourselves unable to assume reasonable risks--and especially when we put other people in jeopardy to shield ourselves from lesser harm. But do we always, or even commonly, fall apart like this in coercive situations? I doubt it. Look again at Dworkin's holdup story: Most victims would, at the time of the incident and later, give their second-order approval of their cautious ground-floor motives. Few will yearn, from their upper-deck tribune, to be stirred by defiant rather than prudent impulses.

    I wonder if we need Dworkin's and Frankfurt's two-layer apparatus even to interpret their hand-picked cases. Continue to contemplate the holdup victim; ask yourself, What is likely to be the primary object of his 'not wanting': the loss of his pocket money, or the "reasons" he has for abandoning it? Surely he "minds" his action, and particularly its financial consequences, more than he "minds" his own motivational state? Surely the former is more "painful" to him? Why, pace Frankfurt, should the compliant holdup victim want to "overcome" his operative desire "if he could"? Either he stratospherically dislikes merely having the desire to comply, or else he opposes it because it "moves him affectively to act". Presumably the latter is what evokes his second-order condemnation. But is he distressed merely because the inclination is on hand while he acts, or because his deed and various consequences result from the inclination? Again, presumably the latter. So it appears that our putative second-order volitional antics are concerned more with our behavior and its effect, than with any first-order desire that engenders our action. Dworkin and Frankfurt must be mistaken, or at least guilty of hyperbole, when they suppose that a constrained person mainly "doesn't want" some desire or other to move him.

We can strengthen this 'superfluity' objection if we turn to a contrasting example which both Dworkin and Frankfurt produce, with fairly similar details, to illustrate how an unconstrained person's first- and second-order desires are in harmony. Instead of the highwayman's victim, who "doesn't want. . . to hand money over . . . for these reasons", Dworkin conjures up someone who "might want to hand over some money to another because he is asked by a relative, or because he is feeling charitable, or because he desires to rid himself of worldly things" (1970, p. 371). Dworkin's "because" clauses bother me. Specifically, I am unsure whether he is merely reporting his protagonist's first-order inclination to give away money "because he is asked", etc.--namely a desire to give that came into being when a relative solicited alms. Or is Dworkin reporting his hero's second-order desire to have a particular reason for his eleemosynary actions? Evidently Dworkin intends the latter. But then I would rephrase my 'superfluity' complaint by inquiring whether the protagonist longs only--or primarily--for one of these unselfish motives. I think there is a more plausible diagnosis: He admires certain forms of behavior--munificence toward kinfolk and the needy; asceticism or the simple life. But he transfers his admiration to the desires that generate such behavior. Anyway, if hierarchical theorists put the accent on a person's second-order desire to be moved "effectively to act" by first-order munificent, charitable, or ascetic inclinations, they again face the dilemma I constructed in the last paragraph.

I admit there may be desires as elevated as those that Dworkin and Frankfurt call "second-order". My grumble is that any prima facie case they give tends to break down. Do you want to have the desire to act generously, or only to do something generous? Can we really distinguish between your being "effectively" stirred by a charitable impulse, and your doing something genuinely charitable--as opposed to something that looks so, but brings you fame and big tax deductions?

At any rate, our authors have trouble maintaining their distinction, and hence proving the need for second-order desires. This emerges from a variant case of first- and second-order harmony imagined by Frankfurt. His hero now "decides to . . . give the money in his pocket to the first person he meets", but he encounters a threatening gunman; frightened, he "loses touch with his original intention . . . and . . . hands over his money in order to escape death" (1972, p. 82). As things turned out, Frankfurt says, the fellow is coerced; but he would not have been if he had relinquished his money "with his original benevolent intention", for then his "motive . . . would have been just the motive from which he wanted to act" (p. 82).

We have already remarked that frequently when someone *is* forced to give up his cash, it is equally true that his "motive . . . [is] just the motive from which he wanted to act", namely the motive of self-preservation. But my present criticism is that we need not burden either constrained or unconstrained donors with an upper-story volition. To make this plain, suppose that Frankfurt's budding philanthropist had carried out his "original benevolent intention". If we wish to differentiate this situation from the outcome Frankfurt imagined, where the man gave under duress, we can do so using first-order desires alone. We can say that he desired to engage in the agreeable activity of giving-without-intimidation, and did not want to engage in the unpleasant activity of giving-under-pressure. If you dislike hyphens, you can suppose that he had a couple of grass-roots desires: the urge to give, and the urge to do so in unmenacing circumstances.

But can we provide a non-hierarchical account of the desires of someone who is coerced? Plainly there is more to be said than that he chooses to submit and minimizes risks. How shall we articulate our basic notion that, as Frankfurt says, a coerced individual also "does something which he does not really want to do"? For a crude start, my non-hierarchical suggestion is rather that "he does not really want to" be in such coercive circumstances. That is confusing, however. The very reason we say he is constrained is that no action of escaping the situation is available to him. Any attempt to flee it would be defiance, which he has rejected in favor of submission. So there is no alternative action, other than complying, that we might say he does "really want to" perform. In what sense, then, is his attitude one of aversion to his setup? My proposal is to say that his top preference would be for a situation in which he is not overwhelmed by threats or irresistible offers. Translated into pragmatic terms, this might mean: If he had been forewarned of this situation, and alerted to a less coercive and otherwise no more disadvantageous alternative, he would have circumnavigated this situation. Now that he has blundered into this one, however, if you asked him to rank compliance, resistance, magical return to the status quo ante, and magical escape simpliciter, he would opt for either of the last-mentioned miracles (see Nozick, 1969, pp. 461 f.). In saying this, I mean nothing occult. My view is that the coercive setting, and not our action or first-order desire, is what we dislike when we reluctantly succumb to threats and offers. This non-hierarchical theory even gets across our pre-analytic notion of what the coerced agent "really wants". Although there is no course of action open to him that he really wants to follow, as conditions stand, his really important attitude is his preference for different circumstances.

Why "really important"? Because if he had been, or were now, in a position to choose, he would not be going along with his oppressors; he would be elsewhere. Uncoerced people who are also doing what they want usually would not prefer turning back the clock or simply getting away.

I have not produced a definitive analysis of coercion, with logically sufficient or logically necessary conditions for saying that a person is forced to do something. Instead I have delineated the crucial pro- and con-attitudes--the 'wanting' and 'not wanting'--that baffled us. Besides being less cumbersome than double-decker theories, my proposal does justice to the vague suggestions of Dworkin and Frankfurt that their protagonists did not "want . . . to hand money over in these circumstances", and "did not want to have to choose" among disagreeable options.

So far, so good; but we still have to tackle the problem of alien desires. By analogy with our results to date, we should try to understand the sense in which a neurotic person, and some individuals who are socialized in certain ways, do what they want, yet perhaps do not really want to. There is no coercive situation they could want to escape, however; so I shall search for bridging examples.

4. <u>Desires produced by hypnosis, secret meddling, and brain-washing</u>. In the larger free-will debate, someone is always bound to parade forth these examples, usually in order to refute the soft determinist's principle that whenever you do what you feel like doing, or what you have chosen to do, you act freely. Among others, Antony Flew has defended that principle, citing as a paradigm of such free action the marriage of two imaginary young people, Murdo and Mairi. Both of them deliberate carefully beforehand, and finally select each other. They are not forced to wed by their families or whatever, and they would not have married if they had chosen not to (Flew, 1955, pp. 149-53).

Challenging Flew's belief that choice brings liberty, Alasdair MacIntyre embellishes the original narrative. MacIntyre informs us that Murdo

> has visited a hypnotist who has [without Murdo's consent] successfully made three suggestions to him . . .: that he shall consider the merits of his female acquaintances, that after due reflection he shall choose [Mairi] . . ., and that he shall forget his visit to the hypnotist . . . [Murdo's] decision is . . . a free act on all Flew's criteria. He considered the . . . alternatives . . .; and if he had chosen otherwise, he would have been able, in Flew's sense, to implement his decision (1957, p. 244).

Has MacIntyre demolished Flew's criteria—not to mention soft determinism generally? Our account of compulsion equips us to deflect MacIntyre's counter-example. The mesmerist provoked Murdo's decision just as inexorably as our highwayman made his victim want to relinquish his money. In fact our holdup victim has more freedom: It is up to him to deliberate; it lies within his power to decide on resistance instead of compliance; and he is aware of the coercive influence shaping his motivational processes, which leaves him in a better position to fight back. There is a broader difference too. Murdo's sudden matrimonial bent, particularly toward Mairi, probably does not spring from his evolving system of beliefs, goals, moods--even from any neurotic impulses that afflict him, or any inclinations he was socially programmed to have. The hypnotist imposed an isolated desire upon him, which may well clash with his dominant proclivities. It is virtually the hypnotist's choice, not Murdo's, that Murdo should settle down with Mairi. Thus I concur with MacIntyre that his expanded story does not illustrate free action. But since it is no longer a _prima facie_ story of Murdo doing what he chooses, it fails to rank as a counter-example against the soft determinist principle that such actions are free.

I would deal similarly with the hallowed fantasy of the "Devil/neurologist", which figured most recently in a symposium between Don Locke and Frankfurt (1975, pp. 104 ff., 120 ff.). There are at least five conceptually interesting variants of this archetypal fiction, not all of them recorded by Locke and Frankfurt:

(1) A Devil, or a diabolical neurologist ("D/n" for short), directly and covertly manipulates all of his victim's (V_1's) attitudes, perhaps by constant tinkering with V_1's brain.

(2) D/n only occasionally, but quite unpredictably, does the same to V_2.

(3) D/n creates V_3 from scratch, inalterably programmed to display just one set of cognitive, affective, and conative responses forever, regardless of what reinforcing or aversive experiences he meets with. No subsequent manipulations by D/n will be necessary.

(4) D/n wires V_4 at 'birth' with some fixed basic drives, emotional dispositions, patterns of reasoning, and Cartesian-Chomskian innate ideas. D/n also endows V_4 with numerous open capacities, to be developed further, or else inhibited, by whatever learning experiences V_4 will undergo. Beyond this, D/n will leave V_4 alone.

(5) The same as (4), except that D/n makes V_5's innate core of attitudes and ideas flexible,

modifiable by learning.

Frankfurt observes, quite correctly, that V_1 is little more than a marionette, and cannot qualify as a genuine person--with desires, thoughts, and so on--however crudely or subtly we define personhood. Therefore V_1 is not a person who is doing what he wants, but unfreely. On the other hand, V_2 is a person with attitudes of his own--as long as D/n stays away. The attitudes produced in V_2 by D/n from time to time are more D/n's than V_2's. They are on a par with the post-hypnotic suggestions inflicted upon Murdo. When V_2 acts in conformity with any implanted desires, he is not doing what he wants, and so once more the question whether he acts unfreely is moot. As for the totally and rigidly programmed V_3, D/n has visited the equivalent of lifelong hypnosis on him. We cannot speak of 'what V_3 himself wants to do'. But V_4 and V_5 strike me as borderline and clear instances, respectively, of people doing what they choose, and able to develop their own tastes. Merely because D/n outfits them with their inalterable or pliable dispositions, we cannot conclude that they lack attitudes of their own--even when they are motivated by D/n-given attitudes. V_4's case seems undecidable, until we discover how dominant or central the attitudes are that D/n built into V_4, and how they mesh or conflict with the outlook V_4 has put together unaided by D/n. Finally, D/n seems to be altogether innocent of gross meddling with V_5's motivation. Hence V_5 is capable of doing what he himself wants, and freely. Naturally if V_5 grows up to be an arch-fiend, or a great benefactor of mankind, some of the blame or credit should go to his maker, D/n. However, we have enough problems on our agenda without considering issues of responsibility.

I intend to compare coercion, hypnosis, and the skulduggery of D/n with the way that neurosis and socialization might curtail our freedom. But first I should situate brain-washing on this continuum. Evidently the term is figurative. Yet we do not lack clear examples of brain-washing. We recall the techniques dramatized in Arthur Koestler's novel Darkness at Noon, where long-time Soviet communists were brought to believe they had betrayed the Party; various types of indoctrination used on American soldiers who were captured in Korea and Vietnam; the re-education of former officials, landlords, and merchants in the People's Republic of China; 'thought reform' of Party bureaucrats during Mao Tse-Tung's cultural revolution. Probably we should include the de-Nazification projects in West and East Germany after World War II. Closer to home, we have read lurid accounts of how mystical and religious groups, such as the Hare Krishna and the 'Moonies', may achieve total mastery over their teen-age acolytes. 'Deprogrammers', hired by distraught parents, often say they must resort to analogous procedures to break the spell. Finally we should mention behavior modification schemes. These may be designed to alter our wicked habits: seriously anti-social proclivities such as child-beating, pyromania, rape, stealing; and such vices as addiction to narcotics, alcohol, or tobacco. I think both voluntary and involuntary programs of this genre count as brain-washing. What I mainly want to exclude is the standard religious and civic indoctrination of children, since that is one of the socializing processes that I hope to elucidate by setting it alongside coercion, hypnosis, the machinations of D/n, and brain-washing.

Before I try to do that, however, I should point out the extent to which choice is, or is not, involved in our cases. While someone acting under duress normally has opted for compliance as the least of evils, but would much rather be in a non-coercive situation, the victims of our hypnotist and of D/n have no such preferences. That is because they are unaware of the hypnotist's or D/n's tampering. A moderately bright victim of brain-washing will realize what is up, and may then decide to cooperate--wholeheartedly or hypocritically--or to resist more or less openly. Even if he has volunteered for behavior modification, he may long for a different scene. Afterwards, if the brain-washing succeeds, a graduate may turn around and sincerely deny that his new attitudes are merely the result of manipulation. He may admit that strong methods were needed to overcome his habits of thought or action; but now his attitudes just seem to him most reasonable.

So much for models; next we should investigate whether they help us understand how neurotic afflictions and some types of social conditioning reduce our freedom.

5. <u>Freudian vs. 'disease' and 'injury' concepts of neurosis</u>. Our task would be easy if the attitudes we consider alien came upon us like fevers or strained

muscles. Our resulting behavior would be akin to symptoms of illness and signs of injury. The situation of a neurotically motivated person would resemble the plight of Murdo, the hypnotized bridegroom, some of D/n's victims, and successfully brainwashed individuals. One's wayward desires would be literally imposed upon one; in this case, however, not by personal, much less diabolical, agencies. This conception may be appropriate to some instances of alcoholism and compulsive drug-taking. Perhaps an irresistible craving resulted from the absorption of enough drug or drink, and the person had no means of knowing that he or she might become 'hooked'. A few of our untoward impulses can be traced to vitamin deficiencies, to low blood sugar, occasionally to a definite and extremely severe childhood trauma. I have not mentioned the major psychoses, and do not plan do, because in such cases the person is often so disturbed that we cannot even begin to contrast his or her attitudes and foreign intrusions. But obviously some of these disorders-- senile dementia, for example--result pretty directly from strokes and brain deterioration. Champions of the 'illness' conception of schizophrenia may be right too. A typical statement of this view comes from psychiatrist E. Fuller Torrey, who writes,

> schizophrenia is most certainly a brain disease . . . [or] several brain diseases . . . [T]hey all affect that part of the brain that handles incoming . . . information, and then hooks up . . . incoming data with the appropriate emotion. In schizophrenia, this central switching system is diseased, so that the person . . . misinterprets the data . . . and hooks up the wrong emotion to the data . . . The part of the brain that is diseased appears to be the limbic system and/or the upper portions of the brain stem (1977, p. 157).

Other experts find no evidence of infections or damage in such cases, and interpret psychotic troubles along Freudian lines, as reflecting tensions and forces at work deep in the person's unconscious. As we noted in the previous chapter, Freud is aware that it often seems to the psychotic and the neurotic individual as if he or she were under attack by hostile agencies. A typical paranoid delusion is reported by a non-Freudian psychiatrist in the United States during the 1950s: his patient imagined that "she has been receiving telepathic messages . . . This experience is denominated, in her language, 'airings' . . . She has received 'airings' from, among other people, President Eisenhower . . . [She says] thoughts were poured on her by some machine done by her enemies" (see Katz, 1967, pp. 431 ff.). Freud cites an equivalent though milder type of neurosis: "the familiar case of sacrelegious thoughts entering the minds of devout persons", as if from without (Strachey, 1953-74, X, pp. 193, 242 f.).

At times Freud encourages us to identify people with their egos, and to cast the id as a foreign invader. We quoted his statement that a psychoanalyst endeavors to "give . . . back . . . command over the id" to the neurotic's faltering ego. His account of how neurosis and psychosis develop has a similar ring. He says that our ego "serves three masters", trying "to bring their claims and demands into harmony . . . [These] masters are the external world, the superego, and the id" (XXII, p. 77). If their "claims and demands" become unbearably insistent, either neurosis or psychosis will ensue, depending upon "whether . . . the ego remains true . . . to the external world and attempts to silence the id, or whether it lets itself be overcome by the id and thus torn away from reality" (XIX, p. 151). But we saw in Chapter Four, and in section 1 of this chapter, that Freud mostly tends to equate our real self with the id and similar dark agencies within us, or anyway to underline their dominant influence upon our lives. Recall his aphorism that the "core of our being . . . is formed by the obscure id". Another significant statement is his response to the view that since your dreams come from your id, you are not to blame for their sometimes outrageous content. Freud protests,

>one must hold oneself responsible for the evil impulses of one's dreams . . . [T]he content of the dream . . . is part of my own being . . .
>
>. . . [In a] sense this bad repressed content does not belong to my "ego" but to an "id" on which my ego is seated. But this ego developed out of the id, it forms with it a single biological unit . . . [and] obeys . . . the id.

> [Psychoanalysts] will leave it to the
> jurist to construct a responsibility that
> is artificially limited to the . . . ego
> (XIX, pp. 133 f., 1925i).

Freud even challenges our common-sense view of situations where another person has a clear role in our misfortunes. Is our external enemy really the source of the harm that befalls us? Freud boldly suggests instead that many people have an unconscious "compulsion to repeat" childhood fantasies and traumas: "their fate is for the most part arranged by themselves . . . Thus we have come across people all of whose human relationships have the same outcome: such as the benefactor who is abandoned in anger after a time by each of his protégés" (XXI, p. 117). The same goes for cases where impersonal hindrances and unlucky contingencies spoil our purposive actions: when we botch tasks we are trying to complete, make slips of the tongue while speaking, 'accidentally' hurt ourselves. Freud reclassifies the mishaps and breakdowns as either "unconsciously intended", or else "compromises" between our warring conscious and repressed desires. Finally, we remember that he thinks the physical symptoms of neurosis—tics, tremors, paralyses, pains—are among our most revealing, albeit unconscious, actions.

The upshot is that if you take a Freudian stance toward neurotic motivation, then you cannot appeal to any of our models. Nothing outside, or alien, to the neurotic can assume the role of coercer, hypnotist, D/n, or brain-washer. In particular, his id and his repressed drives are unsuited for this part, since they are as much, perhaps more, genuinely his as (or than) the desires he acknowledges.

6. Do our values constitute our real pro- and con-attitudes? Aside from the problems I had in the previous chapter making detailed sense of Freud's anthropomorphic and 'mixed' accounts of our mental life, I consider them viable theoretical options, not to be brushed aside without argument. Yet this seems to be a direct consequence of an otherwise promising attempt, by Gary Watson, to distinguish between our own and alien desires, which make us unfree. Watson says,

> [when] actions . . . are unfree, the agent is
> unable to get what he most wants, or values,
> . . . due to his own "motivational system" . . .

> [T]he strength of one's desire may not properly reflect the degree to which one values its object . . .
>
> [I]t is possible that sometimes [one] is motivated to do things he does not deem worth doing. This possibility is the basis for the principal problem of free action: a person may be obstructed by his own will (1975, pp. 206, 210, 213, respectively).

In effect, Watson is equating what one "most wants" and what one thinks morally best. Freudians would immediately object that this begs the question against their doctrine that our moral standards are slyly implanted in us by our elders and other guardians of our social group, and have little to do with the "core of our being". Watson appears ready for this complaint; he even acknowledges that "one may be as dissociated from the demands of the superego as from those of the id" (p. 214). But instead of analyzing the difficult notions of identification and dissociation, Watson takes up a secondary issue. He worries that a person's moral outlook may have "its basis solely in acculturation . . . independently of [his] judgment" (p. 215). He seems to display an intellectualist bias, assuming that our own moral values, as contrasted with the arbitrary rules that society foists upon us, are those we reason out

> in a cool and non-self-deceptive moment . . . That most people have articulate "conceptions of the good", coherent life-plans, systems of ends . . . is of course something of a fiction. Yet we all have more or less long-term aims and normative principles that we are willing to defend . . . [T]hese . . . are . . . our values (p. 215).

The major psychoanalytical objection remains unanswered: Why should we assume that our "life-plans" and "systems of ends"--or, for that matter, the irrational taboos of our moral code--are more representative of us than our most savage, incoherent whims? Perhaps we *value* our disposition toward life-planning, or unquestioning acceptance of our community's rules, and morally condemn our wild, often self-destructive impulses. But that sounds both circular and beside the point. For suppose that we do give the highest moral marks to life-planning, even that it is our worthiest character trait. We cannot infer from this that our values correspond to what each of us "most wants". Thus we still have not explained how a neurotically motivated person acts on alien desires, hence unfreely.

7. <u>Are alien motives those that are inalterable by reasoning?</u> This doctrine originally surfaced more than two decades ago. Alasdair MacIntyre, in the essay I referred to above (section 4), essentially claimed that we act freely when we act rationally. MacIntyre argued,

> Behavior is rational--in this arbitrarily defined sense--if, and only if, it can [in principle] be influenced or inhibited by the adducing of some logically relevant consideration . . . What is logically relevant will necessarily vary from case to case. If Smith is about to give generously to someone who appears to be in need, the information that this man . . . has in fact ample means, will be relevant . . . An impulsive action can in this sense be rational . . . [And] behavior can be reflective without being . . . rational. For a man may spend a great deal of time thinking out what he should do, and yet refuse to entertain a great many logically relevant considerations (1957, p. 248).

One minor difficulty is that MacIntyre neglects to specify whose criteria for "logically relevant considerations" we should invoke to establish a person's rationality or irrationality. Should we rely on his interlocutor's standards? Should we call in experts? This question is addressed in an updated statement of MacIntyre's thesis, by Wright Neely. Like his predecessor, Neely hopes to find "a way of saying that some desires are more intimately related to the self--are more its own"--than others (1974, p. 43). The latter are desires that respond to whatever considerations the person thinks logically germane. Neely illustrates with a thorny example: Socrates' desire to stay in prison and eventually drink the hemlock. Neely admits that Socrates' companions and subsequent readers

> might well feel that Crito presented
> Socrates with good and sufficient reasons

> to escape. Yet . . . Socrates's decision to remain . . . [is hardly] a clear case of an unfree decision . . . This leads us . . . [to suggest]: a desire is irresistible if and only if it is the case that if the agent had been presented with what <u>he</u> <u>took</u> <u>to</u> <u>be</u> good and sufficient reasons for not acting on it, he would still have acted on it (p. 47).

Neely's subjective criterion for "good and sufficient reason" may create some trouble. For instance, what if an agent insists upon absurdly high standards of germaneness or conclusiveness when people remonstrate with him? A defender of Neely may reply that we ought to count only those standards of relevance that a person accepts in a "cool hour". But I find this thermal metaphor unhelpful. Some people are coolly obtuse and pig-headed. Consequently we will have cases where everyone else thinks the agent is irrationally acting on an irresistible desire, but we must accept his word that no decisive or even pertinent reasons were adducted to make him change his mind.

This problem is secondary, however. What really bothers me is an assumption similar to Dworkin's, Frankfurt's, and Watson's. Dworkin and Frankfurt take it for granted that our second-order desires or volitions exemplify what we really want. Our <u>values</u> have the same status in Watson's scheme. MacIntyre and Neely likewise assume that my rational desires—those that seem alterable by reasoning, and hence not "irresistible"—represent the real me. Negatively speaking, if I act on an irrational or irresistible desire, they infer without further evidence that I am <u>not</u> doing what I really want, and thus act unfreely. I reject this kind of inference because it is unsupported by argument and because it seems arbitrarily to rule out a Freudian view of the person, which gives as much, perhaps a lot more, significance to the murky side of our soul.

At this juncture I shall stop trying to explicate our strong hunch that neurotic desires that sometimes act us to move are alien—not really ours—and threaten our freedom. One result of our dialectical exertions should be that we appreciate how recalcitrant the problem is, and specifically why we cannot assimilate this kind of unfreedom to coercion, hypnosis, diabolical meddling, or brain-washing.

I think I can do better with our other problem-case of alien desires: the case of many females whose "motivation to choose" seems to have been undermined by their social conditioning.

8. <u>A contrast between freedom to do what you like and autonomy</u>. The example I took from social psychologists Bem and Bem in section 1 does not illustrate any standard loss of freedom. The women they discuss are not prevented by law, custom, or covert anti-female bias from pursuing careers in science, engineering, and business. When they choose "marriage, children, and living happily ever after" as homemakers, they are not under duress, opting for the least of evils. There is no hypnotist controlling them, and clearly they are not in the same predicament as D/n's victims $\underline{V}_1$, $\underline{V}_2$, and $\underline{V}_3$. Later on we can compare them with $\underline{V}_4$, $\underline{V}_5$, and brain-washed people. In this preliminary narrowing-down process, we may also put aside Watson's explanatory hypothesis about desires that move a person, but conflict with "what he [or she] most wants, or <u>values</u>". We may safely assume that the women in Bem and Bem's sample attach great moral value to domesticity. Perhaps their desire is "irresistible" in terms of MacIntyre's and Neely's rationality criterion. That is, perhaps some or all of these women would stick to their preference even if you presented them with what <u>they</u> "<u>took to be</u> good and sufficient reasons for not acting on it". But this seems to be an empirical question, and it is not in the least absurd to suppose the women's desire <u>is</u> alterable by reasoning. So we might try another approach.

Not long ago, Stanley I. Benn coined the term "autarchy", and defined it as "the condition of being a chooser, presupposed by the standard choice situation". Specifically, Benn's "choosers" manage to "do what they want". Yet Benn considers much of their behavior "unfree" because they seldom bother to "look critically at what they want" (1975-76, pp. 112 f.). To illustrate how people can be "unfree" while enjoying autarchy, Benn imagines a member of some "Spartan or tribal" community "in which the notion of . . . an independent project-maker is poorly developed" (p. 121). Another of Benn's examples is the "slave to convention" in any community, whose desires always mesh with "standards he has accepted quite uncritically", such as norms of "propriety and success absorbed unreflectively from parents, teachers, or workmates" (pp. 123 f.).

According to Benn's lexicon, we progress from this condition of mere autarchy, toward genuine personal freedom--which Benn calls "autonomy"--to the extent that we scrutinize our proclivities, and especially the values and "<u>mores</u>" we have acquired through our socialization. Obviously we cannot do this entirely on our own. As Benn remarks, we must have "criteria and a conceptual scheme for grasping the issues", all of which we get from other people in the conditioning process, if we are lucky (p, 126). We must be stimulated somehow to question folkways and received opinions. Our culture must provide us with the basic tools and methods of reasoning. However this comes about, the fortunate person who acquires the wherewithal to seek autonomy "will appraise one aspect of his tradition by critical canons derived from another"; she or he will "search for coherence", attempting to "resolve by rational reflection, incoherences in the complex tradition" (pp. 126 ff.).

By reference to Benn's account, it might seem that the women in our example have autarchy--freedom to do what they choose--but not autonomy. I am convinced that some such distinction is needed. However, Benn's account will not do the trick. For suppose that the most enlightened of these women "look critically at what they want"; they carefully review the whole ideology in which they have been steeped--the feminine mystique of 'fulfillment', along with supporting doctrines from biology, zoology, psychoanalysis, and the social sciences. Having diligently sought "coherence" in their "complex tradition", the majority of these thoughtful women then decide that on balance their conventional attitudes are reasonable. With a clear intellectual conscience, they enthusiastically plunge into "marriage, children, and living happily ever after". If we adopt Benn's notion of autonomy, must we not say their behavior is autonomous?

9. <u>Autonomy and "identifying with" one's desires</u>. In the hope of articulating a more suitable concept of autonomy, I turn to another related proposal, by Robert Young, which is also "intended to mark off those wants that are truly the person's from those that are alien to him" (1979, p. 361). Young worries that in the final analysis all our thinking is

decisively shaped by

> parents, family, friends, teachers, the media, cultural background and so on . . . [which] makes nonsense of the idea that our convictions, motivations, preferences, principles, ideals and the like are truly ours. [Apparently] they can't be truly ours because where they are not the product of the intentional manipulations of others or of organic causes they are outside our control in virtue of our passive role in our socialization (pp. 367 f.).

Young's main proposal is "to recognize that when a person identifies with certain of his motivations . . . such motivations may legitimately be regarded as his or hers" (p. 373). Young has adapted the notion of "identifying with" one's conative attitudes from passages in Dworkin and Frankfurt that I neglected when I surveyed their split-level theories of coerced behavior in section 3. Essentially, both Frankfurt and Dworkin hold that you identify with a ground-floor desire whenever you have second-order desires to be moved by it. Frankfurt's example involves an "unwilling" drug addict who has a ground-floor disinclination and also a craving for narcotics. From his second-order vantage point he "identifies himself . . . with one . . . of his conflicting desires [namely, his aversion] . . . makes [it] . . . more truly his own and . . . withdraws himself from the other"; consequently the "force moving him to take the drug" anyway must be "a force other than his own" (1971, p. 13). Dworkin tells of a smoker in the same bind: "The part of him that wishes to stop smoking is recognized as his true self, the one whose wishes he wants [on a higher level] to see carried out" (1976, p. 24). More generally, Dworkin asks about a person's desires to act: "Does he identify with them, assimilate them to himself, view himself as the kind of person who wishes to be motivated in these particular ways? If [not] . . . then those [motivations], even though they may be causally effective, are not viewed as 'his'" (p. 25).

Young seems aware of a dubious assumption in the Frankfurt-Dworkin theory, which resembles one I found underlying the 'values' and 'rationality' doctrines. In my terms, the questionable premise is that your second-order desires--or your values and rationally alterable desires--genuinely represent you. Young expresses fairly limited and vague misgivings on this subject. He warns us not to

> run together the reflective self-evaluation manifested in the formation of second-order desires and the notion of identifying with, and thus making one's own, those desires which move to action . . . [O]ne can identify with one's first-order desires. Furthermore where there is a clash between a lower-order and a higher-order desire it would seem possible to identify with the lower-order one. If so, the idea of identification with one's desires is independent of the notion of 'second-order desires' (1980, pp. 36 f.; see 1979, p. 371).

When Young imagines "a clash between a lower-order and a higher-order desire", I think he means that a person disapproves, from his aerie, of some ground-level hankering. How then is it possible for him "to identify with the lower-order one"? Both Dworkin and Frankfurt define this sort of identification as occurring when you give your second-order endorsement to a humble desire. What other meaning does Young attach to "identifying with"? My guess is that Young is bothered by Frankfurt's and Dworkin's tacit belief that what we desire on the second level is what we really desire.

Can we suppose that a person identifies with his or her *second*-order attitude? What might this be like? Would he have to engage in yet higher-level antics—perhaps *ad infinitum*? Frankfurt considers this possibility in several works. His earliest answer is an attempt to tell us what it is for a person to identify with a "decisive" second-order volition. According to Frankfurt, the individual

> has decided that no further question about his second-order volition, at any higher level, remains to be asked. It is relatively unimportant whether we explain this by saying that this commitment implicitly generates an endless series of confirming desires of higher orders, or . . . [that it] is tantamount to the dissolution of the pointedness [sic] of all questions concerning higher orders (1971, pp. 16 f.).

In a later essay, he responds to a challenge: Why can't a person fail to identify with second-order phenomena occurring within himself, and remain a "passive bystander to them? Frankfurt answers,

> it is impossible for him to be a passive bystander to [his second-order volitions]. They constitute his activity--his being active rather than passive--and the question of whether or not he identifies himself with them cannot arise. It makes no sense to ask whether someone identifies himself with his identification of himself . . . [unless we are asking] whether his identification is wholehearted (1975, p. 121).

I shall not try to understand how it can be meaningless to ask if someone identifies with his second-order volitions, while it may be meaningful to ask if "his identification is wholehearted". Instead I shall look at Frankfurt's latest treatment of desires or "passions" that are either "internal", because we identify with them, or "external", because we disown them. Frankfurt argues,

> The fact that a person has a certain [second-order] attitude toward a passion . . . [determines] the internality or the externality of the passion, surely, only if the attitude . . . is itself genuinely attributable to him . . .; it must be one with which he is to be identified. But . . . an infinite regress will be generated by any attempt to account for internality or externality in terms of [second-order] attitudes. For the attitude . . . will have to be . . . internal . . . [by reference to] a higher-order attitude . . .; and so on. This precludes explication of . . . internality and externality by appealing . . . to . . . orders (1976, p. 248).

Frankfurt then says despairingly, "I cannot provide a satisfactory account of what it means to characterize a passion as internal or external". Yet in his final paragraph, he suggests an apparently new account. Frankfurt imagines someone who is torn between the desire to compliment an acquaintance and the desire to hurt the other's feelings. How does he identify with one desire? Frankfurt says,

> By deciding that what he wants after all is to compliment his acquaintance, and that his desire to injure the man is finally to be excluded from the order of candidates for satisfaction, the person renders the second desire external to himself and identifies himself with the first (p. 250).

Frankfurt goes on to concede that "the nature of decision [sic] is very obscure"; but in a footnote he argues that he can escape the regress difficulty because "decisions, unlike desires or attitudes, do not seem to be susceptible both to internality and externality" (p. 251).

I am unsure of this, partly for reasons noted by Dworkin: "A person's . . . identification with his motivations . . . may have been produced by manipulation, the withholding of relevant information", and in general "influenced . . . by others in such a fashion that we are not to think of it as his own choice" (1976, p. 25). If our second-order "decision" may result from such influences, as our workaday decisions to act sometimes do result from coercion, hypnosis, and brain-washing, then I suspect that Frankfurt cannot escape the regress in this manner. Generally, I doubt that multi-layer theories of autonomy will help us explain how social conditioning erodes many females' "motivation to choose". As we remarked earlier (section 8), reflective women--or men--might very well be conditioned to critically examine the received ideology and fully accept it, even approving of their conformist desires. However you define "identifying", and regardless how stratospheric a phenomenon you make it, it does not seem to be enough for the kind of autonomy we are trying to depict.

10. <u>Simpler models of doing what you want but lacking autonomy</u>. I think brain-washing, and the cases of V_4 and V_5, which we outlined in section 4, may provide fruitful hints. The brain-washing analogy is a commonplace, to be sure; but few of its proponents ever get down to the all-important details, the specific points of correspondence and dissimilarity. One troublesome disparity is that brain-washing is normally administered to a relatively mature person, with already formed beliefs, desires, and character-traits. The steering of females toward dependent and

subordinate status begins at birth. Reinforcement never ceases. Moreover, the effects of female sex-role conditioning are peculiarly diffuse, compared with the well-defined credo and attitude of unquestioning loyalty that brain-washed people normally exhibit. To illustrate this diffuseness, here is a passage from a feminist philosopher who wonders about her

> persistent need . . . to make myself 'attractive' . . . [I]s it the false need of a chauvinized woman . . .? Or does it express a wholesome need to express love for one's own body . . . a need which is denied to men in our still-puritan culture? (Bartky, 1977, p. 29).

Along similar lines, you might speculate whether the desire to tidy and beautify one's abode, to care for children, to cook--even to be dependent, and responsive to the expectations or emotions of another--must rank as "false" wants resulting from indoctrination. They might be "wholesome" in moderation. Certainly males have gone overboard on assertiveness and self-reliance. I shall not investigate this "false"-"wholesome" contrast, however, because that would take us into questions of moral value, and away from our conceptual problem of how socialization may threaten personal autonomy.

Just as it is easier to pinpoint the effects of brain-washing than of social conditioning, it is clearer what the brain-washed individual would have been like if he had escaped the experience. When high-spirited young adults become docile votaries of their guru after a long process of fasting and prayer; when hell-raising drinkers are reclaimed by Alcoholics Anonymous; or when a communist regime sends a one-time member of the bourgeoisie through 're-education', you have no trouble distinguishing 'before' and 'after'. You compare the original attitudes of the acolyte, the dipsomaniac, and the capitalist with their outlooks following their edification. You can gauge pretty reliably what their present attitudes would have been if they had not undergone these forms of brain-washing. But with a typical woman, whose role-training began so early, we cannot say, for instance, that had she not been socialized this way, she would have wanted to become an engineer, to cultivate her own tastes, and generally to lead an independent existence. At

best we might locate a sample of young women who
managed to grow up untrammeled and self-directing,
but were then almost literally brain-washed until they
adopted suitable feminine attitudes. Perhaps we
will run across rare twin sisters who were raised
separately, one according to custom, the other in
egalitarian style. No doubt more females of one category will be found engaged in politics, business, the
professions and exact sciences, and disinclined to
submerge themselves in home-making. Then we will
have grounds to say of each traditional twin that
she also would have been more independent if she had
not received the equivalent of brain-washing.

11. <u>Must we assume it is natural for people to
become autonomous?</u> When we extrapolate as I did,
and conjecture that far more females would be self-
directing if only their "motivation to choose" had
not been tampered with, we seem to be taking it for
granted that an independent stance is the natural
outcome, the stance people usually develop as long as
nobody else interferes. A crude physical analogy
for this is the way a cork will naturally float to the
surface of a liquid, unless you hold it down. You need
do nothing to secure its upward motion. A parallel
from botany is the sprouting and blossoming of wild-
flowers and other plants without the help of gardeners.

Do people naturally tend to become their own
bosses? Of course humans, particularly during infan-
cy and childhood, are quite vulnerable to their society's efforts to impose slavish and dependent attitudes upon them. But even with these qualifications,
our 'naturalness' claim is at odds with one widely
accredited principle of the social sciences: what I
call the 'malleability' thesis. Along with countless other writers, the late Margaret Mead propounded
this kind of thesis, often for laudable purposes.
For instance, she attacks the prejudice--which I
reject as firmly as she does--that certain personality
traits always or nearly always belong to males, and
others to women. Mead declares,

> those temperamental attitudes which we have
> traditionally regarded as feminine--such as
> passivity, responsiveness, and a willing-
> ness to cherish children--can . . . easily
> be set up as the masculine pattern in one
> tribe, and in another outlawed for the
> majority of men . . . [Thus] we no longer

> have any basis for regarding such . . .
> behavior as sex-linked . . .
>
> . . . We are forced to conclude that
> human nature is . . . unbelievably malleable,
> responding accurately and contrastingly to
> contrasting cultural conditions (1935,
> pp. 191 f.).

Suppose we accept the malleability thesis. Then we have to consider assertiveness and initiative no more essential, inborn, or natural to human beings of either sex than the contrary attitudes, self-effacement and submissiveness. We should not expect to find either set of personality traits among males or females in the absence of appropriate "cultural conditions".

How does this result square with our hunch that most women who "choose" domesticity do so because of their socialization, and consequently now act as unfreely as the successfully brain-washed person? We seem to be in a quagmire. If we assume malleability, and deny that people naturally become self-directing, what do we say about females? If we only make the negative supposition that females are not conditioned to prefer auxiliary status, we can hardly predict that they will be motivated to take charge of their own destinies. Yet surely women would be far more independent were it not for the conditioning they have undergone?

11. A 'contrast' interpretation. I think we can elucidate the situation that baffles us, and straighten out our conceptual difficulties in a way that does justice to the brain-washing model of unfreedom, and even restores some credibility to the notion of 'naturalness'. My method here will be a constructive application of a technique that I borrowed from Ryle and Wittgenstein in Chapter One. There I asked what theorists of mind could mean when they report that we "have" minds and such mental contents as pains or thoughts. I requested details on their claim that we "perceive", "uniquely own", "have privileged access to" these hidden items or happenings. How do we "refer to" our sensations, "follow private rules for naming" them? What is involved in our supposed "knowledge" of our itches and bouts of emotion? Specifically, I inquired what you exclude when you use these familiar terms to delineate our mental life. There

are distant asteroids that nobody "has"; could pains exist that belong to no contemporaneous sufferer? Ordinary items can be misperceived, jointly owned, inaccessible to everyone; we sometimes refer incorrectly, misname things, unwittingly break rules, fall short of knowledge. Why not in the mental sphere too? If a theory's key terms no longer carry their usual implications and contrasts, we have reason to wonder if it makes any sense. Or so I argued in Chapter One, and its sequel, where I asked what it could mean when followers of Descartes say that mental goings-on are non-physical. Then in Chapter Three I used this approach to rebut charges of meaninglessness that are often brought against the rival claim of materialists: that mental events are also physical. My attempt to clarify Freudian theories yielded other, mostly negative results in Chapter Four. At present I hope to make definite sense of autonomy, as something over and above doing what you want.

Now J. L. Austin was the most influential advocate of a 'contrast' approach to the broader free-will debate. Here is a typical Austinian remark:

> While it has been the tradition to present ['freedom'] as the 'positive' term requiring elucidation, there is little doubt that to say we acted 'freely' . . . is to say only that we acted <u>not</u> unfreely, in one or another of the many heterogenous ways of so acting (under duress, or what not). Like 'real', 'free' is only used to rule out the suggestion of some or all of its recognized antitheses (1956-57, pp. 8 f.).

In the present case, my strategy would be somewhat different, since we do not understand how socialization makes some women--among others--act unfreely. So I would ask what we envisage when we imagine that women are <u>not</u> conditioned as they customarily are. What alternative situation would exist instead? No socialization of any kind? I doubt that we picture anything so nebulous. At any rate, the 'malleability' thesis should remind us that we cannot hope for people with initiative if there are no propitious "cultural conditions". So why not say that the alternative to what females currently get is what exists already-- but so far principally for males? Thus we are implicitly comparing female socialization with what males normally receive.

How does 'naturalness' come into the scenario? A 'contrast' method will encourage us to say that if females were not singled out for special conditioning, what would 'naturally' occur is the kind of socialization that goes on otherwise, the kind that males have hitherto generally monopolized. Here 'natural' is not the antonym of 'conventional', 'artificial', or 'created by human effort'. All forms of socialization are conventional and artificial. The contrast I am trying to delineate is altogether different: We are comparing the way females are now deliberately selected to learn self-effacement, and the upbringing that would remain available to them if only the invidious customary practice ended. Given our admittedly scant knowledge of regularities in human social life, the most likely--and hence 'natural'--outcome is that male-type upbringing is extended to the 'fair' sex. Thus 'natural' is the antonym of 'freakish', 'chance', and 'miraculous'.

Clearly some aspects of typical male socialization either presuppose, or contribute to, the subjugation and the self-effacing attitudes of women. By the same token, there are "wholesome" aspects of female conditioning that do not facilitate their oppression, and which might correct some excesses of the male pattern. So the 'natural' outcome I alluded to could very well combine non-domineering elements of one scheme and "wholesome" ingredients of the other. Of course it is a factual question whether this kind of change would enhance women's "motivation to choose" and thus provide them a wider range of genuine options. But it seems to be a conceptual truth that people who are unmotivated to choose for themselves have less autonomy.

I suspect that my occasionally polemical tone has betrayed my moral bias in favor of individual self-determination. Nevertheless I am far from suggesting that a person who aspires to autonomy should never depend upon others--trust them, become attached to them, and join them in cooperative ventures. What I oppose is wanting to be bossed around, and to have one's identity defined by others. Needless to say, I am against tampering with a male person's attitude for the same reason I dislike the oppressive conditioning of many females; moreover I suppose numerous males are deprived of autonomy by their socialization--for the corporate rat-race or whatever. I have not gone into any of these issues, or tried to justify my moral preference for autonomy. That is because my sole purpose has been to spell out and solve the conceptual problem of alien desires; that is, to explain how a person can do what he or she wants, and yet act unfreely. No model, or theory of wanting--or second-order wanting, for that matter--enabled us to clarify how one's neurotic desires are foreign, not really one's own. Nevertheless we became aware of the crucial elements in this puzzle, and especially why a Freudian theory of the person rules out facile solutions. But I think we have made it plainer how some, though evidently not all, forms of socialization do foist alien desires upon an individual, thereby diminshing his or her freedom. I hope that additional clarity will emerge as we touch on many of these notions in remaining chapters, all of which deal with theories of what it is to act.

CHAPTER SIX

DO WE CONTROL OUR BEHAVIOR THROUGH VOLITION?

1. <u>Willing as the mark of action and the source of power over what we do</u>. In this chapter I shall not grapple with the age-old enigma, What is it to act freely? Instead I want to reason through a challenging and representative answer to a tangle of logically prior questions which have only recently attracted much notice. They concern, first, what it is simply to act; and, second, how we manage to do so--specifically, how we contrive to initiate and regulate the movement or stillness of our body that occurs when we act. Our first puzzle about the 'nature' of action may sound excessively academic; but the second ought immediately to challenge any person of intellectual curiosity. For it is plain that we do not get our limbs to stir, or to freeze, in the way we get a stone or a bicycle to move or to stop. As a matter of fact, could we make a stone or a bicycle roll, or stop rolling, if we were unable to make parts of bodies move and hold still? At least in the cosmos we know, we cannot bring about such events in our surroundings unless there is agitation or immobility of our corporeal frame.

This emphasis upon bodily goings-on may suggest an easy retort to our question about what an action consists of. Perhaps our deeds really are nothing but the gyration or the repose of our limbs. Well, why not? This straightforward equation is unacceptable for several reasons. Our bodies thrash about and remain still when we sleep, but it is doubtful that we are acting. Moreover, while we are fully conscious, and parts of our bodies are in motion or at rest, it is often quite false to say we are performing actions. Suppose I twitch, double over with acute back pain, or sneeze; are these corporeal occurrences actions of mine? Apparently not. In fact, the very same type of bodily happening can take place in one situation where it seems true to say that a person acted, and in another context where it seems untrue. For example, while I am traveling by subway, my elbow suddenly pokes into the rib-cage of a fellow passenger. Did I nudge him? Ordinarily that would be a plausible verdict, but not if I had been thrown off balance as the train lurched around a curve. So it looks as if there is more to action than the bustling or quiescence of bodies. What else does it take?

2. **The standard volitional account.** Until the mid-1930s, when Wittgenstein's influential lecture notes began circulating (see his 1958, pp. 159-67; also 1953, §§588-92, 611-60), we would have received a stock answer to our questions about what action is, how we get our limbs to move or cease moving, and what else there is to action besides this physical motion or immobility. For centuries, philosophers, along with legal and social theorists, had unhesitatingly assumed that our deeds consist of those corporeal events that are engendered by an episode of willing—our volition that such events should take place. As to how we bring about these bodily occurrences, the standard reply was, "By willing them". Naturally our beliefs about our environment, and the probable effect of our alternative limb movements, have a role in these proceedings. But I shall ignore this complication in order to focus on the relationship between willing and doing. Needless to say, willing has no impact on many portions of our anatomy, or on objects that remain at a distance from us. Willing does not make our hair stand up, or make a door open. Yet it seems to give us definite control over some bodily goings-on.

This sketch will need filling in and retouching later on. Historically speaking, what counts is that similar volitional analyses of action were endorsed by such giants as Descartes (1649, §§41, 44), Hobbes (1651, ch. vi), Locke (1690, II, chs. xxi, xxiii), Hume (1748, chs. vii, viii), Reid (1768, chs. v, vii), Bentham (1823, ch. viii, 2), Mill (1843, I, ch. iii, §4), the jurisprudent Austin (1863, lectures xviii, xix), James (1890, II, ch. xxvi), Justice Holmes (1911, ch. ii), and Collingwood (1942, pp. 96 ff.). Berkeley (1713, I, II) mainly expressed misgivings toward the corporeal-motion half of this theory of action.

From the late 1940s through the mid-1960s, however, volitional analyses came under heavy attack. Ryle (1949, ch. iii), Melden (1960), Vesey (1961), and R. Taylor (1966, pp. 49-93) each refined Wittgenstein's critical insights. I believe that at least four of the objections made by these dissenters ought to be taken seriously today. In outline, the objections are these:

(i) Volitionists have not made it sufficently clear to the uninitiated what willing is like. Call this the 'obscurity' charge.

(ii) The doctrine seems to require a thrust of willing for each bodily event that ranks as an action; but even attentive fanciers of volitions seem to have fewer than needed. This is the 'not enough' complaint.

(iii) We must assume that volitions themselves are either mental acts we perform, or else mental happenings of some other, non-active type. If willing is our action--as Descartes *et al*. obviously believed-- then according to the volitional analysis of what it is to act, we must have to will in order to bring about our willing. Our willing to will, in its turn, must require a yet higher level of willing, and so on *ad infinitum*. Now volitionists might try to block this absurd consequence of their analysis by denying that willing is a mental act. But if it is not an act, they should inform us what sort of occurrence it is, and explain how its presence confers the title of action upon the bodily events that it causes. This is the 'infinite regress' objection.

(iv) If volitionists heroically decide to classify willing as a mental performance, then even if they defeat the regress charge, their analysis seems to lead us in a circle. After all, we wanted to learn what makes a bodily event an action, and how people get their limbs moving. The answer in both cases was volition. But now, if we are systematic, we should be just as eager to hear what makes willing our action, and how we get volitions to occur. This is the 'circularity' grumble.

In response to objections such as these, most philosophers discarded the verb 'will' and its cognates. They substituted talk of 'reasons for action', 'wants', 'desires', or 'pro-attitudes'. Goldman has confided that his 1970 book features "a doctrine quite close to the volitional theory"; but he "avoided the term 'volition' partly because of the 'odium theologicum' it has acquired" (1976, p. 67).

Naturally there were die-hards. Prichard (1949) spun out a novel theory of willing that may be invulnerable to some of the objections i-iv. For him, willing alone is our action, and the ensuing movements of our limbs are merely its effects. Volition itself he proclaims "*sui generis* and so incapable of being defined"; in particular, willing is never "desiring", "consenting", "resolving", or any "species of something called conation" (pp. 60 f.). These are bold ideas. Yet since Prichard and other recalcitrant believers in volition made no systematic attempt to rebut Wittgensteinian criticisms, their doctrines must have seemed ready for the curio shop.

    3. <u>Volitions redux</u>. So much for historical stage-setting. What intrigues me is the latest swing: the initially apologetic, and now almost brazen, resurgence of will doctrines. One clear omen is the appearance of an intermediate-level textbook, <u>Theory of Action</u>, by L. Davis (1979), in a widely read series. Davis there elaborates a volitional analysis in the manner of Prichard, and uses it to explain intention, ability, and blameworthiness. An impressive number of other Prichardian volitionists take a similar line, and consider willing our only genuine act. But there is also a more traditional group of will-theorists, led by Goldman, who say that the movements or stillnesses that result from our willing constitute our actions. I see no point in discussing theorists who use the term 'volition' in a purely 'technical' sense. But we should note a further difference of opinion. Most Prichardians, and a few traditionalists, define willing narrowly, as quite unlike desire, intending, deciding, or being favorably inclined. Most traditionalists, though not all, identify one or more of these conative phenomena with willing.

    Whatever form post-Wittgensteinian theories of volition take, I believe we should ask how effectively they withstand challenges i-iv, and how successful they are in overcoming our initial perplexities with regard to the nature of action and our means of producing it. I shall not take time to carp at the antiquated faculty psychology, and the dualistic metaphysics of mind-versus-body, that pervade the earliest and a few of the contemporary will-theories. I shall not worry that Descartes, Locke, Berkeley, Hume, Reid, Mill, and Prichard, among others, regard willing as a non-physical episode beyond the reach of public observation, deep within our consciousness. By the same token, I must neglect the competing ontology of those present-day materialists who say that volitions really are soon-to-be-detected neural processes that trigger our limb movements (see Armstrong, 1968, chs. vi, vii). In any case my Chapters One, Two, and Three dealt with some analogous problems of dualism and materialism.

Besides avoiding these side issues, I shall have to neglect a potentially significant question, viz., What does a person will? Most old-time volitionists, and some of today's speculators, say that an action is what people will. For example, Davis writes, "Volitions . . . have objects. A volition . . . is a volition . . . to do an A for some act-type A" (1979, p. 17). Sellars, a quasi-traditional theorist, similarly holds that "action is essentially the sort of thing that is brought about by volition"; so volition has the "job of getting actions going" (1976, ##10, 8). From these statements I infer that for Sellars action is also the 'object' of our willing. At any rate his frequent follower Aune declares that "we unquestionably do will to act" (1977, p. 67). But not all volitionists agree. McCann asserts emphatically, "What . . . is willed . . . cannot be . . . an action . . . [O]ne does not will to raise his arm. If he did, an infinite regress would obtain: since volition is essential to . . . raising his arm, to will to raise it would be to will to will to raise it" (1974, p. 487). I believe McCann's strictures apply notably to his fellow Prichardians who equate doing and willing, yet also claim that actions are what people will. Davis and Hornsby, inter alia, belong in this category. Davis "regard[s] actions as identical with volitions"; for him, "every action is a volition", an so "volitions are themselves actions" (1979, pp. 41, 45, 39). Hornsby uses the term "conation" instead of "volition", but otherwise apparently concurs with Prichardians that volitions or "conations . . . are identical with actions" (1980, p. 51; see p. 55). Evidently if these analysts say that we will to perform actions, it sounds as though they are committed to saying we will to perform volitions. However, it is possible that Hornsby and Davis really mean 'bodily event' when they speak of action as the object of our willing.

Not all disagreements among partisans of will have this verbal character. For instance, it seems not to be a matter of linguistic preference how we should describe willing itself. This ties in with the 'obscurity' complaint, i, that I invoked in section 2.

4. <u>Restrictive and permissive concepts of willing</u>. If you asked volitionists what kind of mental phenomenon willing is, many would endorse Prichard's view that it is absolutely unique. Thus McCann says "no other mode of thought is quite like it"; its "modality

. . . makes it practical thought, rather than speculative, assertive, desiderative, or wishful. To will is not . . . merely to want . . . Volition <u>is</u> execution: to will . . . a change is to enter upon the act of bringing it about" (1974, pp. 468 f.). Annas likewise believes "volitions . . . must be thoughts", and that "we shall have to follow Prichard and say . . . volitions are <u>sui generis</u> and self-announcing" (1977-78, pp. 208, 211). She confidently denies that willing is "any form of intending" (p. 211). On the other hand, Aune, while agreeing that volition is "practical thought", joins Sellars and assimilates it precisely to intending (Aune, 1974, p. 108; 1977, pp. 65-84). Finally, in opposition to all these experts, Davis judges that we generate only "uncertain illumination" if we classify willing as thinking--even thinking "'in the executive mode' . . . so long as we do not know what thoughts are, or understand what is meant by the executive mode" (1979, p. 17). The same with "practical", I imagine. I would add this: It is a truism that whenever you will X, you must in some way think of X; but that scarcely entitles McCann and others to equate your willing X and your thinking of X, executively or whatever. The identification should be supported by argument. However, that is not our concern here.

We should complete our survey with a look at more traditional, non-Prichardian theories of willing. Goldman considers it a "species of desire or intention" (1976, p. 68). Kenny goes further in a permissive direction; he asserts, "The volition that p . . . [is] something common to hoping that p, wanting it to be the case that p, wishing . . ., being glad that p", even "regretting that not-p" (1963, pp. 214 ff.). Armstrong is the most latitudinarian, stretching our notion of "'the will' . . . to cover every sort of mental [<u>cum</u> neural] process . . . of the conative . . . as opposed to the cognitive . . . or any other sort of process" (1968, p. 131).

In section 7 I plan to ask what difference it makes if we join with McCann, Annas, and Prichard himself, assigning volition to its own niche, or instead say that such lowly events as desiring, resolving, and wishing can be forms of willing. First we ought to test a currently popular characterization of it.

5. <u>Is willing a species of trying?</u> Although Sellars has warned that volitions are definitely "<u>not</u>

tryings"--or "choosings" or "decisions" either (1966, p. 156, my emphasis)--this is a widely favored account. Maybe volitionists think it is difficult to rouse oneself into action; and since we often succeed in carrying out difficult actions by making an effort, perhaps they believe the effort we expend in difficult cases is the same as the volition that gets every action started. However that may be, Annas thinks volitions are special, yet describes them as "acts of trying" (1977-78). Davis repeatedly calls volitions "attempts" (1979, pp. 16 f., 39, 45). Hornsby's theory is somewhat more complex. In section 3 I quoted her Prichardian statement that "conations . . . are identical with actions". She also maintains that "all actions are bodily movements" (1980, p. 1). You might wonder how a volition or conation could be anything so overt. But that is not her view. She argues that our verb "move" may "occur both transitively (i.e., with grammatical objects) and intransitively (without objects)"; deploying subscripts, she offers examples such as "John moved$_T$ his body" and "his body moved$_I$", "Rupert woke$_T$ Rachel" and "Rachel woke$_I$ up" (pp. 2 f., 125). Hornsby's thesis is that our actions "must be movements$_T$, not movements$_I$" (pp. 2 f.). Later she explains that "movements$_T$ occur inside the body", hence they never "reach the surface of the body"; they "are always internal events" (pp. 13, 20, 45). What interests me at this stage is that Hornsby then asserts that "actions [= conations] are tryings to move$_T$ the body" (p. 45). Since she believes actions are identical with conations and with movements$_T$, she must equate movings$_T$ of the body with conations. Does she believe that actions (= conations) are tryings to conate? Evidently not. So they could only be tryings-to-move in a non-technical sense of "move", rather than in her Pickwickian sense of "move$_T$".

What do Annas, Davis, Hornsby, and other volitionists mean when they say willing is trying? Their key term and its near-synonym 'effort' are ambiguous. When I make an effort, or try, to perform an action, or to achieve some result, I engage in an attempt. I try to contact a friend by dialing his telephone number. That is what my attempt, my effort to reach him, consists in. There is also a manner of carrying out some actions and attempts: putting maximum effort into the task, trying one's best, or exerting oneself. Such a zealous manner contrasts with an effortless, easy-does-it style--and equally with a half-hearted, lackadaisical procedure, 'just going through the motions'. The distinction I want to draw is between trying, in the sense of making an attempt, and trying in the sense of exerting yourself; that is, making a strenuous effort, doing something energetically. My attempt to contact my friend is not laborious, frenzied, or energetic. Nor does it seem particularly effortless or indolent. On the other hand, I cannot simply toil: I must exert myself <u>at</u> some task.

Do volitionists mean that willing is making an attempt, or that it is the exertion you put into your attempt or your action? Consider the first alternative. What sorts of attempts can you engage in by willing? Can a swimmer try to cross the Channel merely by willing to do so? If she is restrained just when she has finished willing, and is about to hit the water, has she attempted to swim across? Could I become guilty of attempted robbery, embezzlement, arson, or espionage although I have only willed to commit these offenses? Less dramatically, suppose my fingers are unexpectedly stricken by temporary paralysis, or that the telephone dial jams; does my volition to contact my friend nevertheless count as an attempt?

Volitionists might modify their doctrine. They might explain that willing $\underline{X}$ amounts to attempting $\underline{X}$ just in 'normal' circumstances. These occur when our volition—Hornsby's "conation" or "movement$_T$"—causes our bodies to stir appropriately—Hornsby's "movements$_I$"—and those corporeal happenings in turn produce whatever effects outside our bodies people require for an attempt to swim the Channel, an attempted holdup, or an attempt to telephone somebody. For that matter, when Prichardians equate action with volition, they can explain that they only mean 'normal' episodes of willing, namely those that cause suitable bodily and other events (see Davis, 1979, pp. 16, 20-41). Since I gave cases of volitions that were 'nipped in the bud', before they had a chance to bring about their usual effects, have I really demolished the 'willing is trying' doctrine, much less the 'acting is willing' claim? Perhaps they remain unscathed, but that is because they have taken a very attenuated form. According to the proposal before us, clearly not all volitions are attempts—or actions either. Only those volitions qualify that produce corporeal and other goings-on. There is no attempted burglary—and <u>a fortiori</u> no completed burglary—unless something more than an episode of willing occurs. You cannot disguise this by saying that all we need is a 'normal' thievish volition. So if we interpret 'try' as 'attempt', we should reject the identification of willing and trying.

What if we read 'try' as 'exert oneself'? Here we must consider two of Wittgenstein's examples: "When I raise my arm I do not usually <u>try</u> to raise it"; and "'At all costs I will get to that house'.--But if there is no difficulty about it--<u>can</u> I try at all costs to get to the house?" (1953, §§622 f.). Wittgenstein seems to be implying that when we are in conditions that pose no "difficulty"--because we are unimpeded by fatigue, broken arm-bones, or raging floodwaters between us and the house--we cannot strain to lift our hand, or to reach a nearby dwelling. Since I <u>act</u> when I effortlessly raise my hand, or just go up to the house, then if willing is straining, it seems that willing is <u>not</u> indispensable to action.

McCann evinces some awareness of this snag in the 'willing is trying' doctrine. Nevertheless he insists than whenever people carry out a "bodily action", they do so by "putting forth a physical effort" (1972, p. 240). Indeed he considers it "a matter of physiological fact that, when a person performs a normal act of arm-raising, the upward motion of his arm is caused by the tensing of a set of muscles . . . [and] the tensing of those muscles is the result of an action of physical exertion" (p. 247). I wonder. Has any specialist on matters of "physiological fact" isolated in a laboratory the "action of physical exertion" that McCann alludes to? McCann himself reveals no "physical" characteristics of this "exertion". He only describes its "result": muscular "tensing". While assuring us that every "able-bodied person knows what it feels like to engage in an act of exertion", he concedes that "there is little besides the feeling by which to know [it] . . . for no publicly observable event need occur for the action [of exertion] to be performed" (pp. 244 f.).

I don't understand how exertion could be "physical", a matter of "physiological fact", yet not "publicly observable". My misgiving goes back to the issues of Chapter One, sections 5-9. Initially I want to hear more of "what it feels like to engage in an act" of toil. I am fairly well acquainted with sensations of muscular tension, shortness of breath, and general discomfort--for example, when I lift or push heavy furniture. I suppose I feel the exertion, inasmuch as I am plagued by these sensations, and they occur because I am going about my work so laboriously. They may not be "publicly observable"--though it is unclear what we are denying to be the case when we say this. Nevertheless McCann exaggerates when he contends that "no publicly observable event need occur". Could I be straining energetically with the furniture and yet not be gasping, grunting, turning red, perspiring, wincing, trembling, or showing any rise in blood pressure? Such easily observed occurrences are virtually inseparable from the zealous manner that people exhibit when they are trying their utmost to accomplish a task.

Evidently my strenuous *manner* is not a volition. In correspondence McCann has said that when he discussed exertion, he was not equating it with volition. Nevertheless it seems to do the same job for him--of stirring one's limbs into motion--that willing does in all volitional theories. Since many such theories treat willing as trying in the sense of 'exerting oneself', I shall continue to inquire whether this sheds any light on volition. For instance, McCann speaks of a "feeling by which" able-bodied people "know" they are toiling. If he is talking about the muscular and other twinges I listed above, then I urge him to explain *how* such feelings enable us to "know" this. What *kind* of knowledge is this? How should we go about acquiring it? Could we lack it, as we could lack everyday kinds of knowledge? That is, could we be ignorant of our exertion, mistake it for something else, or merely guess that it is afflicting us?

These obscurities about the "feeling" by which McCann thinks we cognize our exertion are perhaps minor. Another hitch in his doctrine is more fundamental. Even if there are such acts, we have no reason to believe that they, and the feelings they generate, occur during "a normal act of arm-raising". Of course McCann is braced for this Wittgensteinian objection. In his reply, McCann invokes "the average person", and predicts that if

> he were told that normally he just raises [his arm], he would say that if . . . we mean that he does not normally engage in any exertion . . . [then our] analysis is false. In the normal case, too, he would say, he makes an effort; that is one of the differences between cases where one raises

> his arm and cases where the arm goes up
> because someone else raises it . . . To
> [say] a person "just" raises his arm . . .
> is to say the action comes off in the nor-
> mal way, as when a practiced . . . murderer
> says, "There was nothing to it . . . I just
> killed him" (pp. 241 f.).

This seems to beg our question: When our "action comes off in the normal way", do we "engage in any exertion", that is, act laboriously? McCann's example of the skilled assassin hardly bolsters his own thesis. A natural interpretation of "I just killed him" is that the braggart is <u>denying</u> that he exerted himself.

So far, then, we have little reason to believe that the kind of willing that supposedly occurs whenever we act is a species of trying, either an attempt or a toilsome performance. Yet we should not shelve the 'willing is trying' hypothesis until we look at one more popular rationale for it.

6. <u>The Argument from Total Failure</u>. This one has been circulating for decades. Vesey (1961) found a source of it in James's <u>magnum opus</u> (1890, II, p. 105), and rebutted several versions of it. Richard Taylor demolished an enticing reconstruction of it (1966, pp. 79-85). Yet it comes back to haunt us, notably in the work of McCann (1975), Annas (1977-78, pp. 205 f.), and Davis (1979, p. 16). I call it either the Argument from Total Failure, or from Paralysis, because it usually centers on a victim of this misfortune. The idea, in Annas's words, is that "we can try to perform bodily movements, and fail [completely], and nonetheless succeed in doing something" (<u>loc</u>. <u>cit</u>.). To illustrate, imagine that I am reading at my desk. Unbeknownst to me, my right leg has 'gone to sleep', and is temporarily paralyzed. At this moment my unliberated wife is vacuuming; she asks me to pick up my right foot so that she can vacuum under it. Now perhaps I believe--without looking to make certain--that I have elevated my foot. Alternately, I may notice with astonishment that it does not budge, or so much as tremble. In either case, nothing occurs that would justify our saying that I lifted my foot. But didn't I try? And why not say that this trying is my volition?

I am unsure. What would you count as an <u>attempt</u> by me to pick up my foot? Or if you equate straining with trying, what did I do laboriously? That is, what type of exertion did I engage in? Why must we assume that I toiled, or that I did anything when I attempted to lift my foot? Richard Taylor suggests,

> a paralyzed man's subsequent sincere avowal . . . that he tried . . . does not mean that he did something called "trying". It means only that, upon being told to move his leg, he found that he could not . . .
>
> . . . [Nor must we] suppose that he <u>finds it out</u> from . . . the failure of his (purely mental) effort . . . There is no reason to suppose that he succeeds in some purely mental action of trying but fails only in what he is trying to do. He fails completely (1966, pp. 84 f.).

My verdict is that adherents of the 'willing is trying' doctrine have not proven that there must be volitional attempts or exertions in circumstances where we fail totally to act, much less that similar episodes occur every time we successfully rouse our bodies into action. Above all, volitionists have scarcely clarified the nature of willing by their assimilation of it to trying. So the 'obscurity' charge seems warranted. But since future volitionists may develop a more cogent analysis of willing, we should not yet dismiss this approach to action. Accordingly, I shall explore further. Actually the issues I want to investigate concern not only volitional theories, but most other types of causal analysis too. This becomes plain if we take up a question we left unresolved at the end of section 4.

7. <u>Does it matter how narrowly or broadly we define willing?</u> Causal theories, including Prichardian as well as old-style volitionists, believe that when we act, some psychological antecedent or other sparks the movement of our limbs. But how strictly or loosely should we specify this antecedent? We gain one advantage if we insist that only ultra-potent mental occurrences or states like full-fledged willing and 'all-out' trying qualify. For then it should be virtually certain that such antecedents are going to produce appropriate behavior. We cannot rely on mere wanting, intending, even yearning, to always deliver. People often renounce a course of action they want, intend, or long to pursue.

Yet there are serious drawbacks to a restrictive account. We do not seem to be <u>aware</u> of high-powered, <u>sui generis</u> thrusts of willing nearly as frequently as theory demands, namely each time we act. This is the familiar 'not enough' problem, ii, that I invoked in section 2. No doubt you can reformulate your theory to get around it. You can plausibly deny that people must have a distinct volition for each act or bodily movement. Why shouldn't a single mega-volition trigger a plurality of movements--particularly cohesive, temporally extended sequences of behavior? A complementary strategem is to say that we are blessed with numerous <u>unconscious</u> volitions, which only experts have been sufficiently astute to discover. I shall examine these possibilities later if need be.

Perhaps we can avoid both expedients, and the 'not enough' grumble too, if we either let most conative goings-on count as volitions, or else follow ordinary (i.e., non-volitional) causal theorists who talk willy-nilly of reasons for action, desires, wants, drives, motives, and pro-attitudes. It may be immaterial whether or not we describe our favored antecedents as episodes of willing. Thus Brand argues that "the question whether reasons are causes for actions . . . is essentially no different from the question whether the volition theory is tenable" (1970, p. 11). If you seek a compromise, you might endorse Hardie's proposal to use an "open or non-committal . . . vocabulary of willing" because it unifies "the whole field of the voluntary, which includes at one end explicit decision-taking . . . and at the other . . . behavior . . . very like reflex action" (1971, p. 200).

Regardless of whether we hold onto Hardie's "vocabulary of willing", I see trouble at the "reflex" end of his continuum. As the traditionalist Goldman (1970, p. 91) and the Prichardian Davis (1979, ch. i) both remark, no causal theory specifies even relatively 'weak' introspectible antecedents for our habitual but intelligent performances. For instance, when I automatically yet correctly button my shirt, or steer my bicycle around potholes, I am not aware of being assailed by a volition, a reason, or a hankering to behave as I do.

Rote and "reflex" behavior are not the only bothersome cases if we require at least minimally vigorous antecedents for genuine action. Davis's example is someone who spontaneously waves at a passing train, but without "any sort of desire" (1974, p. 133). So broadly causal accounts of action, as well as their austere volitional brethren, seem vulnerable to the 'not enough' charge.

The major shortcoming of a permissive analysis, however, is that it certifies as either a volition or a reason for action many psychological items that are too feeble to do their "job of getting actions going". Frequently we are inclined, perhaps eager, to do something that we have no reason to avoid, and nothing hinders us from going ahead--yet we remain inert. I have no doubt that even people who are said to <u>will that they are going to act straightaway</u> sometimes draw back. We might call this the 'not strong enough' objection. Volitionists and broad-minded causal theorists may defensively tighten up their analyses. They may decide to allow only relatively dynamic goings-on to rank as volitions, or as <u>bona fide</u> reasons for action. But this manoeuvre creates a fresh problem: What shall be our criterion for measuring motivational strength? Felt urgency? Hardly, because quite insistent and annoying urges often do not make us act, or cause our bodies to move. So theorists may resort to a device like one I criticized in section 5. They could say they are exclusively concerned with volitions or reasons for action that have 'normal' potency. Next they could define 'normal' as 'what causes action or movement'. Again my criticism is that this account makes an empty tautology of the claim that whenever we have a volition or a reason of sufficient--that is, at least 'normal'--strength, the result is action or bodily movement.

Thus both volitionists and causal theorists generally face a dilemma. They have a choice between accepting only quite potent conative goings-on as volitions and act-producing reasons, and easing requirements. If they tighten up their criteria, the supply of volitions and reasons is going to seem inadequate. There won't be enough volitions and reasons to trigger all the bodily movements that apparently need a stimulus. But if volitional or causal theorists relax their standards, many of the antecedents that qualify as volitions or reasons are going to seem unreliably weak. Moreover, the prospects for a nontrivial in-between account are discouraging. Consequently we should investigate how strict theorists might increase their stock of sure-fire volitions or reasons.

8. _Could a person will unconsciously?_ The most radical view is propounded by a causal theorist who makes no use of willing in his account. Kent Bach's theory resembles an old-style volitional doctrine, however, since he explicitly defines "actions . . . as behavior caused by executive representations" (1978, p. 367). But what interests me is Bach's statement that his "representations" are "characteristically not . . . conscious" (_Ibid._). I wager that Bach's executive replicas are offspring of James's droll "ideo-motor theory" of how we learn to exercise mastery over our limbs. James himself speculated that we have "memory-images of . . sensations"--usually kinaesthetic ones--which we have previously experienced when "a particular movement . . . occurred in a random, reflex or involuntary way"; James also believed that unless such images come to us now, we shall not be able to produce the same type of corporeal movement (1890, II, pp. 487-92). Bach mainly appends the claim that we are usually unaware of these Jamesian likenesses.

James has other followers, but they do not always share Bach's opinion. Among today's self-styled volitionists, Goldman has elaborated a doctrine of "response images", which he bases partly on the work of contemporary cognitive psychologists (1976, pp. 76-82). As we shall notice, however, Goldman resists the suggestion that such images can go totally unrecognized. On the other hand, Aune challenges the assumption that "willing . . . need . . . involve imagery", either conscious or unconscious (1977, p. 71). If Bach is right, of course, then Aune really has pictures whenever he wills, but he occasionally overlooks them because they remain unconscious. Naturally I must waive all the objections I considered in sections 9 and 10 of Chapter Four, against psychoanalytical and kindred theories of unnoticed mental goings-on. With that proviso, I think I should examine what rival volitionists have to say about the formerly unquestioned premise that we must always be aware of our willing and our imagery.

Is there a rational method of deciding which party to believe? We might test Sellars's approach. As we remarked in sections 2 and 4, Sellars believes that "volitions are a subclass of thoughts"; furthermore, he regards thoughts as primarily "theoretical episodes designed to explain how people can behave intelligently"; and because thoughts have this lofty "theoretical" standing, he says, "what determines the frequency . . .

with which thoughts can legitimately be said to occur is the character of the overt phenomena which they . . . explain" (1966, pp. 150-53). My down-to-earth translation of this is: If there is a lot of "overt" behavior that you want to classify as deliberate, intelligent action, and the only accounts of it that appeal to you are volitional or causal, then you may "legitimately" postulate theoretical occurrences of willing and other forms of practical thinking ad gustam. If people fail to introspect a lot of episodes that your theory demands, you may declare the episodes unconscious.

How many secret incidents of willing should you recruit for your lofty explanatory purposes? Some volitionists oscillate between the cautious strategy of acknowledging little if any unnoticed willing, and the audacious procedure of multiplying clandestine jabs to cause the minutest segments of behavior. Davis, for example, rules that an "agent is not generally aware of [his] willing . . . in itself" (1979, p. 18). Yet he is disinclined to let underground volitions proliferate. So he conjures up high-powered "ongoing processes", such as your continuing volition to chat with some interlocutor. Davis believes that your

> remarks . . . are "controlled" by this volitional process as it "monitors" the . . . conversation. The manner of expression would also be controlled: . . . words and sentence structure, temporary halts . . . It will be possible . . . to treat portions of the volitional process as volitions in their own right, having more specific objects than "conversing". But there may be no single, best way of dividing up the process into such "subvolitions" . . . [We encounter] a similar difficulty in dividing a range into discrete mountains (p. 23).

Unlike Davis, Goldman eschews concealed willing, and declares his "response images" to be "conscious occurrences" (1976, p. 68). But Goldman runs into similar 'How many?' problems. For example, he shifts from the hypothesis that a skilled ballerina's global volition "initiates [an] entire series of leaps", to the conjecture that an expert typist has "volitions for fingers to move" each time he strikes a key (pp. 71, 74). In order to maintain that even these digital volitions are "conscious occurrences", Goldman distinguishes between "focal" episodes which monopolize our "volitional field", and shadowy "peripheral or marginal elements"; this allows him to regard his typist as "at least dimly thinking of the finger movements" (p. 74).

Suppose you prefer to explain behavior without resorting to dim awareness and either conscious or unconscious "subvolitions". You might wonder how much behavior a conscious or an unconscious mega-volition can propagate. Once more theorists seem to have a free hand. In his earlier opus, where he talked of wanting instead of willing, Goldman said, "I cannot execute [an] entire three block walk . . . as a result of a single occurrent want . . . [but] I can, perhaps, take ten or twenty steps" (1970, p. 90). No rationale accompanied his estimate.

Arbitrariness seems to reign in this debate over the presence of "representations" or "response images" when you will, the number of your volitions, the amount of behavior they generate, and your awareness of them. But Davis's remark about "dividing a range into discrete mountains" seems to imply that willtheorists are no more whimsical--in their counting at least--than alpine geographers. Hardie (1971, p. 194) adds the related defense that our methods of tallying volitions seem no less fanciful than those we use to enumerate people's actions. Goldman dismisses the problem of enumerating volitions because "there do not seem to be criteria for counting other categories of mental events"--for instance, the "thoughts one has during a two-minute interval" (1976, pp. 69 ff.).

Are these tu quoque replies effective? Compare the enumeration of mountain peaks and of volitions. My dictionary defines a mountain as "a land mass which projects conspicuously above its surroundings". How much higher should it be to rank as a separate peak? There is going to be some arbitrariness in our pragmatic decision about where to draw the line between a mere outcropping of one mountain, and a distinct summit. Yet once we settle upon a standard--say, projecting vertically at least 100 meters--we have an objective method of reckoning the number of mountains within any specified region of the globe.

As for actions, we must specify how many of a particular kind--for example, how many ascents of

Annapurna. It is not at all capricious to say that as of 1983, there have been four _solo_ ascents: four lone alpinists have climbed from the base to the top of Annapurna. Incidentally, both mountain peaks and actions of scaling them are objective in other ways besides being enumerable. Both may be subjected to public scrutiny--gawked at, filmed, measured. We can establish how the peak affects wind currents, and how climbing speeds up your pulse.

Goldman is probably right that other mental events, such as thoughts, are no easier to count than volitions. My guess is that volitions and similar psychological goings-on lack the sorts of objectivity that I attributed to a mountain-top and the action of scaling it. Goldman implies that since we speak without qualms of people having thoughts, we should be equally tolerant when we hear that people's volitions cause their intelligent behavior. My reaction to Goldman's parallel is that we should be as skeptical toward thoughts as toward volitions.

My goal here is not to cast doubt on theories of mental activity in general. What has concerned me in this section is the response of many volitionists to a pair of criticisms. The first complaint is that their doctrine requires an episode of full-fledged willing each time we act, but we do not seem to be introspectively aware of that many volitions. If theorists attempt to solve this difficulty by allowing wants and lesser hankerings to stand in for volitions, they must deal with a new grumble: that most of these conative states and happenings seem too puny for their assigned task. At this juncture a volitionist may return to a 'high-energy' conception of willing, and then argue along either of two complementary lines. He might assert that there really are enough volitions to go around, but we fail to register many of them because they are unconscious. Or else he might revise upward his estimate of how much behavior a conscious thrust of will can propagate. A mixed strategy is to introduce a minimal number of very brawny unconscious volitions. As I've documented, however, most theorists settle these issues by _fiat_, backing their decrees with little evidence.

As for the notion of unconscious willing, of whatever strength, it may be worse than _ad hoc_. Recall our initial assumption that willing is supposed to give us mastery over our bodily movements and their effects. But how could a volition that I am ignorant of give me such control? Imagine that I find myself stealing people's belongings, or distributing <u>gratis</u> all my own valuables. Am I going bonkers, or laboring under a post-hypnotic suggestion? Am I perhaps acting on unconscious volitions of either a larcenous or an eleemosynary sort? Whatever the cause of my behavior, I would implore passersby to restrain me. If I am engaged in unconscious willing, it seems to diminish my power to act as I please. In fact, how can a volition that I ignore--that sneaks up on me--express <u>my</u> will?

This question brings us to the final pair of problems with volitional theories, and causal accounts generally, that presently deserve attention. For it seems that if my willing represents <u>my</u> will, not only must I be aware of it, but it must be something I <u>do</u>. Then, however, we have to contend with the objections iii and iv that I outlined in section 2: If willing is an action I perform, don't I have to will my willing, and so on <u>ad infinitum</u>? Furthermore, if we have defined action <u>by reference</u> to willing, don't we go in an explanatory circle when we characterize willing as an action?

9. <u>Disputes over the active status of willing</u>. From my survey of Prichardian theorists, notably Davis, Aune, McCann, Annas, and Hornsby, in sections 2-6, it is obvious that these writers believe that willing is an action--according to them, the only genuine action we ever perform. But as usual we find no consensus. The leading dissenters are traditionalists, who say that our action is the movement of our bodies that results from our willing. They tend to deny that willing is also an action. Sellars calls it an "act", but explains that he is using the noun "act" in the Scholastic sense of "actuality" (1966, p. 153; 1976, §§1, 6, 21). Goldman's early doctrine is that "acts [in a non-Scholastic sense] are caused by <u>wants</u>"; and he lays it down that "wants simply are not <u>acts</u>, and hence there is no requirement that they be caused by further wants" (1970, p. 93). In his more recent plea for volitions, Goldman is less categorical, but just as parsimonious with arguments to support his verdict. After remarking cagily that he has "not said whether [a volition] is a mental <u>action</u>", Goldman reminds us that "<u>a</u> dominant view of <u>volitions</u> is that they are a species of desire or intention"; on this he cites the agreement of theorists from Hobbes through Sellars;

as for writers who "have regarded volitions as actions", Goldman thinks them vulnerable to the infinite regress objection; but he says "the easy reply . . . is simply to reject the characterization of volitions . . . as actions" (1976, p. 69). Apparently the "easy reply" satisfies him, since we hear no more on this subject. Nor do we learn why "desire or intention" may not be forms of mental action.

Should we go along with Goldman? The most eminent champion of causal but non-volitional analyses, Davidson, partly disagrees. He suspects that "willing is an act"; nevertheless he is as firmly convinced as Goldman that desire is not an act; however, all he says by way of convincing us is that "the question whether the agent can perform [a desire cannot] intelligibly be asked" (1972, pp. 139, 147 ff.). I have trouble assenting. It makes dubious sense to ask, 'Can the agent perform a walk?'; yet walking is surely an act or activity. Furthermore, not all experts agree with Goldman and Davidson that desiring is inactive. In a passage I quoted earlier (Chapter Five, section 9), Frankfurth says, "A person is active with respect to his own desires when he identifies with them"; otherwise he "is a passive bystander to his desires" and deeds.

At this point we can table the questions whether willing is the same as desiring, and whether it is consequently not an active state or occurrence. We should inquire briefly why Prichardians think willing is an action, and how they react to the 'regress' and 'circularity' problems. I run into many authoritative pronouncements. Aune states that "willing is an activity", and relies on Prichard's word that "willing can result from a desire to will something, but . . . [not] from a further act of willing" (1974, pp. 99 f.). We recall Davis's decree that "volitions are themselves actions", and all "actions are volitions". But how can we get volitions to occur without also willing them to occur, and so on ad infinitum? Davis assures us that this question "has been answered in many different ways and is now of historical interest only" (p. 39). He refers us to such writers as Aune and McCann for the alleged answer. Since I already quoted the principal statement of Aune's on this topic, and it did not seem to be buttressed with any reasoning, I suppose we should consult McCann.

I shall draw upon McCann's original exposition
of his ideas, and his later attempt to clarify them.
As I understand him, he tries to forestall any regress
by distinguishing between two aspects of ordinary
acts--the bodily "change" that must take place, which
he terms the act's "result", and our "bringing about"
of the result (1974, pp. 451 f.). The bringing-about
is a volition. McCann's thesis seems to be that "raising one's arm consists in an act of volition causing
the arm's rising", and "the act of arm-raising would
. . . count as . . . arising [sic] out of the more
basic act of volition"; finally, "volition lacks . . .
a 'result'--that is, it involves no change that is
related to it in the way one's arm's rising is related
to one's raising it" (1979, pp. 592 f.). So "volition
involves no event about which" questions of how we
bring it about may "sensibly be raised" (1974, pp.
463, 466). McCann welcomes this alleged upshot because
he thinks the "threatened regress" of willing can get
started only on the assumption that every act, even
the act of willing, "involves a causal sequence wherein
its [sic] result is caused by a more fundamental action" (pp. 465 f.). Apparently McCann believes it is
impossible to decompose willing further. Yet I fail
to see why his premise that willing "involves no event"
of the type he specifies"--and also "consists" of no
"more fundamental action"--is supposed to halt a regress. We can grant his premise and yet "sensibly
ask how people manage to have volitions at the right
moment--for example, when they think certain behavior
would be advantageous. Can't they will to have a
volition for movement of their limbs? When I pose this
question, I do not think I assume that their limb-moving volition "involves" or "consists in" the added
willing. So McCann's theory that volition is pure
"bringing about", unalloyed with any "result", does
not seem to rule out someone's willing to have a
volition.

In any case, what are the alternatives? Must
people wait around until the type of volition they
long for takes place? That would appear to diminish
their control over their behavior as much as the unconscious volitions I imagined in section 8. Well
then, do the right sorts of volition occur automatically? For instance, when we meet danger, do we will
to flee just as inevitably as our adrenal glands begin
to secrete epinephrine? Again our control is reduced,
inasmuch as automatic volitions would not be 'up to
us'.

Should we take seriously Aune's Prichardian claim that "willing can result from a desire to will something"? I believe that would undermine the whole volitional approach. For suppose--as Aune, McCann, and other Prichardians do--that willing is an action. Now if a desire can produce _this_ action, should it not be able to generate any behavior in our repertoire? If desire alone suffices to get things started, why do volitionists usually make willing an essential intermediary? Volition begins to look superfluous.

Here some theorists may forget about desires, and explain that we manage to have appropriate volitions at the opportune time because we _simply will_ to do such-and-such. But doesn't this clash with the volitional analysis? After all, if you can, without preliminaries of any kind, just engage in the supposed action of willing, why can you not just perform other actions, such as raising your arm? Volitionists beg this question if they retort that unfortunately we only exercise direct sway over our willing, and we must cudgel our body into action by first willing. The regress charge does not seem to have been satisfactorily answered, and Davis is exaggerating when he says it has "historical interest only".

There remains the circularity rebuke: If we bring willing into our account of what it is to act, and of how people control their behavior, aren't we making illicit use of the very notions of agency and power that we claim to elucidate? This circularity is all the more glaring because we must in the end deal with problems about volition that we already had concerning action. For instance, what is it to will, and how do you exercise mastery over your willing?

For purposes of argument, I assume that we have agreed with Davis, McCann, and other Prichardians that willing _is_ an action, thereby parting company from those traditionalists, such as Goldman, who accord nonactive status to willing. Admittedly the reasoning of both sides on that topic was inconclusive. But suppose it makes sense to either assert or deny that willing is an action. Could we say with any plausibility that willing is _not_ something I do--that it merely happens in or to _me_? A volition that sweeps over me, or all of a sudden takes place in me, would not represent my will--much less my goals and my personality-- any better than the unconscious volitions we discussed earlier. We seem forced to categorize willing as something we do. At all events, Prichardian 'activists', while fighting the regress accusation, seem to acknowledge that their procedure would be circular <u>if</u> they believed they had defined action. Thus McCann remarks, "Since I . . . maintain that volition itself counts as action, I cannot argue that it is the key to understanding the nature of action generally" (1974, p. 451). The volitional theory can only tell us <u>which events</u> are things we do, not what makes them actions.

10. <u>A related difficulty</u>. There is another question I have suppressed in order to give volitionists a run for their money. My problem is analogous to those we encountered throughout Chapter One as we tried to make sense of Cartesian theories of mind. I want to ask, What exactly do volitionists, above all Prichardians, mean when they inform us that to will is to act? We have a rich, varied, and multi-dimensional vocabulary for delineating what people do; but how much of it can we use to characterize someone's willing? We already dwelt on the comparison beween our relatively workable methods of <u>counting</u> actions of some type, and the fanciful estimates that volitionists give when asked to enumerate episodes of willing. The same with strength. There are rough-and-ready tests for measuring how hard a boxer's jab is, and how energetically you are pressing a lever. Yet it became quite unclear what volitionists mean when they gauge the behavior-producing strength of our willing. These uncertainties are only the tip of an iceberg. I wonder if <u>any</u> of our action-terminology is suited to describe our volitional capers.

Here are a few random illustrations of this 'intelligibility' problem. I might cook dinner painstakingly or hurriedly. Can willing be done in either of these ways? Your tennis-playing could be graceful or clumsy, daring or inhibited. What could it mean so to portray your willing? Sometimes people do things unwillingly, because they are coerced. What would it be like to will something reluctantly, because you are under duress? Again, we knock things over accidentally, push the wrong buzzer by mistake, absent-mindedly leave the bathtub faucet on. Could a person will something accidentally, by mistake, or in a fit of distraction? If not, do the corresponding 'positive' terms convey anything? A case in point is McCann's statement that "features distinctive of full-fledged action, especially intentionality and responsibility, characterize volition" (1979, p. 593; see his 1974, pp. 471 ff.). McCann goes on to discern these "active" features in the mental event of deciding. He thinks

> we never speak of our decisions as occurring to us . . . because neither at the beginning of the occurrence of deciding nor during it does the relevant content ["the course of action decided upon"] <u>obtrude</u> itself into the decision . . .
>
> . . . [D]eciding . . . is active . . . [I]t is both intentional and . . . controlled. We never hear of anyone unintentionally deciding to do something. It is precisely the opposite. I cannot imagine what it would be to decide . . . to play golf tomorrow, without meaning to decide precisely that . . . [T]he intentionality . . . is essential . . .: to decide is, precisely . . . to intend to decide just as we do (1979, p. 596).

This reasoning begs a significant methodological issue, which came up repeatedly in my first, second, and fourth chapters. Suppose it makes <u>no</u> sense to describe some item or event using one term from a pair or a group of contrary terms. May we then infer, without additional inquiry, that some antonym of the rejected term <u>does</u> apply? From the fact that it sounds unintelligible to report that somebody has <u>misspelled</u> the letter 'A', should we conclude that it makes sense, and may be true, to say that he or she has <u>correctly</u> <u>spelled</u> the letter 'A'? Since it is unintelligible to assert that Linda erroneously took someone else's pain to be her own, may we infer that it is meaningful, even necessarily true, to say she always identifies her own pains, and never mixes them up with anyone else's? If it is nonsense to describe a person as undergoing considerable pain but ignorant that he is in pain, does this prove that we either could or do have knowledge of our pain?

McCann's reasoning parallels these much-debated examples. He "cannot imagine what it would be to decide" unintentionally "to play golf tomorrow"--that is, "without meaning to decide precisely that". Straightaway he concludes that it does make sense, and could be true--indeed must be true--to say that we decide intentionally. "To decide is . . . to intend to decide". Presumably the same goes for willing.

The problem is that we have little if any idea what these familiar terms might mean in such unusual circumstances. We understand what it is to spell correctly a word or syllable--not a letter. It is commonplace for people to identify a stolen car--not a pain. We can explain how spies come to know of secret military exercises--not how a poison-oak victim comes to know of his itches. With regard to intention, we have read about arson for profit--that is, about building-owners who intentionally set their buildings on fire, to collect the insurance money. In this all-too-frequent circumstance, there is not only a contrast with spontaneous and with accidentally set blazes, between the calculating arsonist and the deranged pyromaniac. There are also details to be filled in: how the arsonist planned the conflagration; what materials he assembled; his <u>modus operandi</u>, cover-up, and alibi. But when we consider volition, neither contrasts nor particulars are forthcoming. As a result, I am not at all sure what Prichardians wish to convey when they tell us that willing is an action--perhaps our only action.

11. <u>Lessons</u>. We sustained the longstanding 'obscurity', 'not enough', and 'regress' objections, as well as a conditional variant of the 'circularity' grumble. We added a 'not strong enough' objection against volitionists who define willing broadly, so as to evade the 'not enough' reproach. We saw that some volitionists try to avoid both these complaints by postulating unconscious willing, of whatever quantity and force they need. This defensive measure, like so much contemporary theorizing about volitions, seemed unduly arbitrary. Overall, though it is evident that we are sorely tempted to introduce willing into our analysis of what actions are and how they come about, nevertheless every volitional theory we looked at was riddled with problems. This is hardly proof that willing does not or cannot occur--only that its ingenious and resourceful champions have failed to characterize it adequately. But perhaps we were mistaken to assume, as all volitionists and most of their opponents do, that some antecedent event must take place and get our limbs moving each time we act. My next chapter is devoted to a promising alternative approach that seems to dispense with this seemingly axiomatic assumption.

CHAPTER SEVEN

ARE ACTIONS CAUSED BY AGENTS, NOT BY EVENTS?

The volitional analyses I looked at in Chapter Six are not the only doctrines around that purport to tell us what action is and how it comes to be. A widely respected alternative is the novel theory, most carefully elaborated since the late 1950s by Richard Taylor and Roderick Chisholm, that the cause of our action is not a volition or any other event, but ourselves. The central idea is that an altogether different and unique sort of causality is at work: Our action does not result from anything that happens in us or to us, much less from anything we ourselves do, such as exerting ourselves or carrying out acts of will in foro interno; rather, our deed just springs from us. I'm afraid I will need several pages to exposit this concept of agent-causlity, and several more to decide how satisfactory an account of action it is. Incidentally, the doctrine that we alone agent-cause our action is also designed to clarify ou concept of free, autonomous behavior, which preoccupied us in Chapter Five. It should help us understand the familiar but surprisingly obscure idea, alluded to in the introductory chapter, that what we do is often 'up to us'--by contrast with the way it is never up to inanimate objects what they do. Thus it is up to me whether I go on reading the newspaper, or turn my head and stare out of the window; but it is not up to my radio whether it starts or stops blaring. I believe an agent-causationist would say about this contrast something to the effect that certain actions are within my power because I alone bring them about, whereas the radio's playing or not playing always results from other events, such as my pressing of its 'on' button. Another knot we struggled with in Chapter Five may also yield to agent-causation: the problem of 'alien' desires. For if no events at all cause our actions, then desires do not, and we can stop worrying whether desires imposed upon us by socialization or by neurotic and psychotic disorders rob us of autonomy. In positive terms, how could you exercise more control over your action than by being its sole cause? On the other hand, agent-causationists may have trouble analyzing what it is to act unfreely--for instance, to act under coercion--since your agent-caused behavior would seem, by definition, not to be caused by such events as someone threatening you. Yet isn't this what coercion amounts to?

We can pursue these connections after I set forth the doctrine of agent-causation. Prior to doing that, however, I should remark that the doctrine seems to be neural between various dualistic and materialistic theories of what a person is, such as the analyses we studied in Chapters One, Two, and Three. Presumably if there <u>were</u> immaterial Cartesian spirits ensconced inside our bodies, they could agent-cause agitation of our limbs; nor does anything disbar a 100% physical human organism from carrying out similar stunts, just because it is physical. As for the psychoanalytical theories about the unconscious causes of our behavior, which we examined in Chapter Four, I doubt that they can be squared with the claim that people themselves, not their urges--particularly urges they are ignorant of--trigger their actions. Freudians talk constantly of our unconscious actions, but I cannot imagine agent-causationists ever agreeing that we sometimes agent-cause our limbs to move without realizing it. Finally, I should say that, in line with my approach to theories of mind and free action since Chapter One, I shall be on the lookout for significant nonsense in the doctrine of agent-causality.

1. <u>Three likely sources of Taylor's and Chisholm's theory</u>. The only clear anticipation of Taylor's and Chisholm's idea is C. D. Broad's very tentative, sketchy hypothesis that perhaps we engage in "non-occurrent causation of events" whenever we act (1952, p. 131; see pp. 119-22, 124, 129 f.). Some interpreters believe that Aristotle and Thomas Reid were incipient agent-causationists. Naturally I want to stay out of exegetical disputes here; nevertheless it seems to me that for Aristotle, there is an event in us that triggers our motion when we act purposively, namely our practical reasoning. With Reid, a volition-like event of exercising our "active power" seems to have a similar function. An early twentieth-century philosopher, A. B. Johnson, used the term subsequently adopted by Chisholm, "immanent causality"; but Johnson believed that processes of inanimate nature, as well as human behavior, could display immanent causality (1924, vol. III, pp. xx-xxx, 69, 93-98, 127-42, 171-77). In any case Johnson asserts that our actions result from episodes of willing (pp. xxv, 141).

My guess is that Taylor, Chisholm, and other philosophers who pioneered the notion of agent-causality were convinced by some of the Wittgensteinian and Rylean criticisms of will-theories, and wanted a more plausible account. Certainly Taylor goes out of his way to argue against volitionism (1960, pp. 85-88; 1966, pp. 49, 64-68, 75-79, 88 ff., 113). Taylor also makes it clear that even if we had to will in order to act, the occurrence of our volition would be no guarantee that our resulting behavior was free or autonomous. After all, Taylor imagines, "an ingenious physiologist" might

> induce in me any volition he pleases, simply by pushing various buttons on an instrument to which . . . I am attached . . . By pushing one button, he evokes in me the volition to raise my hand . . . [He] puts a rifle in my hands, aims it at some passer-by, and then . . . evokes in me the volition to squeeze my finger against the trigger, whereupon the passer-by falls dead of a bullet wound (1983, pp. 43 f.).

Taylor remarks that although he would be "acting in accordance with his inner volitions", he would not be "a free and responsible agent". Of course it is doubtful that we should automatically agree that Taylor acted "according to <u>his</u> . . . volition". We analyzed similar cases in Chapter Five, section 4. Yet Taylor is right that the mere occurrence of a volition in me is not logically sufficient for saying that I freely perform the corresponding act.

For his part, Chisholm never explicitly attacks volitional theories of action, though he seems resolutely opposed to the more general view that our deeds result from some antecedent occurrences or other: if not from volitions, then from kindred goings-on. Moreover, in Chisholm's early discussions we find almost nothing analogous to an act of will (but see his 1971b, p. 53). In his latest pronouncements, however, Chisholm gives a place of honor to "undertaking". We read that "a man's undertakings are things he brings about directly", and "anything a man brings about directly is an internal change", which may in its turn "contribute causally to certain changes in [his brain] that we know next to nothing about" (1976a, p. 210). "Undertaking" begins to sound volitional when Chisholm admits that what you undertake to bring about may not in fact happen (pp. 208 f.). This reminds me of willing inasmuch as you can will a movement, and yet the movement may fail to occur. Causing--and surely agent-causing as well--is altogether different in this regard. From the premise that you have caused E, it follows logically that E has taken place.

Whether or not we decide that Chisholm has now countenanced something on a par with volition, we shall see that his theory of agent-causlity, like Taylor's, must be at loggerheads with any doctrine that makes our action the result of earlier or concurrent happenings and states, volitional or otherwise. More important, we can see how easy it is for agent-causationists to dispense with willing and its ilk. They need not suppose that I have to exercise my conative faculty, or start out by "undertaking" to set my limbs in motion. Instead they can postulate that I "directly" make some or all of my body budge, without preparatory inner jabs.

2. <u>The need to distinguish between action and mere bodily happenings</u>. So far I've described only one probable source of agent-causality doctrines. The second is precisely the main riddle that motivated Chapter Six: What is an action? More specifically, if we agree that whenever people act, their bodies move, what else is there to people's action? For brevity I follow contemporary philosophical custom and interpret our key verb 'move' quite broadly, so that even if a person is holding still, and his or her limbs are motionless, it will be true that his or her body moves (see Davidson, 1971, p. 11; Honderich, 1972, p. 187). To avoid characterizing action in a circular manner, we must also interpret 'move' as what Hornsby calls an "intransitive" verb (see her 1980, pp. 2 ff., discussed in section 5 of Chapter Six). That is, we should <u>not</u> equate the movement of someone's body with that person's action of moving her or his body. For then we would be answering the general question, 'What is it to act?', with a barely less general action-verb, saying 'To act is to move one's body'. Such truisms bring us no closer to analyzing action.

Besides my limbs' movement--understood broadly and intransitively--what then constitutes my action? Obviously I do not act every time my limbs move. They occasionally twitch or tremble; when I sleep they flail about; and these goings-on are not deeds of mine. We cannot any more designate a volition as the 'something more' that engenders the movements of my body and transforms them into actions. At this point we should be receptive to Taylor's proposal. He argues that

> the beating of my heart and the growth of my hair . . . are motions and changes of my body, but in a familiar though somewhat baffling sense they are not things with which I have anything to do . . .
>
> My arms and fingers sometimes move, on the other hand [sic], or my body moves from place to place, carried . . . by my legs, and these motions seem clearly to be events of a wholly different kind . . . [I]f they happen at all it is because I make them happen. And this seems manifestly different from my body, or my brain and nervous system making them happen.
>
> . . . [W]e can say that . . . I cause the motions of my fingers but not those of my heart (1966, pp. 57 f.; see Chisholm, 1971b, pp. 68 f.).

Who does not feel an urge to deploy causal terminology in thus marking off action from bodily movement? Even if we withhold the overworked verb 'cause' itself, we will at least want to brandish one of the related expressions that Taylor considers: "make happen", "initiate", "bring about", "originate" (1966, pp. 111, 113, 262; 1983, p. 49). For diversity, we may enlist verbs such as Chisholm's "endeavor" (1971b, p. 53) and "undertake".

Before we go on, I should mention a snag in all this, which we are going to encounter repeatedly. Remember that our concern is with circumstances in which a person is supposed to bring about movements of his own limbs. Yet normally when there is some event that a person is said, in any down-to-earth sense, to have caused, you can always distinguish between the occurrence that he or she brought about, and whatever he or she did to make it happen. We bring about a reconciliation between an estranged husband and wife by talking separately with them. We cause a panic in the commodities market by circulating rumors. Our causing of E is a separable performance, A, which produced the event E. But when we move our limbs in the standard way--that is, when our limbs are not broken, paralyzed, frozen, or otherwise incapacitated--there is no distinct performance that we can set alongside their movement, and say that this is what we did to cause their movement. Since it is part of what we ordinarily mean, when we talk of people causing E̲s, that they did something that caused the E̲s, therefore we should ask for details of the agent-causationist's new usage of the expression 'So-and-so caused such-and-such a movement of his body'. By reference to my objection in Chapters One and Two that Cartesian theories of non-physical minds or mental happenings make no sense, we should urge the agent-causationist to go beyond the minimally illuminating negative statement that we do no̲t have to engage in any separate high-jinks when we "directly" bring about everyday movements of our unhampered limbs. So be it; nevertheless it is surely legitimate for us to inquire what one do̲es have to do, or what does have to happen in circumstances where one agent-causes movement of one's body. We understand well enough, at least in particular situations, how such events as our deliberate and accidental behavior work to bring about their effects. Until the proponent of agent-causality divulges some corresponding data on his alternative, how can it be intelligible to us? The appearance of our shopworn verb 'cause' only gives us the illusion that we comprehend what it is to agent-cause movements of our limbs.

Broad's early discussion touches on this problem with his "non-occurrent" causality (1952, p. 131). In one book, Taylor seems to brush aside any meaning problems; he says the notion of agent-causality is more "archaic", "primary", "original", and "natural" than that of one event resulting from others (1966, pp. 10, 14 f., 18, 21, 111). Yet elsewhere he remarks that his "conception of the causation of events by beings or substances [i.e., agents] that are not events is . . . so different from the usual philosophical conception [of what it is for something to cause events] . . . that it should not even bear the same name" (1983, p. 43). Examining statements like "A brick caused that window to break", Taylor reminds us that

> objects or substances seem to be referred to as causes . . . [b]ut this is simply a common manner of speaking . . . It is not . . . just the brick as such that causes the window to break. It is, rather, the impact

158

of the brick against the window; and this impact is not itself a substance, but a change . . . [I]n all typical cause-and-effect situations, the causal connections are between changes or states of substances, and only indirectly between the substances themselves (p. 81).

I would add a similar misgiving. In typical contexts where we learn that event $\underline{A}$ caused event $\underline{B}$, we are in a position to explain and predict. You can account for B: It happened because $\underline{A}$ took place immediately or a while beforehand. If you observe an $\underline{A}$-ish event going on now, you are entitled to expect something $\underline{B}$-ish. However, in the cases of someone moving her or his body, which preoccupy agent-causationists, there is no analogue for the $\underline{A}$-ish event that justifies our forecast of someone's bodily motion. Evidently the mere existence of an agent at some given time does not justify our predicting that her or his body will move at the time, much less how it might move. Nor does the fact that he exists then enable us to explain why or how his body moved at the time (see Taylor, 1966, pp. 218 ff.).

Similar questions about what agent-causationists mean are going to surface no matter what causal verb we select: "make happen", "originate", "initiate", "endeavor", "undertake". Should we then abandon causal verbs, as Taylor suggests at one juncture, and say instead that an agent merely "does" or "performs" the movement of his limbs? (Taylor, 1983, p. 43; see Danto, 1970, pp. 110-13, and 1973, pp. 7, 38 f., 50-60, 119). I'm skeptical. The verbs "do" and "perform" are, syntax aside, virtual synonyms for the verb "act"--and scarcely better understood. Therefore it will not help us separate action from bodily happening if we say one acts when one "performs" the movement of one's body. Incidentally, if we specify a corporeal movement in certain quite standard ways, for example as 'the rising of my hand', it will be ungrammatical for us to say that I do or perform it, viz., do or perform the rising of my hand. It is a fairly reliable sign that a metaphysician is in deep trouble if he thereupon declares our ordinary grammar inadequate to express the real nature of agency or what-not.

I said earlier that agent-causationists may have had three reasons for developing their admirably unorthodox view. I have considered their likely wish to escape the criticisms made against volitional theories, and their probable need to distinguish action from mere movement of the body. Before I cover a third source of agent-causality doctrines, I want to state my sympathy both for these metaphysicians' impatience with the limits of grammar and for their obsession with causal terminology. I also share Taylor's reluctance to say that my actions are just corporeal goings-on which result from events in "my brain and nervous system". This last point brings me to what I regard as the fountainhead of agent-causality: the perennial conundrum over determinism, indeterminism, free will, and responsibility.

3. <u>Does agent-causality avoid both determinism and indeterminism?</u> Chisholm and Taylor each believe, as I do, that sometimes a human being exercises power over his or her own behavior, and is free to act in alternative ways. Chisholm believes, and I agree heartily, that such free agents are sometimes justly held accountable for harm they have wrought. The metaphysical conundrum is, How can these homespun beliefs be true, if it is also true that every event--including our bodily movement when we act, and any volition or other mental caper that is supposed to produce our movement--has resulted from antecedent or contemporaneous events? For Taylor and Chisholm, it does not matter whether determinists say that electrical activity within our cortex makes our limbs gyrate, or that in favored circumstances our own decisions, impulses, ambitions, and more or less reasoned thoughts are what do the trick. Chisholm and Taylor each argue that by a determinist's account, ultimately we have no control over these "inner" causes of our behavior. I am unsure what Taylor and Chisholm mean when they contend that we lack such mastery. In line with the methodology of my first, second, fourth, and fifth chapters, I would ask what these philosophers think it would be like for us to be in command of all the important causes of our behavior. By the same token, I would ask for particulars on how they think all causes of our action--our neural, attitudinal, even cognitive states and processes--operate to curtail our freedom. For example, are these causal antecedents on a par with sudden disabilities, or with the sorts of interferences we tried to analyze in Chapter Five--coercion, madness, neurotic compulsions, brain-washing, hypnosis, and certain forms of socialization? At any rate both Chisholm and Taylor seem

convinced that ordinary causation of our deeds by earlier or simultaneous events will take away our autonomy. Here is a characteristic passage in which Taylor insinuates that all causes leave us equally powerless to choose among alternatives:

> Whether a desire which causes my body to behave in a certain way is inflicted upon me by another person [such as the ingenious physiologist] . . . or derived from hereditary factors, or . . . from anything at all, matters not . . . [I]f it is in fact the cause of my bodily behavior, I cannot but act in accordance with it (1983, p. 44).

Chisholm worries specifically about someone whose action is determined by his own cognitive and conative states. Chisholm declares that

> if these beliefs and desires . . . caused him to do just what he did do, then, since <u>they</u> caused it, <u>he</u> was unable to do anything other than just what he did do. It makes no difference whether the cause of the deed was internal or external; if the cause was some state or event for which the man himself was not responsible, then he was not responsible for what we have been mistakenly calling his act (1966, p. 13; see pp. 23-28; also 1964b, pp. 24 f.).

    Would it comfort Taylor and Chisholm if determinism proved altogether false--if, for instance, scientists discovered significant numbers of totally uncaused bodily motions, or perhaps movements resulting from uncaused decisions, volitions, and thoughts? That would only vindicate "simple indeterminism", of which Taylor jibes, "We . . . avoid picturing a puppet . . . but the conception that emerges is . . . that of . . . an erratic and jerking phantom, without any rhyme or reason" (1983, p. 45; see Taylor, 1958, p. 225).

    What if we follow Libertarian theorists of an earlier generation and postulate a noumenal Self, which barges into the causal order of events, thereby overpowering our "character as so far formed"? (see Campbell, 1951, p. 170). On such occasions we would experience random breaches of "causal continuity", and these gaps would somehow coincide with our "effort of will" to "'rise to duty' in the face of opposing desires" (ibid., pp. 166, 169; cp. Chisholm, 1966, p. 25). Taylor plausibly interprets this reference to a Self as an obscurantist way of emphasizing that it is the person herself or himself who performs an action. Otherwise, as Taylor suggests, the Libertarian variety of indeterminism seems to imply that we are in constant danger of losing command over our behavior to an unpredictable though miraculously dutiful Self which we somehow "possess" (Taylor, 1966, pp. 134 f., 263).

Chisholm incisively sums up the apparent failure of both indeterministic and deterministic outlooks. Neither of them explains how an individual can control what he does, and how we can justify our practice of holding anyone accountable on the grounds that he or she had within his or her power to follow alternative courses of action. Chisholm's précis goes,

> 'Human beings are responsible agents; but this fact appears to conflict with a deterministic view of human action (the view that every event that is involved in an act is caused by some other event); and it also appears to conflict with an indeterministic view . . . (the view that the act, or some event that is essential to the act, is not caused at all)'. To solve the problem . . . we must make somewhat far-reaching assumptions about . . . the agent (1966, p. 11; see 1969, p. 199).

4. A qualified endorsement of Chisholm's and Taylor's position. I intend to examine those "assumptions" in a moment. For now I want to emphasize that I share many of Taylor's and Chisholm's discontents. Take indeterminism. How could anyone be said to exercise power over uncaused movements of his limbs-- or movements engendered by uncaused decisions, desires, and beliefs? How can the mere absence of events that produced my behavior guarantee that I act freely? I would certainly not be in charge of movements, or volitions, inflicted upon me at random by a will-of-the-wisp Self which is supposed to be "mine".

So much for indeterministic theories. The stock deterministic model of action generally, and of free action in particular, seems hardly more adequate. But my reasoning on this topic diverges from Taylor's and Chisholm's. I dissent from their repeated but largely unsupported claim that a person's own motivational state destroys her or his freedom whenever it causes his or her bodily movement. I would block Chisholm's hasty inference, "since <u>they</u> caused it, <u>he</u> was unable to do anything other than just what he <u>did</u> do". Why should we conclude, without evidence of duress, paralysis, insanity, ignorance, or the like, that the person did <u>not</u> have the power to act differently? Taylor's approach is subtler, but open to the same challenge. From the premise, "existing conditions are causally sufficient for my not moving my finger", Taylor says "it follows that it is causally impossible for me to move my finger" (1960, p. 86). What sort of hindrance is Taylor describing? Imagine that among "existing conditions" there figured prominently my wish to test the breeze for velocity and direction, and my belief that I could do so by holding my moistened finger upright in the wind. My finger is now motionless as a result of these undramatic "existing conditions". Suppose we straightaway deduce that it is "impossible for me to move my finger". Aren't we assuming that digital motion is beyond my power, although we have no indication that I am disabled or that my finger is impeded from moving? Where is the impossibility? I suppose we should pay attention to Taylor's modifier, "causally". All right, then: Does "it is causally impossible for me to move my finger" mean anything more worrisome than that my finger is <u>caused</u> not to bend? This is a far cry from proving that my own motivational states, along with other "causally sufficient" conditions, leave me <u>unable</u> to crook my finger.

    I do not share Taylor's and Chisholm's belief that if our behavior is causally determined we are powerless to act otherwise than we do act. But I join them in rejecting the standard deterministic picture of motivated action. As I reconstruct things, an agent is portrayed as a field of causes. He or she is comparable to an arena where calculations, perceptual judgments, noble and base inclinations, surges of emotion, maybe also repressed fantasies and a conscious sense of duty--all of these somehow "his" (or "hers")--manage to contend or blend with each other. Even if the upshot of this <u>mélée</u> is agitation of his limbs, why should we call that "his act"? I would echo Chisholm's phrase, "<u>they</u> caused it". Movement has resulted from the protagonist's "beliefs and desires", but _he_ seems to have virtually nothing to do with it.

Now determinists may retort that, after all, it is the person who calculates, desires, and so on; consequently we do not merely have cause-effect sequences running through him. Moreover, since these mental goings-on are clearly his, the bodily motions they produce--at least the ones he wanted or expected--should in turn rank as his deeds.

I admit that this re-drawing of the deterministic tableau connects up the agent with various mental states which allegedly bring about his corporeal movement, thereby making him look more active--more in command. I shall put aside questions about what it might mean to say we are active or passive in regard to our psychological states; this will occupy Chapter Eight. But my immediate response to the modified deterministic scenario is that it sounds oddly Prichardian. As soon as determinists emphasize that the agent does her or his practical thinking, desiring, and so on, I wonder if they can say he or she does anything else. Isn't the resulting limb motion simply an effect of his real action--what he does mentally? I shall not pursue this question any further, since I only wanted to illustrate why it was reasonable for metaphysicians such as Taylor and Chisholm to propound a new theory of action.

5. <u>What do we agent-cause?</u> Before we decide whether agent-causality is what we need to overcome the aforementioned difficulties about volition, the distinction between action and mere corporeal movement, as well as the enigma of determinism, we must briefly peruse both Chisholm's and Taylor's writings. They differ on a few crucial points--for instance, on what it is that an agent alone brings about. Taylor nominates concrete, individual, ephemeral events, specifically those events that are motions of our bodies. I get the impression that he thinks we agent-cause our hands, legs, and so on to move, <u>without</u> first getting neural events to occur that <u>will</u> bring about motion of our extremities in the ordinary way. Chisholm's approach is more complicated. In one recent discussion of these matters, Chisholm asserts that "there are no such things as . . . events", and especially no "'concrete events' in addition to states of affairs" (1976b, p. 115). It will save space if we abbreviate here, using the acronyms "SAs" and "SA" for the plural and singular, respectively. Then we

can explain what Chisholm means when he denies that there are concrete events in addition to SAs. To begin with, Chisholm's examples of SAs are such items as "Socrates being mortal", "there being unicorns", "Brutus killing Caesar", "Truman being re-elected president", "Brown being elected mayor", "Jones being robbed", and "Smith being ill" (pp. 117-36). According to Chisholm, these

> are abstract entities which exist necessarily and which are such that some but not all of them occur, take place, or obtain . . .
>
> . . . [They] are in no way dependent for their being upon the being of concrete, individual things. Even if there were no concrete, individual things, there would be indefinitely many [SAs] (p. 114).

Although in this sense Chisholmian SAs are aloof from particular worldly items, they seem in another way to be tailor-made for the cognitive, affective, and conative antics of people. For Chisholm declares, "The mark of an [SA] is . . . that it is capable of being accepted"; and he goes on to encapsulate this "mark" in a definition: "$\underline{p}$ is a [SA] = $\underline{Df}$. It is possible that there is someone who accepts $\underline{p}$", and more generally, "A[n SA] is whatever may be considered or entertained" (p. 117). An astute reader will guess that it is only a short step from entertaining to agent-causing SAs. But we are getting ahead of ourselves.

Unlike the supposed "private objects" of a Cartesian mind, which we poked fun at in Chapter One, Chisholmian SAs are designed to be publicly accessible. For instance, Chisholm says that the SA "Brown being elected mayor" is the "intentional object" of both Jones's fear and Smith's efforts--which is to say that Jones is apprehensive toward the SA, while Smith is acting with the goal of "bringing . . . about" the SA (pp. 116 f., 164 f.). Their opposed attitudes and purposive behavior--Jones's con-attitude and Smith's precinct work--"would have this common [intentional] object even if Brown were not elected mayor"; in the latter case "Jones's fears would have been unfounded and Smith's efforts unsuccessful" (p. 117; see p. 123).

On Chisholm's view, SAs make "concrete events" supernumerary, because when SAs occur, take place, or obtain, we already have concrete events. But what is it for SAs to do this? Chisholm's position in the recent book I am quoting from is that a given SA occurs, takes place, or obtains, whenever the "concrete, individual" things that figure in the SA acquire the relational or non-relational "property" that also figures in the SA. Chisholm says the concrete thing or things "concretize" the SA. His illustration runs, "that [SA] which is Brutus killing Caesar was concretized in 44 BC by the set consisting just of [the concrete human individuals] Brutus and Caesar" (p. 125). Of "that [SA] which is Smith being ill", Chisholm writes that it "implies Smith to have the property of being ill", and the complete SA gets "concretized" when poor Smith is afflicted with "the property of being ill" (ibid.)

In his earlier work Chisholm sometimes refers to events and to occurrings or obtainings of SAs, but never to concretizations of SAs. He also draws a sharper contrast between agency and ordinary causation. We have the latter, or "transeunt" causation, when one SA, in occurring, makes another take place (1966, pp. 17-20; 1971b, p. 42). Agency is a different kettle of fish. Chisholm sees it only when "there is some event, or set of events, that is caused, not by other events or [SAs], but by the man himself, by the agent" (1966, p. 17). As I remarked above, Chisholm's term for this is "immanent" causation. He emphasizes the negative point that we immanently "cause certain events to happen" just in case "no other events--or agents--determine [i.e., transeuntly cause] us to [immanently] cause those events to happen" (1971c, p. 34; but see 1976a, pp. 201-205). Presumably Chisholm would also not allow the events themselves, which we immanently cause--that is, the SAS we immanently make occur--to have transeunt ancestry as well. Interestingly enough, some such principle appears to underlie an argument that leads Chisholm to conjecture that we immanently cause only various neural happenings, and these have the job of transeuntly bringing about our peripheral movements. His reasoning goes,

> A responsible act is an act [that] . . . the agent . . . had . . . within his power . . . not to perform . . . But what . . . he thus accomplishes is [transeuntly] caused by certain physiological events. (The man raises his arm; yet certain cerebral events

cause his arm to go up.) Hence it [seems to be] false that it is within his power not to perform the act, and therefore he [seems to be] not responsible . . .

. . . The things he makes happen directly may well be certain cerebral events . . . he is likely to know nothing about . . . [and] these . . . made his arm go up (1964a, pp. 19 f.; 1969, p. 216; 1971c, p. 38).

In his most famous exposition, Chisholm generalizes without hesitancy: "whenever a man does . . . <u>A</u>, then (by 'immanent causation') he makes a certain cerebral event happen, and this cerebral event (by 'transeunt causation') makes <u>A</u> happen" (1966, p. 20). Unfortunately Chisholm does not take up a further question: Is the "cerebral event" we immanently bring about <u>transeuntly uncaused</u>, or might it just possibly be a transeunt effect of other preceding or contemporaneous brain events? Neurophysiologists would be surprised to learn that the cortical goings-on that transeuntly make our extremities move are <u>without</u> transeunt causes.

To gain perspective on this difficulty, we should formulate Taylor's position in Chisholmian terminology. Besides holding that we immanently bring about movement of our limbs rather than mere cerebral events, Taylor allows a single limb-movement to have transeunt as well as immanent origins. He illustrates transeunt-immanent co-existence with regard to the transeunt efficacy of our beliefs and desires. Taylor imagines that

I am the [immanent] cause of . . . a motion of my finger . . . Further, . . . there are [transeunt] conditions causally sufficient for my doing just that--such as, among other things, my conviction that only by doing so can I save my life . . .

. . . [W]hat is entailed by . . . [the doctrine that] men are the [immanent] initiators of their own acts, is that for anything to count as an act there must be an essential reference to the agent as the [immanent] cause of that act, whether he is,

> in the usual [transeunt] sense, caused to
> perform it or not (1966, pp. 114 f.).

One advantage of Taylor's co-existence principle is that it enables him to distinguish between actions in general and those actions that are free. Taylor modestly concedes that "there are doubtless other and indeed more adequate meanings [sic] for the expression 'a free act'"; still, he proposes that

> we . . . define . . . 'a free act', not as
> an uncaused bodily motion . . . but as [a
> transeuntly] uncaused act . . . not as some-
> thing that just happens from no cause, but
> rather as something that is in fact [imma-
> nently] caused to happen by some agent,
> but under circumstances . . . such that
> nothing [transeuntly] causes him to do it
> (pp. 127 f.,; see pp. 34 f.).

Admittedly this passage is not easy to decipher. The first appearance of the term "uncaused", and the phrase "from no cause", both sound ambiguous. At the same time it is unclear whether Taylor wishes to contrast "bodily motion" with "act", and "something that . . . happens" with something an agent does or performs. Is the "bodily motion" he alludes to both transeuntly and immanently "uncaused"? Is this "bodily motion" identical with the transeuntly "uncaused act" that he is defining as a free act? The previous quotation suggests no difference between immanently caused bodily motions and immanently caused acts. So I shall interpret Taylor as holding that a free act is an immanently but not transeuntly produced bodily motion. Unfree acts would be transeuntly as well as immanently generated agitations of the body.

Earlier I quoted Chisholm's statement to the effect that we act only when we immanently cause an event and no other events transeuntly cause the event in question. If this is Chisholm's view, he cannot distinguish between free and unfree acts using Taylor's criterion. N. L. Ranken sees the problem clearly:

> Immanent causation is understood [by Chis-
> holm] in such a way as to preclude any
> change happening to the agent in his causa-
> tion of the act . . . [T]here is no foreign

> [transeunt] causal influence . . . [But a] man is free with respect to an act, and, therefore, responsible, says Chisholm, if he has the power both to perform and not to perform that act. <u>Immanent causation</u> [and the absence of transeunt causation] <u>accounts for</u> . . . <u>that power</u>. Now if all our actions are immanently caused by us [but not transeuntly caused by events]--and this is analytically true [for Chisholm]--then all our actions are free, and we are, all of us, equally responsible for all our actions (1967, p. 405).

Obviously it would be wiser for agent-causationists to side with Taylor on this topic, and allow for the possibility of unfree acts--which will have transeunt plus immanent ancestry. This implies that what we agent-cause may be overdetermined, since it may also result transeuntly from our beliefs, desires, or other event-like goings-on.

    We noticed two additional issues on which Chisholm and Taylor disagree about what people agent-cause. My hunch is that it is simpler for agent-causationists to follow Taylor, and say we immanently produce events, thereby blocking charges of nonsense against Chisholmian SAs and their mysterious occurrings--not to mention the concretizing of properties by concrete individuals. We also wondered if agent-causationists should say that the happenings we immanently bring about are movements of our extremities--Taylor's candidates--or that they are the "cerebral events" of which Chisholm admits we are "likely to know nothing". If agent-causationists join with Taylor, and if the movements of our limbs result transeuntly from cerebral events, then Taylor's account of unfree action entails that we always act unfreely. If agent-causationists take Chisholm's line, they can at least hope that the neural happenings of which we are "likely to know nothing" have no <u>known</u> transeunt causes, and perhaps lack transeunt causes altogether. I make this last recommendation with little confidence, however. For suppose we indeed "know nothing" of the neural goings-on that Chisholm thinks we agent-cause. Why should we assume, as he does, that they nevertheless transeuntly make our limbs move? Furthermore, the doctrine that we go around immanently producing brain events of which we are totally ignorant surely is vulnerable to accusations of nonsense. After all, agent-causationists can tell whether the limb-movement they wanted to bring about has taken place, or whether it has failed to occur. How would they decide if they have succeeded in agent-causing unknown cerebral occurrences? Agent-causationists can pinpoint various hindrances upon our limbs, and say with some plausibility that these interfere with our immanently bringing about certain large-scale bodily motions. But what analogues of this could there be in the case of our neural processes? That is, what impedes us from generating this or that cerebral happening? Agent-causationists might say that we exercise our limbs, and make our bodies thinner by dieting, so that we will be able to immanently produce graceful or otherwise demanding movements that are not yet in our repertory. What could be the cerebral equivalents of knee-bends, push-ups, <u>cuisine minceur</u>, and Weight Watchers? I conclude that there seem to be serious problems for agent-causationists who accept Chisholm's view that we immanently bring about neural occurrences --<u>and</u> also for those who defend Taylor's position that we directly call forth movements of our limbs.

 I shall leave the matter unresolved, because I want to discuss two even more fundamental questions about agent-causing. First I shall ask,

 6. <u>Is agent-causing act-like?</u> My present worry is connected with the <u>prima facie</u> difficulty we noticed in section 2. Ordinarily when we say of a person, rather than of an event, that she or he caused an uproar, a flood, a traffic accident, or what-not, this is not the end of the story. The person must have done something--must have screamed, left on the water tap, or stopped his car without signaling--and this action helped greatly, along with various other circumstances, to produce the uproar and so on. I'm not so much interested in what <u>else</u> the person did when he or she caused an event; what seems particularly significant to me is that such transeunt causing by a person is <u>active</u>. So I want to inquire now whether immanent causing is similarly active.

 What if it is? Well, suppose its champions are right that we do nothing else, and no conative, cognitive, or other goings-on have to occur antecedently when we agent-cause our brains or bodies to move. Consequently agent-caustionists do not have to face an infinite regress--for instance, of causing an uproar by screaming, and causing the scream by somehow plucking one's vocal cords, and causing one's vocal cords to twang by . . . But agency-theorists are not out of the woods. For if immanent causing is nevertheless comparable to standard forms of action, then the proposed analysis of action--as immanently bringing about peripheral or cerebral movements--is bound to be circular. All types of action will then be equated with the one rather occult species, namely agent-causing.

If it were not active, what would agent-causing be? Could it be like a mere event, to which we are either witnesses or ignorant bystanders? Chisholm actually says that agent-causing *is* an event, but not exactly a mere happening. He says this while struggling with the puzzle we alluded to in section 3, that both deterministic and indeterministic outlooks seem to invalidate our belief in responsibility. Chisholm imagines "that . . . a man does [immanently] cause a certain event e to happen". Then Chisholm wonders,

> What now of *that* event--the event which is his thus [immanently] causing e to happen? . . . [Was] it . . . not caused by anything? . . . [If so,] then we cannot hold *him* responsible for his [immanently] causing e to happen. What we should say, I believe, is that . . . if a man contributes causally to the occurrence of . . . e, then he contributes causally to his contributing causally to the occurrence [of e] . . .
>
> . . . [He] will . . . be a causal contributor to that event which is his being a causal contributor [to e] (1971c, pp. 40 ff.; see 1969, p. 214; 1976a, pp. 205-207).

I shall not worry about the prospect of an endless array of simultaneous agent-causings of agent-causings, nor about distinctions that Chisholm might draw between agent-causing and being a causal contributor (1971c, pp. 44 f.; 1976a, pp. 200 f.). Deeper problems should be apparent. The first is quite general: In familiar situations where one or more events $C_1, \ldots, C_n$ *transeuntly* bring about some result, R, would we reify "*that* event--the event [TC] which is [their transeuntly] causing" R? Suppose we acknowledge TC as a separate occurrence, over and above $C_1, \ldots, C_n$ as well as R. What would TC be like? How might it be related to $C_1, \ldots, C_n$ and R? Could TC result from

$C_1,\ldots,C_n$, and could it help them propagate R? Then there would have to be another causing-event TC_1, which is that event that is $C_1,\ldots,C_n$'s transeuntly causing TC; and similarly for that further causing-event TC_2, which is $C_1,\ldots,C_n$'s and TC's joining up and transeuntly bringing about R. Obviously these consequences are unacceptable, and we should not make transeunt causing into a separable occurrence. Why then does Chisholm accord such a privileged status to immanent causing?

Perhaps the major reason we should not reify immanent causing is that we would thereby undermine the novel contrast we started with between immanency and transeuncy. Forget about regresses, and imagine that there is a Chisholmian "event" of agent-causing, followed by e—either a "cerebral event" or a bodily motion. Why should we not assume that the agent-causing-event transeuntly brought about e? We could bank upon an e-like occurrence whenever we meet displays of immanency resembling this "event which is [someone's] thus causing e to happen". We could investigate whether such agent-causing of e-like events have any regular antecedents themselves. Most important of all, once we rank agent-causing as an event, it will be incorrect to say of a person's actions that they are "caused, not [transeuntly] by other events . . . but [immanently] by the man himself". Thus e would being to seem like an ordinary transeunt upshot of a simultaneous or somewhat earlier display of immanent causality. The only contrast left in our metaphysical analysis of action would be relatively unexciting. Previously we could distinguish between the relation that agents bear to their deeds, and the relation that events bear to their effects. Now we would have only a minor disparity between two types of events which transeuntly bring about other occurrences. We would have garden-variety events—for instance, cerebral processes—and also dark episodes of people's agent-causing. But both would be events that produce movements of people's limbs and similar effects.

If we were on the lookout for nonsense, we could ask what kind of event agent-causing might be. How long does it take to unfold? Could a single episode of it be intermittent, like a storm? Must it be instantaneous? What sort of location does it have? How is it spatially related to the brain process or limb movement that it presumably causes? Chisholm neglects to say what species of event he thinks it is, and Taylor does not so much as consider the possibility that agent-causing is an event in its own right.

Actually I prefer to drop this line of questioning, and instead to return to our central problem in this section: Is agent-causing act-like? We began inquiring if it might be an event, in the sense of 'mere event' that a person might live through, witness, or ignore; then we latched onto Chisholm's talk of "the event which is [someone's immanently] causing e̱ to happen". Since we made little headway in that direction, I want to try another tack. I believe it might be worthwhile to ask if any event that is not an action can serve as a model for agent-causing. In speaking of a 'model', I mean to leave it open whether agent-causing is literally an event, or just significantly like one.

There seem to be roughly three alternatives. Our model could be some occurrence on the order of freezing weather. Masses of cold air roll in from the mountains. You could be related to this cold spell as someone who is affected by it, because it makes you uncomfortable, gives you frostbite, or maybe invigorates you. Alternatively, perhaps it fails to affect you; it does not even catch your attention. Neither of these situations seems comparable to what Taylor and Chisholm mean by agent-causality. We surely do not just put up with our agent-causing. Even less could we be on hand when it takes place, yet remain oblivious and unmoved. All we have left is an active model, such as an event we control--for instance the brewing of our afternoon tea. We are active because we sprinkle tea leaves into the china pot, boil some water, and pour it over the leaves. When we see that the mixture is dark enough, we fill our cup with it. We are not just affected by the tea's brewing, and we are certainly not ignorant bystanders while it occurs. We are aware and in charge of it. But for the analytic purposes of agent-causationists, this kind of example is worthless. They first informed us that acting really is immanently bringing about certain processes in your brain, or else movements of your limbs. Then they explained how vastly different this form of causation is from the familiar transeunt variety. Yet when we became bold enough to ask for a more positive characterization of agent-causing, we only learned how similar it is to brewing tea and other humble actions that were supposed to be analyzed for us in terms of agent-causality.

Defenders of immanent causation may quash this charge of circularity, but not without sacrifice. They can reiterate that acting is agent-causing, and then announce that the latter phenomenon is primitive--totally uncharacterizable and without everyday analogues such as the brewing of tea. An equivalent strategy is for agent-causationists to offer their doctrine as a purely formal calculus of definitions, postulates, and rules of inference. Evidently we should not expect to learn much about the nature of action when action is proclaimed to be an unanalyzable relation between agents and their brain states or limb movements--or when we are confronted with an uninterpreted, technical system of notation. Neither approach is likely to furnish us an alternative to volitional theories--or to help us deal with determinism, and distinguish between action and mere bodily agitation.

No doubt the proponents of immanency are undaunted, and still feel an overpowering urge to brandish the philosopher's enchanted verb 'cause'. So I shall attempt to exorcise the doctrine of agent-causality by setting out one last problem I find in it. A question should bring the issue into focus:

7. <u>Why do people immanently cause events to occur?</u> I am alluding to the beliefs, the knowledge, the emotions, plans, decisions, and impulses upon which people are ordinarily said to act. I am uninterested in our reasons <u>for</u> doing this or that, because we often do not get around to doing what we have reasons for doing. My inquiry now is about the reasons <u>on</u> which, and presumably because of which, we sometimes act. My question is this: Are the reasons we seem to act on in any way connected with our agent-causing and the cerebral or bodily events that our agent-causing produces? I choose the vague term "connected" because, in fairness to partisans of immanency, I wish to provide for other than transeunt causal relationships between the event of our having reasons, and either our agent-causing or its immanently engendered effects. One issue I am raising is whether our cognitive, affective, or conative state ever amounts to--or constitutes a vital part of--causally sufficient conditions which transeuntly bring about our brain processes or limb movements.

Now, as we have noticed in preceding sections, there seems to be no way of singling out a person's exercise of immanent causation, and separating it from the cerebral or bodily event that supposedly results from it. Therefore I shall assume that any transeuntly sufficient causal condition of this cerebral or bodily effect will be just as much a sufficient condition of one's agent-causing. However, my dilemma about reasons does not hinge upon this assumption.

What sort of causal role, if any, do agent-causationists assign to the reasons on which we apparently act? Chisholm's most definite pronouncement reads, "If our actions, or those for which we are responsible, are not causally [i.e., transeuntly] determined, then they are not causally determined by our desires" (1966, pp. 23 f.). One might infer from this that immanently caused bodily or cerebral events, particularly those that take place when we act freely, cannot be influenced at all by our so-called reasons. But other statements belie this interpretation. For instance, Chisholm begins one discussion by informing us,

> the agent's undertaking of [his] act . . . is not preceded or accompanied by any set of events constituting a sufficient causal condition for it . . . [I]t is caused by the man . . . [Yet] his causing . . . need not have been capricious. For there is a [SA] such that he caused these things to happen in the endeavor to make that [additional SA] happen. Making that [additional SA] happen, therefore, was one of his reasons for acting as he did. And he may have had other reasons; perhaps he desired that that [SA] happen, or perhaps he thought he ought to make it happen (1969, p. 214; my emphasis).

How can we harmonize the assertion quoted earlier, that our deeds--anyway, those we should answer for--are "not causally determined by our desires" with this story of someone who is not "capricious" perhaps desiring to make an SA happen? The best reading I come up with is this: Despite suggestions in the passage above, and in Chisholm's argument that I quoted in section 3, Chisholm does not believe that our operative desires are causally sufficient for our behavior when we have those desires. This exegesis gains some support from Chisholm's brief allusion to Leibniz' doctrine that one's "motive for making $\underline{A}$ happen . . . <u>inclines</u> <u>but</u> <u>does</u> <u>not</u> <u>necessitate</u>" (Chisholm, 1966, pp. 23-28). Chisholm appears to take it for granted that transeuntly sufficient conditions do "<u>necessitate</u>". This is more explicit in a later essay; there Chisholm says that if "$\underline{c}$ is a sufficient causal condition of $\underline{e}$, then it is physically <u>necessary</u> that if $\underline{c}$ occurs then $\underline{e}$ occurs" (1976a, p. 201). Chisholm also says that "lawlike generalizations . . . express laws of nature--the physical necessity of certain [SAs]" (pp. 200 f.; see 1971c, pp. 44 f.). What relationship of our desires, and associated beliefs, to our behavior would fall short of such necessitation?

Chisholm's analogy is the way we influence another person's behavior, not by forcing her or him to carry out a specified action, but by restricting "his options"; in this manner we "prevent him from making choices he otherwise would have made", and thereby "cause him to act in a certain general way and leave the further particulars up to him" (1976a, p. 203). The idea is that our own desire "inclines but does not necessitate" us by narrowing down the courses of action available to us, just as one individual may cause another "to act in a certain general" manner. Chisholm kindly sent me a manuscript that illustrates his comparison. An adventurer is on top of a pedestal. It is safe for him to jump off toward the west, the east, the north, or the south. He believes that the landing on the west side is the hardest and most likely to give him a painful jolt. While he ruminates, you heat up the pedestal. The heat becomes unbearable to him. As a result of your machinations, he must leap, and so you have deprived him of the option of staying put. His belief that a westward plunge would be disagreeable, and his desire to avoid suffering, eliminate another alternative. Now there is a causally sufficient condition for his generally leaving the pedestal, and for his slightly more specific action of departing in a non-westerly direction. Perhaps it is one of the "laws of nature", and therefore a "physical necessity", that anyone who is like the pedestal-squatter, in similar circumstances, with similar operative desires and beliefs, will take a non-westerly hop. But "the further particulars" are not thus necessitated. For suppose he agent-causes his brain or legs to behave in such a manner that he leaps <u>eastward</u>. Although your heating of the pedestal, together with his cognitive and conative state, transeuntly brought about his jumping, and his avoidance of the west side, Chisholm's point is that neither your thermal skulduggery nor his own motivational state forms a transeuntly sufficient condition of his eastward plunge. There might not be any such condition.

Maybe so; but my grumble against this exemplary tale of inclining without necessitating is that, in Chisholm's own terms, it seems "capricious" for his jumper to go east. It was not arbitrary for the man to leap in a non-westerly direction. His behavior was rational to this extent. But "the further particulars" do strike me as whimsical; he might just as well have plunged northward or southward.

Chisholm's story may be exposed to the opposite kind of attack. Can you be sure that his jumper had no supplementary reason at all to select the east side, and to shun the north and south landings? You say the desire you induced in him by warming up the pedestal, and the attitudes he already had toward the west side, necessitated his acting "in a . . . general way", but only <u>inclined</u> him to select the eastern landing. Yet why should we halt our search for necessitation there? Isn't it a good methodological bet that additional factors--perhaps further beliefs and desires of our saltimbanco--necessitated his behavior all the way? Can't it be a law of nature that anyone like him with such reasons would, in parallel circumstances, hop eastward?

These objections make me uneasy about the 'inclining without necessitating' analysis of how our motivational state is connected with our deeds. But I should mention a variant theory that Chisholm has propounded. Once again he denies that anything transeuntly necessitates our action, at least when we act freely. As he says in the vocabulary of his later work, a person's undertaking--which I take to be roughly the same as agent-causing--"has no sufficient causal conditions", but nevertheless has "indefinitely many necessary causal conditions . . . each of which is a <u>sine qua non</u> of his undertaking what he does" (1976a, p. 204). In particular, Chisholm lists "our reasons and motives" among these transeuntly necessary causal conditions.

I assume that his necessary conditions neither incline nor necessitate our antics. A stock example of a necessary condition, in many circumstances, is the presence of oxygen; without it, matches will not ignite. But of course matches may be in an oxygen-filled environment without bursting into flame. Nor does oxygen <u>incline</u> a match to start burning. Finally, it is unintelligible to say that the presence of oxygen restricts a match's options, or prevents the match from making choices it otherwise would have made. So Chisholm's distinction between necessary and sufficient conditions is not equivalent to his contrast between conditions that incline and conditions that necessitate. However, I foresee once again a pair of worrisome counter-arguments.

First, should we rely so heavily upon the problematic concepts of causally necessary and causally sufficient conditions? Something like this dichotomy has been under siege ever since John Stuart Mill denied that there was "any scientific ground for the distinction between the cause of a phenomenon and its conditions" (1843, p. 214). Among all the critiques of this dichotomy, H. L. A. Hart's and A. M. Honoré's made the deepest impression upon me. They convincingly illustrate the many "ways of distinguishing the cause from other necessary conditions", and how very "relative to the context of any given [causal] inquiry" these different methods will be (1959, pp. 30, 33). Plainly I cannot here attempt to vindicate these authors, or to develop a knock-down argument myself against the 'necessary'-'sufficient' antithesis. But I warn agent-causationists that they are building their analytical edifice on unstable ground. I believe they take a great risk if they deny that the reasons we act on are a sufficient condition of our agent-causing, or even "parts" of one (Chisholm, 1976a, p. 201; 1971c, p. 45), and at the same time admit that our reasons are a causally necessary condition. Their distinction may vanish.

In any case their position will be attacked by those metaphysicians who accept the 'necessary'-'sufficient' dichotomy, yet demand a rationale for Chisholm's edict that our beliefs and desires only rank as necessary conditions of our immanent highjinks. All I find is assertion, but no proof of this claim.

There is an alternative strategy for agent-causationists. They could drop the 'necessary'-'sufficient' antithesis with regard to transeunt causes.

Then they could admit that when we immanently bring about happenings in our brains or limbs, we have—even act on—reasons; however, they could repudiate their previous assumption that our reasons must be transeuntly connected with our agent-causing and its products. I can imagine two variants of this manoeuvre. An agency-theorist may argue that our reasons are the right sort of events or states to serve as transeunt causes of our immanent capers; however, as a matter of hard, empirical fact, no reason of ours ever has transeuntly caused, or helped cause, our agent-causing. Taylor's argument is more daring than this. He contends that our desires, beliefs, and other motivational goings-on cannot possibly be transeunt causes of our deeds. If his reasoning convinces us, we can inquire what sort of non-transeunt—perhaps altogether non-causal—relationship our motives bear to our motivated behavior.

8. <u>Taylor's denial that reasons may transeuntly bring about action</u>. By Taylor's definition of "a free act", which I quoted in section 5, a free act cannot have transeunt causes; yet there should be some way for it to be "rational". Taylor suggests that "an action that is both free and rational . . . must be such that the agent who performed it did so for some reason, but this reason cannot have been the [transeunt] cause of it" (1974, p. 55). Perhaps; yet a thoughtful reader might wish to understand how we can act <u>for</u>, or <u>on</u>, a reason without the reason playing a transeunt causal role. All Taylor manages to prove is that our <u>statements</u> ascribing reasons to someone do not entail that the reasons were causal factors. Hence we do not contradict ourselves if we deny that they were. Thus Taylor remarks that when we explain people's behavior "by reference to the aims, purposes, or goals of the agents", our account <u>need</u> <u>not</u> contain "any references, hidden or otherwise, to any causes" (1966, p. 141; see pp. 216, 222). He adds that "the question, 'why did you do that?' . . . is almost never a request for a recital of causes". Taylor is right. Our linguistic and epistemic practice of searching for and constructing what I would call a <u>teleological</u> or 'why' explanation differs significantly from our practice of ferreting out and reporting transeunt causes. But what can we infer from this? Although our teleological and causal methods of explaining what goes on are unlike each other, does it follow that we <u>cannot</u> make "references" in each of them to the same events, namely to our "aims, purposes, or goals", and

to our behavior <u>cum</u> agent-causing?

    I rely upon a hotly disputed assumption here, which I tried to spell out more fully in Chapter Three. I take it for granted that we cannot report and characterize the very same events, often using non-synonymous terms from quite disparate vocabularies. For example, consider those states or episodes that we refer to and describe--as states or episodes of desire, belief, bodily motion, perhaps immanent bringing about--when we produce a teleological account of someone's deed. I assume that we can pinpoint and delineate these very same goings-on when we shift to more scientific idioms, and indulge in transeunt causal explanation. Nothing said by Taylor and others of his persuasion seems to rule out the possibility that in this latter context, the very same events that we had previously called "reasons" and "actions" or "agent-causings" now have the status of transeunt causes and effects.

    But suppose my assumption is erroneous. Suppose teleological and transeunt causal accounts are so incommensurable that a single occurrence may not be named in both. Does this prove that the occurrence itself--say, the event of N desiring and believing such-and-such during time interval t--cannot engender movement of N's limbs during t? How could our linguistic customs impose this sort of restriction upon what transeuntly causes what?

    I suspect more dubious reasoning when Taylor declares, "Purposes do not <u>cause</u> one to do anything; they only render intelligible whatever it is that he does" (1966, p. 142). Why "only"? Why can't our cognitive, conative, and affective goings-on help produce motions of our limbs, and also deserve to be mentioned in teleological accounts that make sense of people's behavior? My response is similar when Taylor concentrates on the example of precautionary activity. He contends, "A purpose, end or goal is not part of the <u>cause</u> of preventive action. It is part of the very <u>concept</u> of such an action, just as being a sibling is part of the concept, but no part of the cause, of being a twin" (1966, p. 199; see pp. 223, 252, 255; also 1960, p. 88). Again we ought to be shown this. We can grant that one concept--our concept of someone having a purpose--is "part of" another--our concept of her or him taking preventive measures. Does this entail that the corresponding events--my wishing to avoid mosquito bites when I go on a hike, and my use of mosquito repellent--are never related as cause and effect? The inference certainly is not <u>obviously</u> valid.

I think another of Taylor's examples will bring out the unspoken issue. This time he denies that an episode of deliberation can "itself be one of the causes of . . . actions . . . that result from deliberation" (1966, p. 182). Why not? That is, how can a logical or part-whole relationship among concepts stand in the way of a causal relationship between events? There is something special in this case. Taylor explains,

> To say that some agent does something as a result of deliberation is very far from saying that he is caused to do [it] . . . by his deliberation . . . It is part of <u>the</u> <u>very</u> <u>concept</u> <u>of</u> <u>deliberation</u> that it applies to situations in which there are, or are at least believed to be, alternative courses of action, and that as a result of one's deliberation he might do either one (pp. 192 f., emphasis mine; see pp. 147 f., 176 f.).

Taylor seems to be suppressing a crucial premise: If any antecedent of your immanently caused behavior, such as the ruminating you engaged in before acting, were a transeunt cause of your behavior, then you would be robbed of freedom, unable to act otherwise than however it made you act. Essentially this is the dogma we keep encountering, most recently in sections 4 and 5. But do all transeunt causes of your behavior, including your deliberations as well as your desires, force you to act as you do, and close off "alternative courses of action"? This assumption has not been elucidated--or justified. So Taylor's claim that our reasons cannot cause our deeds is questionable in its own right, and partly depends upon another dubious principle.

Suppose I have failed to appreciate the cogency of Taylor's argument that reasons cannot transeuntly produce our actions. Assume Taylor is correct, and the act-motive relationship is entirely "logical and semantical", not in the least causal (Taylor, 1966, p. 223). For that matter, we could grant to agent-causationists either of the conjectures we discussed in section 7: that a person's motivational state

"<u>inclines</u> <u>but</u> <u>does</u> <u>not</u> <u>necessitate</u>"; or that it is only a transeuntly necessary condition of what he does. Would any of these concessions help agency-theorists analyze the reason-action hookup?

Ironically, it seems to me that these doctrines, singly and combined, are as inimical to the theory of agent-causality as old-fashioned views that make our reasons into transeuntly sufficient conditions. I mean that whatever causal or non-causal status you ascribe to reasons, they will overshadow agent-causality. To illustrate, imagine that the body of a sane, waking adult has moved. Partisans of immanency will hasten to inquire, Did the person alone, without the help of any transeunt factors, directly bring about this corporeal motion? All right, let us assume so. Is that all we wish to learn about the incident? Do we not want to discover <u>why</u> the person immanently made her or his limbs move? Does it matter that his reasons are conceptually though not causally tied up with his behavior; that they inclined him to behave as he did, without necessitating his antics; or that they are transeuntly necessary but not sufficient conditions for his deed? Questions about the course of his deliberations, if any, or what he wanted, feared, believed, and so on, are surely at least as important as the agent-causationist's inquiry. If it emerges that the person did immanently produce his deed, yet was in no way influenced by reasons, his performance surely ought to seem rather "capricious" to us.

9. <u>A stunning but flawed metaphysical construction</u>. The doctrine that each of us alone immanently produces movement of our limbs, or perhaps occurrences in our brain, thus appears to defy consistent elucidation. Of course it is no more problematical than the volition theories we canvassed in Chapter Six. But there are fundamental uncertainties about it. Its champions seem unable to tell us what this sort of causing is like, by analogy with the sorts of things we do when we transeuntly cause a disturbance. They disagree on what we immanently bring about--particular, concrete events or SAs, cerebral or peripheral goings-on--and we discovered few decisive considerations favoring any view. Although one of agent-causationists' primary goals is to articulate a clear, viable concept of acting freely and having the power to engage in alternative courses of action, we noticed many difficulties in their treatment of these topics.

As we've seen, they never explain why they believe that if _any_ event is a transeuntly sufficient causal condition--or part of one--then our resulting behavior is unfree, and we are powerless to act differently. Recalling what we said of "alien desires" in Chapter Five, I have sympathy for this outlook. Some of our urges, impulses, even moral rules and life-plans have been foisted upon us, inasmuch as they have been produced by festering traumas, morbid fixations, tyrannical socialization, maybe even by hypnosis or secret tampering with our brain. But could it make sense to describe _all_ our motivational states as alien: to say that no matter what their origin, whether they come from indoctrination or from permissive, warmly supportive upbringing, they are imposed upon us, and do not represent what we really want? If none of your deliberations, aims, and beliefs can possibly be called 'domestic'--authentically yours--then 'foreign' ceases to mark a distinction. So Taylor and Chisholm cannot mean this when they say that if our desires and deliberations transeuntly bring about your behavior, then you had no power to act differently. Since these and other proponents of agent-causality are taciturn about what they do mean, a central claim of theirs is fatally unclear. For instance, they owe us an account of how it gives us autonomy if our desires and deliberations do _not_ constitute all or part of a transeuntly sufficient condition of our deeds.

Generally speaking, one of the major problems for agent-causationists is that they admit there must be a role for the reasons on which we presumably act, yet they have so far furnished us only a vague, negative characterization of it as not transeunt sufficiency. An equally serious difficulty for them is the circular appearance of their doctrine. For they define action as immanent causing, and then have to concede that this is itself a further sort of action--which I assume we have to understand on the model of those more familiar actions we started with.

Despite these and other misgivings I have expressed toward Chisholm's and Taylor's theories of agent-causality, I am firmly convinced that such doctrines are imaginative, systematic attempts to deal with the most profound riddles about human behavior and freedom. Our appreciation of bold theories of this high intellectual caliber should only increase as a result of the critical scrutiny I devoted to them. Another welcome result should be that we notice new issues. One that emerges from our study of agent-causality doctrines, as well as our struggles with the notion of autonomy and with volitional theories of action in Chapters Five and Six, has to do with mental activity. I already argued, in Chapters Two and Three, that it is gratuitous to assume that mental goings-on are non-physical, and especially that this might be true because of the way speakers of English and cognate languages define the adjective 'mental'. So I am concerned with such mental events as we have been discussing under the rubric of 'reasons': processes of calculation; flare-ups of anxiety; states such as bearing a grudge against someone; and of course agent-causing, if it occurs. The basic question I am provoked to ask is, What do we mean when we classify some of these goings-on as active, others not? What sort of control, power, or freedom does a person exercise over some of them? In what sense do we lack dominion over the others? This cluster of enigmas will occupy us in the next, final chapter.

CHAPTER EIGHT

CAN OUR MENTAL STATES BE ACTIVE OR PASSIVE?

1. A neglected conundrum. We have periodically run into disputes about the active or passive character of various mental goings-on. In Chapter Six and Seven, we inquired at length whether or not willing and agent-causing should be seen as forms of mental activity. A major issue of Chapter Five was the status of so-called alien desires, which presumably overwhelm us and shove us around like passive victims. In the same chapter we considered Frankfurt's assertion that we can be either active or passive vis-à-vis our first-order desires, depending upon whether or not we have a second-order desire to be stirred by them. Earlier, in Chapter Four, we probed some of Freud's admirably unorthodox theories of the repressed forces and agencies which he thought crucial to our neurotic and other troubled patterns of behavior, as well as our 'normal' functioning. A difficulty that surfaced from time to time had to do with the seemingly active nature of these denizens of our mental apparatus. The more traditional dualistic and materialistic theories of mind that we examined in the first three chapters also provoked questions of this sort. For instance, what activity might be involved when, according to Cartesian dualists, we perceive or acquire knowledge of our thoughts or aches--or when we unerringly assign the right names to our private sensations? Although we have frequently run across such activity-passivity puzzles in our exploration of issues concerning mind and freedom, there is hardly any philosophical literature on this distinction among various mental events. In my introductory remarks I cited some of Descartes', Locke's, and Berkeley's blandly self-confident assertions about our supposedly active "assent" to some ideas, and about how other ideas "force themselves" on our passive minds, while our imagination can actively "excite" a wide range of ideas in us "at pleasure" Only fairly recently has any theorist asked what basis, besides whimsey, we have for this method of categorizing psychological occurrences and states. In a paper written more than a decade ago, Richard Wollheim mused,

> Is there . . . any way . . . of determining the passivity or otherwise of our inner life, apart, that is, from how it strikes

> us[?] . . . [M]uch of the time our feelings, our emotions, our inclinations are as fluctuating or as imperious as if they were not totally under our control. We are elated: we are dejected: we get angry, and then our anger gives place to a feeling of absurdity: . . . we see a stranger . . . who is poor or crippled, and we feel guilt: someone does something wrong or foolish, and we are unaccountably transported by laughter . . . and then, as unaccountably, we are thrown down (1968, p. 227; see Wollheim, 1967-68, pp. 17, 23 f.).

I want to search for criteria other than "how it strikes us", which may help us with troublesome cases of the sort I mentioned above. But initially I should make sure my key terms are not misunderstood. I shall deploy the expression "mental event" as a blanket term which covers relatively enduring states, short-lived occurrences, as well as processes of change. The mental goings-on that primarily interest me are those that have comparatively few salient physical characteristics. Aching, having after-images, fantasizing, worrying, hoping, quietly deliberating, settling on a plan are all examples. In order not to prejudge our main issue--namely, whether the person who figures in these events is a doer or something else--I only say, non-committally, that such mental events "occur". And since my concern is exclusively the active, passive, or other status of mental happenings, I must now pretend that I am neutral in the controversy between Cartesian mind-body dualists and their materialist opponents. For purposes of this investigation of mental activity and passivity, it makes no difference whether my attacks on Cartesian doctrines, and my version of "whole person" materialism (in Chapters One, Two, an-Three), were successful or not. Thus I leave it open whether the psychological events that are supposedly active or passive can be identical with various corporeal happenings--with events in the nervous system alone, or with states of a complete human being. I would of course be implicitly favoring dualists if I took the adjective 'mental', and its cognate 'psychological', to mean 'non-physical' or 'immaterial'. As I documented in Chapter Two, this definitional tactic has been used by Cartesians, and even at one time by the "eliminative materialist" Richard Rorty. Although I can stand by the objections I lodged against equating 'mental' with 'non-physical', I must temporarily retract my further claim that 'non-physical' and its synonyms have no clear meaning whatsoever. In sum, then, my position in this chapter is that the mental events I am going to scrutinize might be 100% physical, or altogether immaterial, or possibly some curious blend of both.

My concept of activity or action has to be similarly open-textured. Clenching one's fist might be one comparatively overt, and apparently physical, analogue for a mental activity. You would scarcely nominate fist-clenching as an example of mentally doing something, but you might agree that some mental performances are _like_ clenching one's fist. However, exertion--hustle and bustle--is not an indispensable feature of activity. For suppose that a game of hide-and-go-seek is in progress at a children's birthday party. A girl holds perfectly still behind the drapes. Although she is not straining, or moving busily about, she is engaged in a sort of activity: concealing herself.

I made a few tentative remarks about passivity in section 6 of the previous chapter. As I hinted, there seem to be at least two distinct forms of this stance toward an event in your vicinity: you may be a victim, to whom something happens; or you may be a bystander. Here are crude illustrations: (i) a cloudburst occurs in the mountains, and a hiker gets drenched by it; (ii) another more fortunate climber is safely inside a refuge, and either watches the deluge quite helplessly, or perhaps manages to sleep right through it. The victim of this downpour is passive in getting soaked, even though he or she may be dashing wildly toward a shelter. As for the passive observer, he or she might be observing carefully, and conscientiously recording on film or in a diary what goes on. Nevertheless, in his relation to the storm, he is passive. We can say of both the victim and the spectator that no action they perform has any effect upon the rain and sleet. Whatever the victim does, he continues to be soaked, though he may limit the damage by putting on rain-gear. Similarly, nothing our onlooker does will have any impact on the rainfall.

Both these examples reveal that we must specify clearly what kind of event, or what particular aspect of an event, we are considering when we assert that

a participant's role in it is passive. The victim
of our imaginary storm is passive only inasmuch as
he is caught in it, or drenched by it. The witness is
passive with regard to the rainfall because he exercises no mastery or influence over it. In both cases,
passivity is defined by reference to the fact that
any actions these people carry out will be to no
avail--that is, will not affect the storm. There is
an additional element in victimization: a natural
force, or in other examples a personal agency--some-
times an animal--is <u>acting upon</u> the victim. This is
not true of spectators, except insofar as a perceiver
must be visually, auditorily, or otherwise affected
by the event or object he perceives. Furthermore,
an ignorant bystander may be totally unaffected; his
sense-organs may not be stimulated, and the storm
may not give him a chill, or even nightmares.

I've wasted few words on unobservant bystanders.
This sub-category seems to hold no metaphysical enigmas. And probably it is otiose for me to add that
some overt human goings-on will be found that do not
fit under the rubrics that I have indicated on the
active-passive continuum. But we will be busy enough
trying to sort out predominantly psychological events
such as those I mentioned.

2. <u>Are the mental antecedents of behavior themselves actions?</u> In Chapters Five, Six, and Seven I
paraded forth, quite unsystematically, most of the
contending analyses of what an action is, and some
leading theories of what it is to act freely or unfreely. It should not oversimplify things too much
if I say that all these doctrines agree that an action
occurs when there is bodily behavior of the right
kind, antecedent or concurrent mental occurrences of
the right kind; and the behavior results in the right
way from these mental events. I speak vaguely of
"the right kind" and "the right way" in order to
avoid some very troublesome side-issues. One is connected with our disinclination to rank sneezing,
perspiring, the growth of our hair, or the beating of
our heart as actions or as behavioral elements of our
deeds. Another, more widely discussed riddle was
brought to the notice of contemporary action-theorists
by Chisholm (1964, p. 616) and Davidson (1972, p. 153).
This is the so-called problem of lunatic causal
chains: Should we say that a person has acted when
appropriate behavior occurs, but in a freakish, altogether unanticipated manner? (See my 1984.)

Circumnavigating those questions, I want to say a little more about the best-known analyses of action. The forefathers of contemporary action theory--Locke, Hume, Bentham, Austin the nineteenth-century jurist, and J. S. Mill--all seem to have believed that we produce our bodily behavior by willing, and that <u>both</u> our volition and our resulting behavior count as our actions. The only major present-day figure who seems to get stuck with a similar 'double-action' theory is Frankfurt. At any rate we saw in Chapter Five, section 9, that Frankfurt believes a person can be "active with respect to his own desires when he identifies with them", and "without such identification the person is a passive bystander to his desires and to what he does". Frankfurt also seems to classify as an action the behavior that is produced by one's desires (but see his 1978). If we do this, we are not a step nearer to analyzing action. For even if we define overt bodily action by saying that it is behavior suitably engendered by one's desires, all our curiosity will shift to desires, particularly those "with respect to" which Frankfurt says we are active. He must mean that sometimes we actively desire such-and-such, while at other times the desires that afflict us seem alien. If so, we will ask Frankfurt to tell us what it is like to actively desire.

There are alternatives to a double-action theory. In section 9 of Chapter Six, we looked critically at a thesis defended by two eminent authors who frequently disagree. Yet Goldman and Davidson both declare that our bodily behavior is our action, and that its antecedents, our beliefs and desires--the latter dubbed "volitions" by Goldman--simply are not actions. Davidson seems momentarily to promise us what I called in Chapter One an "argument from nonsense". Davidson announces that beliefs and desires "are not themselves actions or events about which the question whether the agent can perform them can intelligibly be raised". As I noted in section 9 of Chapter Six, this is much too strict a test for action. Walking is clearly an action, though we cannot intelligibly ask if an agent "perform[s]" his walking. we need an account of why walking should go into the "active" basket while desiring and believing should not.

Perhaps we will manage to develop such an account. But in the meantime I should recall the most popular

alternative to double-action views, and also to
Davidson's and Goldman's dictum that only behavior
is an action. In Chapter Six, particularly sections
9 and 10, I had a go at contemporary Prichardians;
they decree that when we act, our willing is the antecedent that generates our bodily behavior, yet, they
say, only our willing should receive the title of
'action'.

    I shall not rehearse all the complaints I made
against volitionists who say willing is active, and
those who say it isn't. I would rather pinpoint a
tension that underlies both types of volitionism as
well as the doctrine of agent-causality, which emerged
as an alternative to volitionism. On the one hand,
volitionists and agent-causationists are inexorably
driven to compare their favored phenomenon with everyday bodily actions. Certainly willing and agent-causing must not be like events that just happen to
or around you. But on the other hand, besides the
familiar dangers of regress and circularity, if volitionists or agent-causationists say that their pet
phenomenon is the mental equivalent of a bodily caper,
they might be asked for details: How long does it
take to will or to agent-cause? Is it difficult or
easy? Does practice make perfect? Can you get rusty?
Can you start to will or to agent-cause something,
but leave the job unfinished? Might you will or agent-cause something accidentally or by mistake, or unwittingly? Can you presently will or agent-cause something to take place several hours, days, or weeks in
the future, as you might now set a time-bomb to
explode, and then forget about it, confident that
things will happen on schedule?

    These and similar questions are bound to elicit
nonsense. Consequently it is going to seem that
volitionists and agent-causationists mean nothing
very intelligible when they compare willing or
agent-causing to acting. How about volitionists who
deny that willing is active? They are unlikely to
meet with any greater success by picturing volitions
as things that simply occur, even inside you. But
agency theorists may be in the worst predicament; for
their distinctive claim is that in order to immanently
bring about bodily or neural events, we do not have
to do anything else beforehand, nor must there be any
neural or other antecedents to pave the way. Now,
ironically enough, our agent-causing begins to resemble
a preliminary act.

I have only examined the influential doctrines of Frankfurt, Davidson, and leading volitionists and agent-causationists. I found no clear rationale for the mutually incompatible views that they hold, or seem committed to, regarding the active or passive status of desiring, willing, agent-causing, and similar antecedents of behavior. Perhaps other experts have dealt more convincingly with this topic. However, as things stand, I would say that until some theorist develops a stronger case, and explains away the prima facie nonsense we encountered, we should refrain from saying that people are active or passive when they desire, will, or agent-case. Admittedly, "it strikes us" often that we actively want or decide to do something--or that alien impulses are sweeping over us. But so far I do not understand what we mean when we speak this way about ourselves.

In the hope of getting a better grasp of what mental activity is, I shall turn briefly from the conative antecedents of behavior to cognition, which may or may not by itself generate overt behavior.

3. Is thinking a paradigm case of mental activity? In section 9 of Chapter Six, I criticized an argument by the Prichardian volitionist McCann which was designed to justify an activist conception of willing. As a matter of fact, McCann's thesis was much broader. For he believes that willing is a unique "executive" or "practical" species of thought, and that thinking is an active phenomenon. He even suggests that it is "preferable to speak of most mental behavior as action" (1974, p. 473). Since there are elements in his discussion of thought that had no place in his defense of willing as action, I shall risk some redundancies, and have a look at his more general argument. My purpose is not to beleaguer McCann. He deserves praise for having bothered to offer reasons for his position in a debate where most contributors seem content to proclaim their doctrines ex cathedra.

The cornerstone of McCann's reasoning about thought as well as volition is his analysis of overt "bodily actions" into a pair of component events: a "result" and a "bringing about" of the "result". I said before that in McCann's technical use of the term, a "result" is an event of some type which must take place if you perform the corresponding bodily action, by virtue of how we define the type of bodily action. His example is the rising of your arm, which he labels the "result" of your action of lifting your arm. Obviously the rising of your arm does not result causally from your raising it, in the way that perspiration or weight-loss might result from your jogging. These latter occurrences would not be "results" in McCann's sense. It is logically possible that you should jog without sweating or losing weight, but not that you should raise your arm without your arm rising. Conversely, your jogging causes your perspiration and weight-loss, but your action of lifting your arm does not cause your arm to rise. We can meaningfully ask how jogging brings about these effects, and other, less welcome side-effects, such as injury to vertebrae. What could we be after if we inquired how your lifting of your arm made your arm go up? Certainly the levitation of your arm is not an unwanted or a welcome side-effect of your lifting it.

That should explicate McCann's "results" of bodily action. His other ingredient is what he call your "bringing about" of the "result". Although your raising your arm does not causally engender its "result"--your arm's rising--McCann assumes that the "bringing about" component of your action of raising your arm does produce, in the standard causal manner, your arm's rising.

How does McCann use this "result"-"bringing about" analysis in his activist theory of non-volitional as well as volitional thinking? His thesis is that all forms of thinking are only bringings-about; furthermore, a bringing-about may not itself be split up into a "result" plus an additional bringing-about. So McCann is denying that when we think, there must be some "result" event comparable to the levitation of our arm when we lift it. In other words, he believes there is no thought process that we either actively bring about, or else passively undergo. How does he eliminate the latter possibility? At first he seems to acknowledge the familiar

> distinction between cases where a thought occurs to me by happenstance, and cases where I think of something deliberately. For example, the thought of the number 1 might occur to me as part of a reverie about my first day in school . . . or I

might think of 1 purposely, in constructing
. . . [an] example (1974, p. 464).

McCann's treatment of this apparent contrast is so perplexing to me that I shall have to quote most of it. He asserts that

> while these examples do illustrate a need for a distinction between two types of thinking, they do not undermine the claim that thinking does not have a result, for the distinction [we need] is not to be drawn in those terms. The word 'thought' . . . can mean either the actual process of thinking of some content . . . or the content itself [here, the number 1]. Now since the content is not an event and so cannot be brought about, the only sense that can be attached to the claim that I bring about my thought of 1 in the second example is that I bring about my <u>thinking</u> <u>of</u> <u>1</u> . . . [W]hat is brought about can only be the action itself . . .
>
> . . . [W]hat occurs to me [in the first case] is only the number, not my thinking of it, and the case could as well be described as one in which I <u>come</u> <u>to</u> the thought of 1, which sounds a good deal less passive (pp. 464 f.).

It would be a digression to ask for details of the "reverie" case, particularly of the claim that "what occurs to me is only the number, not my thinking of it". Does this mean that no thinking of the number takes place in me? Is it possible that "the content itself" somehow "occurs to me" although no episode, process, or state of cognizing that "content" is to be found?

These are comparatively trifling obscurities. The major flaw of McCann's attempt to prove that thinking is active seems more obvious. He has simply ignored the tough cases for a mental activist: situations where we <u>cannot</u> <u>stop</u> thinking of some traumatic incident, where frightening, morbid, loathsome, or sad thoughts haunt us, despite our efforts to think of something else.

Some earlier writings by Richard Taylor ought to have provoked McCann to fill this lacuna in his argument. But we can derive benefit from Taylor's discussion now, because, like McCann, he believes that some mental goings-on are active. What Taylor says conflicts with what McCann says because Taylor discerns "a clear difference between the thoughts that merely occur within me and those which are within my control" (1966, p. 58). Taylor gives examples of "entirely passive" cognition: "dreams, reveries, and thoughts that are simply evoked by external stimuli" (p. 155). The last illustration may be questionable--unless we overemphasize the "simply"--because explorers, detectives, and scientific researchers often seem to have quite controlled thoughts in response to the "external stimuli" that they confront. However, the subject of perceptual stimulation is much too complicated for us to deal with in this ground-floor investigation of mental activity and passivity.

A virtue of Taylor's contribution is that he tries to spell out what he means by saying that thoughts are "within" or outside one's "control". A mark of control he suggests is that if it "were . . . not for my actively thinking" certain thoughts, "they would be most unlikely to occur at all" (p. 59). Taylor might well have added that one characteristic of the disturbing thoughts that seem to plague me at times--or to "merely occur within me"--is that they are "unlikely" to vanish when I try to focus on pleasanter topics instead. Of course both these characterizations already presuppose that we understand what mental activity is, since we are told that it is a sine qua non for the occurrence of certain thoughts, and that in the case of haunting thoughts, our active efforts to get rid of them are useless.

However that may be, Taylor does produce some helpful cases of psychic activity and passivity. First he supposes that he has a luncheon appointment for tomorrow with a man whose name ("Shilling") has eluded him for several days. Now if the name "just comes to mind suddenly, unsought, when I am entirely preoccupied with other things", then this cognitive episode does not seem to be an instance of mental activity (1970a, p. 273). We would have a partly analogous situation if another person asked Taylor, out of the blue, "Are you lunching with Shilling?" Taylor says this "utterance . . . would simply cause the name to occur to me"; and consequently his own role is passive (<u>ibid</u>.). Taylor also imagines an instance of active cognition. This time he is aware that the elusive name has something to do with British currency. Therefore he runs through the names of British coins, with the express purpose of unblocking his recalcitrant memory (<u>ibid</u>.). No doubt this story of active rumination would suit McCann; but he made little effort to deal with promising cases of passivity like those described by Taylor, and his general argument did not seem to rule them out.

Taylor's work definitely advances our inquiry. Yet the vital question is whether he enables us to formulate criteria of active and passive musing. I am afraid that he does not. Like some of his remarks on controlled and uncontrolled thinking, which I quoted earlier, Taylor's examples appear to take it for granted that we know how to classify thinking one way or the other, and also that the active kind does occur. Thus when Taylor describes himself as "entire preoccupied with other things", that sounds like active reflection--which is interrupted when the fugitive name "just comes to" his notice. In Taylor's second illustration of passivity, we have to assume the opposite: that he is <u>not</u> actively cognizing, not "entirely preoccupied", at the moment when somebody's question "simply cause[s] the name to occur to" him. If we leave out this premise, our thinker may not seem altogether passive when he recalls the wayward name. Finally, Taylor's story of actively remembering the name clearly depends upon the very assumption we are debating here: whether there are such apparently active forms of cognition as reviewing the names of British coins.

Taylor himself admits some of these difficulties. In fact he says "there is no good non-question-begging analysis" of action generally (1966, p. 153). Consequently he is not especially bothered by doubts over the classification of mental events. Taylor concedes,

> it is difficult to see how thinking can [sometimes] be an <u>act</u>, but . . . it is no more difficult than seeing how just raising one's arm . . . can be an act. The metaphysical peculiarities [<u>sic</u>] are not produced by regarding thought as an activity; they are only duplicated (1970a, p. 282).

Maybe overt and mental deeds are equally shrouded in mystery. But with respect to psychic passivity, I am fairly certain we will encounter "peculiarities" that do not surround its outward counterpart. More of that shortly. For the moment, I will draw an important negative conclusion, which bears on the problems we encountered in almost every chapter regarding those mental goings-on that seem to be linked with action and freedom. The negative upshot is that we have failed to discover any rational grounds for classifying either conative or cognitive states and events as things we do. Nor have we articulated reasons for calling any passive. But the significant point is that <u>some</u> of the supposed antecedents of behavior--some of our desiring, deciding, and willing, if indeed we will--really strikes us as being under our command. Likewise for at least some of our thinking. Yet we are unable to elucidate or justify our hunch. Perhaps we can achieve a breakthrough with some favorite candidates for passive status: the unconscious mental processes of repression, transformation, resistance, and so on, that we discussed in Chapter Four; and the less exotic family of conscious emotions, which we have only touched on fleetingly here and there. I shall take the latter first, because the doctrine that we passively undergo emotion is very ancient and relatively easy to assess.

4. <u>Are we passive when we have emotions?</u> Recall how faculty psychologists of earlier centuries divided up the person into Reason, Will, and Passion or Emotion. Desire usually got shunted between volitional and emotional jurisdictions, but that was a minor problem. Overall, the consensus was that we do our thinking and willing, but in some sense we are afflicted with our terrors, joys, rages, and probably our cravings and baser appetites, if not our nobler desires--our purposes and ambitions. On this traditional view, our emotions operate like surging floodwaters, violent winds, uncontrollable forest-fires, unruly saddle-horses, or mutinous citizens trying to seize power from their government. Our emotions seem to overcome us, and tug or propel us along willy-nilly. The passage I quoted from Wollheim in section 1 reflects this archaic imagery, for example when he says we are "unaccountably transported" by mirth, and just "as unaccountably . . . thrown down".

My concern is not stylistic or antiquarian, however. What intrigues me is that some very astute contemporary philosophers of mind cling to fragments of this picture of emotion. Richard Peters gives it a clear formulation when he writes that we typically deploy

> the term 'emotion' and its derivatives . . . when we speak of judgments being disturbed, clouded or warped by emotion, of people being not properly in control of their emotions, being subject to gusts of emotion, being emotionally perturbed. The suggestion in such cases is always that something comes over people . . . Emotions, like the weather, come over us (1961-62, pp. 119 f.).

Peters's conclusion is that "we naturally use the term 'emotional' and its derivates to pick out our passivity" (p. 121).

Richard Taylor expounds a similar thesis in an ethics book. He asserts,

> One can do certain things . . . but emotions can only . . . be "suffered" . . . One can . . . move his limbs, voluntarily, or even pursue a certain train of thought, voluntarily; but one can in no similar way feel elation or dejection . . . [O]ne could be commanded . . . to swing his arms (an action) but could not intelligibly be commanded to love or hate (passions) (1970b, p. 241).

The upshot is that "love and compassion are passions, not actions, and are therefore subject to no rule or command, and can in no way be represented in terms of duties or moral obligations" (p. 252).

As our earlier coverage of debate on the active or passive status of wanting and desiring might lead one to expect, some theorists reject Peters's and Taylor's view of emotion. Robert Solomon has championed a thesis, which he claims to extract from Kant, Scheler, and Sartre, that in some sense "emotions are judgments" and, "as judgments, are a species of activity, and thus to be included on the 'active' side of the all-too-simple 'active-passive' disjunction according to which we evaluate most human affairs" (1980, p. 276). Solomon draws together themes from his previous writings:

My central claim is that emotions are defined primarily by their constitutive judgements, given structure by judgments, distinguished as particular emotions (anger, love, envy, etc.) as judgments, and related to other beliefs, judgments, and our knowledge of the world, in a 'formal' way, through judgments . . .

. . . I argued in [1973] that emotional judgments are essentially nonreflective and prior to deliberation. This was . . . an [overstatement] and in [1976] I discussed several examples of deliberate emotions, for example, making oneself angry . . . I also stress the affinities between my notion of judgment and Kant's concept of 'constitutive judgment', but what is 'constituted' in emotions is not knowledge but meanings. In my more recent work, I prefer to talk more in terms of emotions setting up 'scenarios', within which our experiences are endowed with personal meaning. Each emotion, so characterized, is a specifiable set of judgments constituting a specific scenario. Anger, for example, is to be analyzed in terms of a quasi-courtroom scenario, in which one takes the role of judge, jury, prosecuting attorney and, on occasion, executioner . . . The object of anger is the accused, the crime is an offense, and the overall scenario is one of judgmental self-righteousness . . .

My most cavalier move in [1973] was my easy inference from 'emotions are judgments' to the idea that we 'choose' them . . . I am sure that it makes little sense to ask whether perceiving something is voluntary, much less a matter of choice. Intractable emotions must be treated similarly; they are still matters of judgment, and as such activities . . . But they are surely neither voluntary nor chosen (pp. 274-77).

En passant, Solomon says that "it is the heart of my argument that 'feelings' and physiology and, with qualifications, dispositions to behave, do not play an essential role in the constitution of emotions" (p. 274).

In the context of my attempt to understand what mental activity and passivity are, I shall not explore the minutiae of these diametrically opposed accounts of our affective life. Rather, I shall first look back at our preliminary characterization of passivity, in section 1, and ask what Peters could mean when he alludes to "something [that] comes over people". What sort of "something" might this be, when I am grieving or ashamed? Is it enlightening to say, with Taylor, that emotions such as grief and shame are "suffered"? Generally, how do these passivity theorists imagine we are acted upon when we have emotions? The same for Solomon's contrary, activist interpretation, which evidently depends on the unspoken premise that judging is a mental performance. We need not consider how our negative assessment of McCann's doctrine, that thinking is an act, should influence our reception of Solomon's theory about judgmental thinking. Solomon has no similar argument.

In our discussion of mental passivity thus far we have mostly toyed with cases of some natural force acting upon people, or simply 'acting up' while onlookers stare helplessly or fail to notice. As we search for mental analogues of victimization and bystanding, we should not embroil ourselves in the side-issue whether tidal waves, blizzards, and falling trees can be said, literally, to <u>act</u> upon human agents. Certainly they do not deliberately--or unintentionally--carry us off, bury us, or hit us; but they do affect us in many of the ways that another person might. However, we can avoid further speculation on that subject if we concentrate on settings where human beings act upon each other.

Visualize a kidnapper whisking his (or her) prey into a getaway car. In what sense is he acting upon his victim? At least part of the answer should be causal: the victim's change of location--from sidewalk to automobile--is principally an effect of the gangster's energetic pommeling and shoving. As for bystanders, this episode of evil-doing has no effect on them, beyond stimulating the eyes and ears of those who notice it, and thereby causing some spectators to react with fear, indignation, or indifference. Their passivity, unlike the victim's, consists in the fact that they do nothing that aids or impedes the abductor. They do not facilitate his task, as they might by holding open the car door. And no action they do perform makes his task harder.

Needless to say again, victim and bystanders do not have to be totally supine. What matters is that their behavior should not affect the event in which they play a passive role.

If our notion of mental passivity is going to be made intelligible, we should be able to specify counterparts for all or most of the elements we discerned in the kidnapping. But can we? Suppose that we are victims of our moods. What, in the psychical realm, might "come over" us, after the manner of abductors who grab us, or rain that drenches us? It is fairly evident how, causally speaking, kidnappers and raindrops bring about various changes in a victim's situation. Yet even if we postulate internal forces and quasi-agencies at work beneath our skins--enveloping fogs of gloom, gnawing envy, swelling impatience--we have no idea of how they operate on us. It remains fatally unclear what old-fashioned and contemporary theorists mean by saying that we are victims of our own emotion.

Do our models of bystanding take us further? What would it mean if we supposed that I am just on hand when I emote? Presumably this is what Frankfurt envisages for some of our desires when, in the passage I reproduced earlier (section 2), he claims that if an individual does not identify "with the desire that moves him", then he is only "a passive bystander to his desires and to what he does". But are overt and sub-cutaneous bystanding sufficiently comparable? We said that the passive witness and the ignorant person both fail to influence the kidnapping or the natural disaster. Still, we can intelligibly suppose that they might do so; in which case, it goes without saying, they would not be bystanders any more. The significant disanalogy is that it is altogether uncertain what might go on if we decided not to gape at, or turn away from, our emotions any more, and if we became involved, either promoting or inhibiting them. Of course these images--of throwing off one's lethargy and taking a stand toward one's emotion--are quite graphic. However, they are entirely based upon the model of an external bystander who is capable of intervening. What I question is precisely whether it makes sense to suppose that, although we are only bystanders to our affects, we could try to control them instead. I realize "it strikes us" that this is possible. I deny that it has been shown. So as things stand, the traditional doctrine that we passively undergo or sit out our rage, fear, and grief has no definite meaning. Even the more moderate claim that only some emotions are passive has not been adequately elucidated; for no theorist has given us criteria by which to recognize the passive instances, or told us what is passive about them.

How should we deal with Solomon's contrary view that "emotions are judgments" of some kind, and "as judgments, are a species of activity"? One prima facie objection would parallel a complaint I made against McCann: Sometimes we seem to be obsessed or tormented by anxiety, resentment, and remorse; thus we do not seem to have active control of our feelings. Solomon does no better than McCann with such apparent counter-examples. He has one terminological advantage, however: initially it sounds more plausible to say that we act when we make "judgments" than to say, with McCann, that "thinking" generally is an activity. It is not flagrantly absurd to suppose that sometimes we think compulsively, and find ourselves unable to stop; but what would it be like to judge in this way, or to have unwelcome judgments plague us? Nevertheless Solomon's catchword may become a serious liability, as soon as we ask why he is so emphatic that judging, rather than some other variety of cognizing, takes place when we are emotionally stirred up. Must we always be engaged in that conscientious and solemn a procedure when we are suddenly elated or amused? If careful pondering is not essential to the sort of cognition that Solomon calls a "judgment", what do we gain by so labeling it? All I get from the long passage I quoted six paragraphs ago is that Solomon is attached to the term. Nor does any rationale emerge from another discussion where Solomon explains,

> by 'judgment', I do not necessarily mean 'deliberative judgment'. Many judgments . . . are made without deliberation. (One might call such judgments 'spontaneous' as long as 'spontaneity' isn't confused with 'passivity'.) But . . . many emotions are deliberative judgments. We literally 'work ourselves up' to anger or love. . . but whether deliberative or 'spontaneous', getting angry or 'falling in' love are things that we do . . . (1977, p. 46).

I would say that Solomon's activist theory of emotion is menaced by a straightforward dilemma: Either we must take him literally when he describes an emotion as being or involving "judgment", in which case there are counter-examples such as surprise and hilarity; or else he is using the term "judgment" so broadly that it is uncertain whether emotional judgment must be active. Either way, it does not seem to be an obvious truth that emotions are judgments and therefore instances of mental activity.

We have not yet managed to unpack, or to justify, widely held beliefs regarding the active or passive character of the most familiar mental occurrences and states: conative goings-on such as desiring or willing; cognition; and emotion. One more test case remains: those radically different unconscious occurrences and states postulated in psychoanalytical theory. Since by hypothesis we standardly cannot know anything about these events, it seems that we cannot control them, and that insofar as they shape our behavior and our conscious mental life, we must be passive in relation to them. So our final test case looks promising. Furthermore, the misgivings I expressed in Chapter Four about Freud's models of mind should not prejudice this investigation. Even if, alongside his many brilliant, unorthodox suggestions, Freud produced some irrelevant or nonsensical doctrines, psychoanalytical theory might still yield an adequate illustration of mental passivity.

5. <u>Are we victims or ignorant bystanders of our unconscious mental processes?</u> First off we should note that Peters, in his account of emotion, says there are "affinities" between his outlook and some central Freudian doctrines (1961-62, p. 129). For instance, Peters believes that his own

> passivity model would explain [defective or faulty] actions and performances (e.g., characteristic errors and distortions of thought, perception and memory, motor slips and breakdowns) and goings-on like dreaming and hysteria which do not rank as performances or actions at all (p. 133).

As an example, here is Peters's view of unconscious repression and projection:

> In repression . . . the traumatic experience just passes out of the sufferer's mind; he does not wittingly put it out of his mind. Similarly a man who projects his fears onto something does not wittingly rig his environment. He just comes to see the world under an aspect such as that of threat. The phenomena . . . are indubitably mental . . . but fall into the category of passivity (p. 131).

How is Peters's subject passive with regard to these unconscious events? As far as I can tell, Peters only represents him as _not active_: not purposely driving a traumatic memory from his consciousness, not deliberately making his surroundings look dangerous. But you beg our question if you go from the premise that _he is not active_ during repression and projection, to the conclusion that _he is passive_. We wonder precisely whether it makes sense to describe him as _either_ active _or_ passive; so from the assumption that he is _not_ the former, you are scarcely entitled to deduce that he is or could be the latter.

We should attempt to learn what Peters or anybody else might mean by asserting that unconscious occurrences like repression "fall into the category of passivity". Are they making the historical claim that Freud so conceived of unconscious phenomena? Then we should have to discover what Freud's notion of mental passivity was. On the basis of my study of Freud, I suspect that this approach would be mistaken. My general impression is that Freud rarely classifies unconscious goings-on as passive. One atypical instance I have come across I reproduced already in section 3 of Chapter Four. In an early work, Freud seems uncertain what to make of the violent symptoms displayed by a hysteria-sufferer. The patient's "state . . . bears all the signs of a painful affect-- weeping, screaming and raging". Freud conjectures that "a process is going on in him of which these physical phenomena are the appropriate expression". At this juncture Freud describes the hysteric as "_overcome_ by an affect about whose cause he asserts that he knows nothing", although the man is "behaving as though he _does_ know about it" (first emphasis added).

I believe that Freud very seldom says that deep processes "overcome" or otherwise victimize us. More often than not, he seems to consider both aberrant and so-called normal states of mind to be situations of dynamic conflict. As I documented lavishly in Chapter Four, the tension Freud envisages is either between quasi-physical items, or forms of energy, within the "mental apparatus", or else between various anthropomorphic "agencies". On my reading of Freudian theory, the person herself or himself is not a party to either the conflicts modelled on a clash of physical forces, or the conflicts that Freud depicts in terms of social interaction such as censorship and rebellion. These contests affect his behavior and conscious mental state, but he is not a participant in them, not even a victim or so much as an ignorant bystander. I would say that the participants are either the inanimate forces or the homunculi that supposedly lurk within each person.

Perhaps I should illustrate briefly how the individual does not get embroiled with the animistic denizens of his mental realm. According to later Freudian doctrine, we recall, each person has an ego, whose "task" is "representing the external world to the id" and ministering to the id's "instinctual needs". As I said in Chapter Four, Freud also compares our "ego's relation to the id . . . with that of a rider to his horse . . . [O]ften . . . the rider is obliged to guide the horse along the path by which it itself wants to go". Remember too that when "following the dictates of its superego, the ego turns against its id" and repressively denies "motor discharge" to an "instinctual impulse" from the id, psychic trouble may ensue. The repressed impulse may create "for itself substitutive gratification (a symptom)", which the ego must attempt to stifle along with the impulse--"and all this together produces the clinical picture of a neurosis".

What I must underline in all these Freudian mini-dramas is that the person does not figure in them. His or her ego deals with, and may be victimized by, his or her id. The super-ego issues "dictates" to the ego, not is owner. The ego vainly attempts to get rid of the symptom, and only when the ego is defeated is there neurosis. At this stage only, the person has a role. He or she--not her or his ego-- becomes neurotic, as a result of discord which he failed to notice between his ego and its compatriots. The person, unlike his ego, superego, id, instinctual impulse and symptom, is not passively acted upon by anything; and since there seems to be no possibility of intervention by him in the struggle, we can assume he is not a bystander to it, either observant or unobservant.

I am summarizing Freudian <u>theory</u>, of course, and not Freud's many fascinating case histories which report the doings and undergoings of whole human beings, as well as the capers of their psychical agencies. When Freud recounted the lives and sufferings of such people as Elizabeth von R., Anna O., Dora, Little Hans, Dr. Schreber, the Rat Man, and the Wolf Man, the individuals are usually represented in an active stance, unconsciously yet still in some sense intentionally arranging their own misfortunes. So almost the only kind of passivity we encounter in Freud's world-picture involves not the people he is studying but their ego or whatever--and, as I remarked in section 1 of Chapter Four, we should not equate people with their egos.

The kind of inertness Freud ascribes to the tenants of our mental edifice is nearly always victimization. One exception is a passge I quoted toward the end of section 3, Chapter Four. Here Freud records the testimony of patients recovering from hallucinatory confusion. It had seemed to them as if "in some corner of their mind . . . there was a normal person hidden, who . . . watched the hubbub of illness go past him". The "normal person" referred to cannot be the patient, since he or she was hardly "normal" while in a demented state; so this must be a Lilliputian observer. The only case of ignorant bystanding that I noted earlier was the "sleeping" or heavy-lidded ego who figures so prominently and enigmatically in Freud's account of dreaming (see section 6, Chapter Four). But the point worth repeating is that Freud's view of our unconscious processes seems to cast the inhabitants of our mind, not us, in a passive role--usually that of being acted upon by another resident. We cannot analyze mental quiescence --or activity--by describing the interplay of these midgets, since they are only diminutive copies of full-sized <u>Homo sapiens</u> engaged in familiar types of overt social behavior. Our mental life bears some resemblance to conflict among individuals, but each one of us is not literally a collection of opponents struggling to dominate or accommodate. All told, then, we have failed to explain the meaning of an apparent truism: that unconscious goings-on "fall into the category of passivity". We had similar difficulties with the more traditional claim that we passively undergo our emotions, and also Solomon's refreshing contrary view that your emotion is essentially a "judgment" you actively make. Prior to these investigations, we were unable to find rational grounds to agree or disagree with volitionists and other causal theorists of action--including believers in agent-causality--about whether or not you are active when you will, want, or immanently produce your behavior. In between, we considered the rather extreme thesis of McCann that we actively do all our thinking, and we at least dredged up counter-examples. But when we tried to spell out Taylor's quite moderate assertion that some of our thinking is under our control, and some is not, once again obscurities prevented any definite answer.

    A critic may try to neutralize this upshot with a *tu quoque* argument. In section 8 of Chapter Six, I mentioned Hardie's and Goldman's reply to the complaint that if willing is the kind of event its proponents say it is, then we should be able to count the number of volitions we have during the next hour. Hardie's retort was that we experience just as much trouble computing how many overt actions we performed. Goldman's example was the number of thoughts we have over a stretch of time. Taylor reacted similarly in a passage I quoted at the end of section 3 above. Noticing problems with his claim that there is "a clear difference between the thoughts that merely occur within me and those which are under my control", Taylor argued that as a matter of fact we cannot do any better analyzing the difference between overt behavior that is and overt behavior that is not an action. What I anticipate now is the very general rejoinder that our notions of active and passive outward behavior are no less muddled than our concepts of mental activity and passivity.

    Fortunately there is a short answer to this counter-charge. I have already introduced many clear-cut examples of overt activity, victimization, attentive and ignorant bystanding, particularly in sections 1 and 4. I also made a stab at characterizing the victim as someone who is acted upon, and the bystander as someone who is present during an occurrence, although her or his actions have no effect on it. Naturally if a person is acted upon--knocked off his feet by winds during a tornado--he is not a mere bystander. As for outward action, I have only discussed some of the contending analyses, but have not myself tried to lay bare its essential features. If challenged, I would propose a very rough criterion, formulated by reference to what we can meaningfully say, an approach I have developed since Chapter One. I would suggest that human behavior qualifies as action if, and only if, you can intelligibly describe it with a reasonable number of terms such as the following: 'deliberate', 'accidental', 'premeditated', 'impulsive', 'reluctant', 'whole-hearted', 'conscientious', 'irresponsible', 'well-intentioned', 'malevolent', 'polite', 'thoughtless', 'awkward', 'skilful', 'strenuous', 'effortless', 'successful', 'bungled'. It is significant, I believe, that we can describe few, if any, of the mental phenomena discussed in this chapter with adjectives and corresponding adverbs of this extended family. In fact we remarked constantly how uncanny it sounds if we depict our inner life in the terms that should be appropriate, according to various official theories. What would it mean to say we carefully or distractedly observe the aches and other contents of our minds? that we correctly or mistakenly identify our sensations of dizziness? that we try strenuously to will, desire, or agent-cause something, but botch the job?

That is secondary, however. What matters is that, by comparison, our concepts of overt activity and passivity are fairly unproblematical, whereas our classification of a mental event as one or the other seems to depend largely on "how it strikes us". Indeed we have met with a similar--and philosophically significant--kind of arbitrariness, an insistence that this is the way things must be, in almost every one of our forays into a current debate about some aspect of mind and freedom.

6. <u>Final perspectives on this and foregoing chapters</u>. Throughout I have investigated only live controversies and recalcitrant unsolved puzzles. The questions I tried to deal with were, by preceding chapter, (1) What did Ryle, Wittgenstein, and their sympathizers mean when they attacked the Cartesian theory of mind as nonsensical though illuminating? (2) What exactly do Cartesian dualists mean by their claim that minds and mental events are non-physical? (3) How insuperable are some of the favorite objections

against the view of present-day materialists that
mental events are physical? Could these events be
simply brain processes? (4) Among the alternatives
to both Cartesian and standard materialist theories
of mind, how cogent is Freud's influential and revolutionary account? (5) Turning to the conative side
of our mental life, how should we analyze the obvious
but elusive relationship between doing what one wants
and acting freely? If all our desires, goals, scruples, and so on are shaped by our socialization, and
perhaps by unconscious forces beyond our control,
is genuinely autonomous behavior possible for us at
all? (6) How clearly do we understand action itself?
What sort of event is an action? Do we exercise con-
trol--and thus some freedom--over the motions of our
body by willing them? Have today's neo-volitionists
answered the famous criticisms--particularly the
charges of nonsense--made by Wittgenstein, Ryle,
Melden, and their allies? (7) Instead of clinging
desperately to some patched-up volitional account
of action and free action, should we hold that agents
directly, or immanently, bring about their behavior--
without willing, desiring, or any other preliminaries?

Except for achieving some needed clarification
of the nonsense indictment in Chapter One, I think I
mainly reached negative conclusions there, and in
Chapters Two, Four, Six, Seven, and Eight. But I
hasten to add that these are not trifling outcomes.
It is significant, and I hope philosophically liberat-
ing, to realize that we are attracted to a theory of
the person as an immaterial consciousness dwelling
within a complex organism, but we have not so far even
managed to intelligibly formulate the theory. Both
the general outlines and the specifics--for example,
what it means to say we have knowledge of our pain--
seem resistant to clarification. Dualists, and their
most avid opponents, have not so much as provided us
with clues about what they are claiming or denying
when they debate whether minds and mental events are
non-physical.

But mind-body dualism is not the only popular
doctrine that is flawed by such obscurities. Freud's
boldly imaginative and resolutely anti-Cartesian
accounts of our mostly unconscious mental life are
also difficult to articulate. Nevertheless I believe
these mysteries are not so imposing that we ought to
abandon Freud's novel approach. I am less sanguine,
however, that we can ever make sense of those

eternally fashionable volition theories whose latest guises I studied here. As for the comparatively recent doctrine of agent-causality, I suppose that some of my grumbles are directed at an assumption that need not be part of an agent-causationist's <u>credo</u>--namely, the assumption that if our behavior <u>results</u> from any antecedent or contemporaneous events, we do not act freely, and perhaps do not act at all. Most of my remaining objections have to do with the overworked verb 'cause', and how we should understand the central positive claim of agency-theorists that we alone cause our behavior. In what sense of our tired but still familiar verb? Are there virtually no parallels between the situation where events--including our conative and cognitive states--are said, in the standard sense, to cause our behavior, and the situation where an agent is now said to immanently cause his or her behavior? We looked in vain for significant resemblances. Perhaps, then, we should attach no definite meaning to the verb 'cause' here. Instead of talking as if they had analyzed what it is to act, agency-theorists should say that the relationship between person and behavior is deliberately left unanalyzed. Hence we should expect no more enlightenment from the assertion, "People immanently cause their limbs to move", than from "People move their limbs".

This conclusion may be something of a shock; but it cannot be as disconcerting as our failure to make intelligible the common-sense contrast between active mental goings-on--for instance deciding, thinking, possibly agent-causing or willing--and passive ones like being overcome by jealousy. Yet I think we can live with this result, for there are plenty of other aspects of our conscious and unconscious mental career that are worth study after we reluctantly stop describing it as active or passive.

Naturally these negative verdicts are open to counter-argument. But they, and the reasoning in support of them, shift the burden of proof to dualists, Freudians, volitionists, agent-causationists, and mental activists, who must now do more than just proclaim their visions. Their doctrines have to be exposited more fully, and shored up by non-question-begging arguments.

My positive conclusions, mainly in Chapters Three and Five, should be easier to encapsulate. I

contended that if we identify mental events with
physical states of the entire person--not only states
of her or his brain--then we can successfully defend
materialism against three widely repeated objections.
At the same time we can explain why so many materialists have dwelt obsessively upon the role of our
brain in our mental career. I agree that it has a
crucial part to play, though not a solo performance.
It is the whole human being who thinks--whose location is where her or his thinking takes place, whose
thinking is directed toward objects, whose authority
regarding his or her thoughts and their objects may
be unimpeachable. No doubt it is also the complete
woman or man who acts more or less autonomously. But
our other positive results had to do with a different
aspect of the free-will issue. People who are not
doing what they want can hardly be exercising control
over their behavior. On the other hand, if their
behavior or their decision-making is warped by alien
desires, they also seem to act unfreely. To compli-
cate matters, it is unclear what we mean when we distinguish between the individual's own conative
attitudes and foreign ones that were imposed upon
him or her. Although we failed to make good our
hunch that unconscious motivational forces are alien,
we did make considerable progress toward criteria
for saying that sometimes an individual's socialization has implanted desires in him that curtail his
autonomy. Along the way we attained a sharper understanding of how people who are coerced into doing
something act unfreely while nevertheless doing what
they want to do, given their unwanted coercive
situation.

REFERENCES

Abbreviations will be as follows: 'A' for Analysis; 'APQ' for American Philosophical Quarterly; 'JP' for Journal of Philosophy; 'PAS' for Proceedings of the Aristotelian Society; 'PASSV' for Proceedings of the Aristotelian Society, Supplementary Volume; 'PQ' for Philosophical Quarterly; 'PR' for Philosophical Review; 'PS' for Philosophical Studies.

Ackerman, R. J. (1972) Belief and Knowledge. Garden City, N.J.: Doubleday.

Annas, J. (1977-78) "How Basic are Basic Actions?", PAS, LXXVIII, pp. 195-213.

Armstrong, D. M. (1968) A Materialist Theory of the Mind. London: Routledge.

Aune, B. (1961) "Knowing and Merely Thinking", PS, XII, pp. 53-58.

_____ (1967) Knowledge, Mind, and Nature. New York: Random House.

_____ (1974) "Prichard, Action, and Volition", PS, XXV, pp. 97-116.

_____ (1977) Reason and Action. Dordrecht: Reidel.

Austin, J. (1863) Lectures on Jurisprudence. Reprinted, London: Murray, 1911.

Austin, J. L. (1946) "Other Minds", PASSV, XX; reprinted in C. Landesman, ed., The Foundations of Knowledge. Englewood Cliffs: Prentice-Hall, 1970, pp. 124-59.

_____ (1956-57) "A Plea for Excuses", PAS, LVII, pp. 1-30.

Ayer, A. J. (1954) "Can There Be a Private Language?", PASSV, XXVIII; reprinted in Ayer (1963), pp. 36-51.

_____ (1959) "Privacy", Proceedings of the British Academy; reprinted in Ayer (1963), pp. 52-81.

Ayer, A. J. (1963) *The Concept of a Person and Other Essays*. London: Macmillan.

Bach, K. (1978) "A Representational Theory of Action", PS, XXXIV, pp. 361-80.

Bartky, S. L. (1977) "Toward a Phenomenology of Feminist Consciousness", in M. Vetterling-Braggin et al., eds., *Feminism and Philosophy*. Totowa, N.J.: Littlefield Adams, pp. 22-34.

Bem, S. L. and D. J. (1975) "Homogenizing the American Woman", in K. J. and P. R. Struhl, eds., *Ethics in Perspective*. New York: Random House, pp. 197-213.

Benn, S. I. (1975-76) "Autonomy and the Concept of a Person", PAS, LXXVI, pp. 109-30.

Bentham, J. (1832) *The Principles of Morals and Legislation*. Reprinted, New York: Hafner, 1949.

Berkeley, G. (1708?) *Philosophical Commentaries*. Discovered and first published by A. C. Fraser, ed., in *The Works of George Berkeley*, 4 vol., London: 1871.

_____ (1709) *The Principles of Human Knowledge*. Reprinted, Indianapolis: Bobbs-Merrill.

_____ (1713) *Three Dialogues between Hylas and Philonous*. Reprinted, Indianapolis: Bobbs-Merrill.

Binkley, R., et al., eds. (1971) *Agent, Action, and Reason*. Toronto: University of Toronto Press.

Brand, M., ed. (1970) *The Nature of Human Action*. Glenview, Ill.: Scott-Foresman.

_____, and Walton, D., eds. (1976) *Action Theory*. Dordrecht: Reidel.

Broad, C. D. (1952) "Determinism, Indeterminism, and Libertarianism"; reprinted from Broad, *Ethics and the History of Philosophy*, in Morgenbesser and Walsh (1962), pp. 115-37.

Brodbeck, M., ed. (1968) *Readings in the Philosophy of the Social Sciences*. New York: Macmillan.

Bruner, J. S. (1968) "The Freudian Conception of Man and the Continuity of Nature", in Brodbeck (1968), pp. 705-711.

Campbell, C. A. (1951) "Is 'Freewill' a Pseudo-problem?"; reprinted from *Mind* in J. Margolis, ed., *Introduction to Philosophical Inquiry*. New York: Random House, 1968, pp. 154-72.

Castañeda, H.-N. (1964) "The Private Language Argument", in C. D. Rollins, ed., *Knowledge and Experience*. Pittsburgh: University of Pittsburgh Press, pp. 88-105.

Chisholm, R. M. (1964a) "The Descriptive Element in the Concept of Action", JP, LXI, pp. 613-25.

_____ (1964b) "J. L. Austin's *Philosophical Papers*", *Mind*, LXXXIII, pp. 1-25.

_____ (1966) "Freedom and Action", in Lehrer (1966), pp. 11-44.

_____ (1967a) "He Could Have Done Otherwise", JP, LXIV, pp. 409-18.

_____ (1967b) "Brentano on Descriptive Psychology and the Intentional"; reprinted from F. Lee and M. Mandelbaum, eds., *Phenomenology and Existentialism*, in Morick (1970), pp. 130-49.

_____ (1969) "Some Puzzles About Agency", in K. Lambert, ed., *The Logical Way of Doing Things*. New Haven: Yale University Press, pp. 199-217.

_____ (1970) "Events and Propositions", *Nous*, IV, pp. 15-24.

_____ (1971a) "States of Affairs Again", *Nous*, IV, pp. 179-83.

_____ (1971b) "On the Logic of Intentional Action", in Binkley *et al.* (1971), pp. 38-69.

_____ (1971c) "Reflections on Human Agency", *Idealistic Studies*, I, pp. 36-46.

_____ (1976a) "The Agent as Cause", in Brand and Walton (1976), pp. 199-211.

Chisholm, R. M. (1976b) *Person and Object*. LaSalle, Ill.: Open Court.

Collingwood, R. W. (1942) *The New Leviathan*. Oxford: Oxford University Press.

Danto, A. C. (1970) "Causation and Basic Actions", *Inquiry*, XIII, pp. 108-25.

―――― (1973) *Analytical Philosophy of Action*. Cambridge: Cambridge University Press.

Davidson, D. (1971) "Agency", in Binkley *et al*. (1971), pp. 3-25.

―――― (1972) "Freedom to Act", in Honderich (1972a), pp. 139-56.

Davis, L. (1974) "Actions", *Canadian Journal of Philosophy*, Supplementary Vol. I, Part II, pp. 129-44.

―――― (1979) *Theory of Action*. Englewood Cliffs: Prentice-Hall.

Descartes, R. (1648) *Les passions de l'âme*. Translated in N. K. Smith, ed., *Descartes's Philosophical Writings*. London: Macmillan, 1952.

Dworkin, G. (1970) "Acting Freely", *Nous*, IV, pp. 367-83.

―――― (1976) "Autonomy and Behavior Control", *Hastings Center Report*, VI, pp. 23-28.

Eccles, J., and Popper, K. (1977) *The Self and its Brain*. Berlin: Springer.

Feigl, H. (1960) "Mind-Body Identity", in Hook (1960), pp. 15-32.

Feinberg, J. (1970) *Doing and Deserving*. Princeton: Princeton University Press.

Flew, A. G. N. (1955) "Divine Omnipotence and Human Freedom", in Flew, ed., *New Essays in Philosophical Theology*. London: SCM Press, pp. 144-69.

Flew, A. G. N., ed. (1964) *Body, Mind, and Death*. New York: Collier-Macmillan.

Frankfurt, H. (1971) "Freedom of the Will and the Concept of a Person", JP, LXVIII, pp. 5-20.

───── (1972) "Coercion and Moral Responsibility", in Honderich (1972a), pp. 72-85.

───── (1975) "Three Concepts of Free Action" (symposium with D. Locke), PASSV, XLIX, pp. 113-25.

───── (1976) "Identification and Externality", in A. O. Rorty, ed., *The Identities of Persons*. Berkeley: University of California Press, pp. 239-51.

───── (1978) "The Problem of Action", APQ, XV, pp. 157-67.

Goldman, A. I. (1970) *A Theory of Human Action*. Englewood Cliffs: Prentice-Hall.

───── (1976) "The Volitional Theory Revisited", in Brand and Walton (1976), pp. 67-84.

Grünbaum, A. (1971) "Free Will and the Laws of Human Behavior", APQ, VIII, pp. 299-317.

Gunner, D. L. (1967) "Professor Smart's 'Sensations and Brain Processes'", in C. F. Presley, ed., *The Identity Theory of Mind*. St. Lucia: Queensland University Press, pp. 1-20.

Hardie, W. F. R. (1971) "Willing and Acting", PQ, XXI, pp. 193-206.

Hart, H. L. A., and Honoré, A. M. (1959) *Causation and the Law*. Oxford: Oxford University Press.

Hobbes, T. (1651) *Leviathan*. Reprinted, Indianapolis: Bobbs-Merrill, 1954.

Honderich, T., ed. (1972a) *Essays on Freedom of Action*. London: Routledge.

───── (1972b) "One Determinism", in Honderich (1972a), pp. 187-215.

Hook, S., ed. (1960) *Dimensions of Mind*. New York: Collier.

Hornsby, J. (1980) *Actions*. London: Routledge.

Hume, D. (1748) *Inquiry Concerning Human Understanding*. Reprint, Indianapolis: Bobbs-Merrill, 1955.

James, W. (1890) *The Principles of Psychology*, 2 vols. Reprint, New York: Dover, 1950.

Johnson, W. E. (1924) *Logic*, 3 vols. Reprint, New York: Dover, 1964.

Katz, J., et al., eds. (1967) *Psychoanalysis, Psychiatry, and Law*. New York: Free Press.

Kenny, A. (1963) *Action, Emotion, and Will*. London: Routledge.

Kris, E., et al., eds. (1954) *The Origins of Psychoanalysis*. London: Hogarth.

Lehrer, K., ed. (1966) *Freedom and Determinism*. New York: Random House.

Locke, J. (1690) *Essay Concerning Human Understanding*. Reprint, New York: Dover, 1959.

Lurie, Y. (1979) "Inner States", *Mind*, LXXXVIII, pp. 241-57.

MacIntyre, A. (1957) "Determinism", reprinted from *Mind*, in B. Berofsky, ed., *Free Will and Determinism*. New York: Harper and Row, 1966, pp. 240-54.

McCann, H. (1972) "Is Raising One's Arm a Basic Action?" JP, LXIX, pp. 235-48.

_____ (1974) "Volition and Basic Action", PR, LXXXIII, pp. 451-73.

_____ (1975) "Trying, Paralysis, and Volition", Review of Metaphysics, XXVIII, pp. 423-42.

_____ (1979) "On Mental Activity and Passivity: Reply to Thalberg", *Mind*, LXXXVIII, pp. 592-96.

Mead, M. (1935) *Sex and Temperament in Three Primitive Societies.* New York: Morrow.

Melden, A. I. (1960) "Willing", PR, LXIX, pp. 475-84.

Mill, J. S. (1843) *A System of Logic.* Reprint, New York: Hafner, 1950.

Morgenbesser, S., and Walsh, J. J., eds. (1962) *Free Will.* Englewood Cliffs: Prentice-Hall.

Morick, H., ed. (1970) *Introduction to the Philosophy of Mind.* Glenview, Ill.: Scott-Foresman.

Nagel, T. (1965) "Physicalism", reprinted from PR, in C. V. Borst, ed., *The Mind-Brain Identity.* London: Macmillan, 1973, pp. 210-25.

Neely, W. (1974) "Freedom and Desire", PR, LXXXIII, pp. 32-54.

Nozick, R. (1969) "Coercion", in S. Morgenbesser et al., eds., *Philosophy, Science, and Method.* New York: St. Martin's, pp. 440-72.

Peters, R. S. (1961-62) "Emotions and the Category of Passivity", PAS, LXII, pp. 117-34.

Place, U. T. (1956) "Is Consciousness a Brain Process?", reprinted from *British Journal of Psychology,* in Flew (1964), pp. 276-87.

Prichard, H. A. (1949) *Moral Obligation.* Oxford: Clarendon Press.

Putnam, H. (1960) "Minds and Machines", in Hook (1960), pp. 153-60.

_____ (1967) "The Mental Life of Some Machines", in H.-N. Castañeda, ed., *Intentionality, Minds, and Perception.* Detroit: Wayne State University Press, pp. 177-200.

Ranken, N. L. (1967) "The Unmoved Agent and the Ground of Responsibility", JP, LXIV, pp. 403-8.

Reid, T. (1768) *Essays on the Active Powers of Man.* Extracts in Brand (1970), pp. 236-46.

Rhine, J. B. (1960) "On Parapsychology and the Nature of Man", in Hook (1960), pp. 74-79.

Rorty, R., ed. (1967) *The Linguistic Turn*. Chicago: University of Chicago Press.

―――― (1970) "Incorrigibility as the Mark of the Mental", JP, LXVII, pp. 399-424.

―――― (1980) *Philosophy and the Mirror of Nature*. Princeton: Princeton University Press.

Ryle, G. (1931-32) "Systematically Misleading Expressions", reprinted from PAS, in Rorty (1967), pp. 85-100.

―――― (1949) *The Concept of Mind*. London: Hutchinson.

―――― (1970) "Autobiographical", in G. Pitcher and O. P. Wood, eds., *Ryle*. Garden City, N.J.: Doubleday, pp. 1-15.

Searle, J. R. (1969) *Speech Acts*. Cambridge: Cambridge University Press.

Sellars, W. (1966) "Thought and Action" and "Fatalism and Determinism", both in Lehrer (1966), pp. 105-74.

―――― (1976) "Volitions Re-affirmed", in Brand and Walton (1976), pp. 47-66.

Shaffer, J. (1966) "Persons and their Bodies", PR, LXXV, pp. 59-77.

Sherrington, C. (1950) Introduction to P. Laslett, ed., *The Physical Basis of Mind*. Oxford: Blackwell, pp. 1-4.

Smart, J. J. C. (1959) "Sensations and Brain Processes", PR, LXVIII, pp. 141-56.

―――― (1963) "Materialism", JP, LX, pp. 651-62.

―――― (1964) "Causality and Human Behavior", PASSV, XXXVIII, pp. 43-48.

Solomon, R. (1973) "Emotion and Choice", Review of Metaphysics, XVII, pp. 312-48.

───── (1976) The Passions. Garden City, N.J.: Doubleday.

───── (1977) "The Logic of Emotion", Nous, XI, pp. 41-49.

───── (1980) "Emotions and Choice", in A. O. Rorty, ed., Explaining Emotions. Berkeley: University of California Press, pp. 251-81.

Strachey, J., ed. (1953-74) The Standard Edition of the Complete Psychological Works of Sigmund Freud, 24 vols., London: Hogarth Press.

Strawson, P. F. (1966) "Self, Mind, and Body", reprinted from Common Factor, in Morick (1970), pp. 89-96.

Sussman, A. N. (1981) "Reflections on the Chances for a Scientific Dualism", JP, LXXVIII, pp. 95-118.

Taylor, C. (1976) "Responsibility for Self", in A. Rorty, ed., The Identities of Persons. Berkeley: University of California Press, pp. 28-49.

Taylor, R. (1958) "Determinism and the Theory of Agency", in S. Hook, ed., Determinism and Freedom in the Age of Modern Science. New York: Collier, 1961, pp. 224-36.

───── (1960) "I Can", reprinted from PR, in Morgenbesser and Walsh (1962), pp. 81-90.

───── (1966) Action and Purpose. Englewood Cliffs: Prentice-Hall.

───── (1970a) "Thought and Purpose", in Brand (1970), pp. 267-82.

───── (1970b) Good and Evil. New York: Macmillan.

───── (1983) Metaphysics. Englewood Cliffs: Prentice-Hall.

Teichman, J. (1974) The Mind and the Soul. New York: Humanities Press.

Thalberg, I. (1971) "Singling Out Actions, their Components and Properties", JP, LXVIII, pp. 781-86.

_____ (1973a) "Constituents and Causes of Emotion and Action", PQ, XXIII, pp. 1-14.

_____ (1973b) "The Ingredients of Perception", A, XXXIII, pp. 51-59.

_____, and Weil, V. (1974) "The Elements of Basic Action", Philosophia, IV, pp. 111-38.

_____ (1975) "When do Causes Take Effect?", Mind, XXXIV, pp. 583-89.

_____ (1977) Perception, Emotion and Action. Oxford: Blackwell.

_____ (1978a) "The Irreducibility of Events", A, XXXVIII, pp. 1-9.

_____ (1978b) "A Novel Approach to Mind-Brain Identity", PS, XXXVI, pp. 255-72.

_____ (1980) "Can We Get Rid of Events?", A, XL, pp. 25-31.

_____, and Weil, V. (1981) "Basic and Non-basic Actions: 'Same' or 'Different'?", A, XLI, pp. 12-17.

_____ (1984) "Do our Intentions Cause our Intentional Actions?", APQ, forthcoming.

Torrey, E. F. (1977) "Schizophrenia: Sense and Nonsense", Psychology Today, XXV, p. 157.

Vesey, G. (1961) "Volition", Philosophy, XXXVI, pp. 352-65.

Watson, G. (1975) "Free Agency", JP, LXXII, pp. 205-20.

Wilkes, K. (1975) "Anthropomorphism and Analogy in Psychology", PQ, XXV, pp. 126-37.

Wisdom, J. (1936-37) "Philosophical Perplexity", reprinted from PAS, in Rorty (1967), pp. 101-10.

Wittgenstein, L. (1953) Philosophical Investigations. New York: Macmillan.

_____ (1958) The Blue and Brown Books. New York: Harper and Row.

_____ (1967) Zettel. Oxford: Blackwell.

_____ (1969) On Certainty. Oxford: Blackwell.

Wollheim, R. (1967-68) "Thought and Passion", PAS, LXVIII, pp. 1-24.

_____ (1968) "Expression", Royal Institute of Philosophy Lectures, vol. I. London: Macmillan, pp. 227-44.

_____ (1971) Sigmund Freud. New York: Viking.

_____ ed. (1974) Freud: Critical Essays. Garden City, N.J.: Doubleday.

Young, R. (1979) "Compatibilism and Conditioning", Nous, XIII, pp. 369-81.

_____ (1980) "Autonomy and the 'Inner Self'", APQ, XVII, pp. 35-43.

INDEX

Ackerman, R., 211

activity vs. passivity, xvi, 116 ff., 127-51, 154-57, 170-74, 185-210

agent-causation, xiv f., 153-84, 190

Annas, J., 132-51, 211

Anselm, Saint, xii

Aristotle, 154

Armstrong, D., 28, 49, 54, 60, 130, 132, 211

Augustine, Saint, 33

Aune, B., 20-23, 132-51, 211

Austin, J., 128, 189, 211

Austin, J. L., 122 ff., 211

autonomy and "autarchy", 114-25, 208

Ayer, A. J., 14-21, 211 f.

Bach, K., iv, 141, 212

Bartky, S., 120, 212

Bem, S. and D., 94 ff., 114, 212

Benn, S. I., 94 f., 114 ff., 212

Bentham, J., 128, 189, 212

Berkeley, Bishop, 1 f., 128, 130, 212

Bernheim, H., 89 f.

Binkley, R., 212

brain, 45-61, 72 ff., 164-70

Brand, M., iv

Brand, M., and Walton, D., iii, 212

Broad, C. D., 154, 212

Brodbeck, M., 64, 212

Bruner, J., 71 ff., 213

Campbell, C. A., 161 f., 213

Carroll, L., 4

Castañeda, H., 15-24, 213

cause, xiv f., 46 f., 49, 153-84, 209

Charcot, J. M., 85

Chellas, B., iii

Chisholm, R., xiv, 154-84, 188, 213 f.

coercion and similar impediments to free action, 96-112

Collingwood, R. W., 128, 214

Danto, A., 159, 214

Davidson, D., 146, 156, 188 f., 191, 214

Davis, L., 130-51, 214

Descartes, R., vii, xii, 29, 31, 33, 42, 63, 128 f., 214

dualism

    of instincts in psychoanalytical theory, 65 f., 69 f.

    of mental and physical, vii f., x-xii, 27-43, 63 f., 130, 154, 185 f., 207

Dworkin, G., 98-104, 113-119, 214

Eccles, Sir J., and Popper, Sir K., 27, 214

ego, Freudian concept of, 66, 72, 77 ff., 86 f., 108 ff., 204 ff.

epistemological solipsism, 12-25, 47 ff.

Feigl, H., 47 ff., 214 f.

Feinberg, J., 96, 214

Flew, A., 33, 104 f., 214 f.

Fliess, W., 64

Frankfurt, H., 99-104, 105 f., 113-19, 185, 189, 200, 215

free action and freedom to act otherwise, xiii, 93-125, 153 ff., 160-64, 175-79, 209 f.

    hierarchical theory of, 97-125

French, P., iii

Freud, S., iii, xii-xiii, 60, 63-91, 94, 108 ff., 202-208, 219

Goldman, A. I., 129-51, 190, 206, 215

Grünbaum, A., 96, 215

Gunner, D., x, 215

Gustafson, D., iii

Hamlyn, D., iii

Hardie, W., 139, 206, 215

Hart, H. L. A., and Honoré, A. M., 178, 215

Hobbes, T., xii, 128, 145, 215

Holmes, Justice O., 128

Honderich, T., 156, 215

Hook, S., 216

Hornsby, J., 131-51, 156, 216

Hume, D., 128, 130, 216

incorrigibility, xii f., 18-25, 34 ff., 50, 56 f.

intentionality, xi f., 51 f., 58 f.

James, W., 128, 137, 141, 216

Johnson, A., 154, 216

Kant, I., xii

Kasher, A., and Lappin, S., iii

Katz, J., 109, 216

Kenny, A., 132, 216

Koestler, A., 106

Kris, E., 64, 216

Lehrer, K., iii, 216

Leibniz, G., xii, 55

Levison, A., iv

Locke, D., 105

Locke, J., 1 f., 128, 130, 189, 216

Lurie, Y., 29, 216

MacIntyre, A., 104 f., 112 ff., 216

McCann, H., iv, 131-51, 191-94, 201, 206, 216

Mead, M., 121 f., 217

Melden, A. I., 128, 217

mental events as physical, xi f., 34 ff., 39-43, 45-61, 63, 208 ff.

mental life

    and free will, vii, 93, 97-125

    mechanistic and anthropomorphic models of, xiii, 66-92

Mill, J. S., 128, 130, 178, 189, 217

minds

    and their contents, 6 ff., 23 ff.

    and their contents as somehow perceived, 9 f.

    and their contents as 'owned', 10, 23 ff.

Morgenbesser, S., and Walsh, J., 217

Morick, H., 217

Nagel, T., 52-56, 217

Neely, W., 112 ff., 217

non-physical, viii-xii, 27-43, 45-46, 207

nonsense (unintelligibility), 1-26, 30 f., 50 ff., 71 f., 86-93, 123, 144-50, 172 ff., 200 ff., 206 f.

    distinguished from unverifiability, 5 f.

Nowell-Smith, P., 64

Nozick, R., 103, 217

Peters, R. S., 197, 201-207, 217

Place, U., 28, 47 f., 217

Plato, xii, 1, 36, 42, 68

Prichard, H., xiv, 129-51, 217

privacy of mind and its contents, 10 ff., 35

private language, including private rules of reference, 12-18, 48 f.

Putnam, H., 58, 217

Ranken, N., 168 f., 217

Reid, T., 128, 130, 154, 217

Rhine, J., 27 f., 218

Rorty, R., 28 f., 31-32, 38-42, 186, 218

Ryle, G., xiv, 1-26, 128 f., 207, 218

Sartre, J.-P., 197

Scheler, M., 197

Searle, J., 21 ff., 218

Sellars, W., 131-51

Shaffer, J., ix, 27, 218

Shaftman, S., iv

Sherrington, Sir C., ix, 27, 42, 218

Smart, J., ix f., 28, 47, 52, 58, 218

socialization and 'alien desires', 93 f., 97 f., 110 ff., 209 f.

Solomon, R., 197 ff., 201 f., 206, 219

spatial location of mental and physical events, 50, 52 f., 172

Stocker, M., iv

Strachey, J., iii, 219

Strawson, Sir P., viii, 219

superego and "values", 81, 110-25

Sussman, A., 29 f., 32, 38 f., 219

Taylor, C., 99, 219

Taylor, R., 42, 51 f., 128, 137 f., 154-84, 194-97, 206, 219

Teichman, J., 28, 220

Thalberg, I., 59 f., 220

Torrey, E., 108, 220

trying
>   as attempting and as straining, 132-39
>   and total failure, 137 f.

unconscious, xiii, 70 f., 84-92, 196, 202-207
>   willing, 139, 141-45

universals, including numbers, 2-4, 36 f.

Vesey, G., 128, 132, 220

Watson, G., 110 ff., 114 f., 220

Weil, V., 220

Whittemore, R., iii

Wilkes, K., 81-84, 220

willing or volition, xiv, 127-15, 154 ff., 208 f.

Wisdom, J., 1, 221

Wittgenstein, L., xiv, 1-26, 31 f., 128, 207, 221

Wollheim, R., iii-iv, 63, 71 ff., 185 f., 196, 221

Young, R., 115 ff., 221